Originally

Pacific Beach

Looking Back at the Heritage

of a Unique Community

John Webster
2013

Table of Contents

1 The Pacific Beach Company......................3

2 The College 19

3 The Railroad....................................52

4 The Racetrack...................................70

5 The Asbestos Works.............................94

6 Lemons...110

7 The Scripps and Braemar.......................146

8 The Military Academy..........................168

9 Kate Sessions.................................193

10 The Housing Projects........................205

References......................................220

Illustrations...................................245

Acknowledgements

Most of the information about the Pacific Beach past which appears in this book was derived from original source material; contemporary newspapers and other periodicals, city directories, maps, public records and photographs. Local newspapers on microfilm dating to the 1860s are available in the California Room at the San Diego Central Library and the Geisel Library at the University of California, San Diego. These libraries also hold original copies of other early periodicals and city directories, as well as special collections relating to San Diego history. Microfilm records of property transfers going back to 1846 and other official records and maps can be viewed in the Office of the San Diego County Recorder at the San Diego County Administration Center.

The research library at the San Diego History Center also has many of these resources as well as other archives including transcripts of Superior Court cases, articles of incorporation, marriage certificates, maps and Lot Books, the ledgers in which the ownership and assessed valuation of each lot in San Diego County was recorded in the late nineteenth and early twentieth centuries. Thanks to Jane Kenealy, Lauren Rasmussen and Muriel Strickland for their knowledge and assistance identifying and interpreting these resources. Thanks also to Chris Travers and Carol Myers for their help with the History Center's extensive collection of historical photographs.

Outside the Pacific Beach Company office, Fifth and E Streets, San Diego, 1888.
(SDHC #3797)

Settlement of San Diego began with the establishment of a Spanish presidio or military outpost on today's Presidio Hill in 1769 and the gradual growth of a civilian population around the presidio in what is now called Old Town. Mexico gained independence from Spain in the 1820s and in 1834, the population having grown to nearly 500, the Mexican government granted San Diego the status of 'pueblo', which included rights to the surrounding lands. When California was taken over by the United States in 1846, and became a state in 1850, San Diego was incorporated as a city and acquired the rights to the pueblo lands of San Diego. These pueblo lands, the property between National City and Sorrento Valley lying west of a line which is approximated today by the route of Interstate 805[1], were subdivided into

Pueblo Lots, generally a half-mile square and 160 acres. Pueblo Lots 1783 to 1803 covered the area from the Pacific Ocean and Mission Bay (then known as False Bay) to the Mount Soledad foothills and Rose Canyon, the area we now know as Pacific Beach. By the mid-1880s the city had sold the Pueblo Lots in the Pacific Beach area[2] but there was little incentive for the buyers to improve them and they remained almost entirely undeveloped before 1887.

In 1885 a transcontinental rail link finally reached San Diego. Competition among railroad companies forced ticket prices down and

[1]The land east of the line had belonged to Mission San Diego.

[2]Except for the eastern 86 acres of Pueblo Lot 1785 which was 'set apart' for the city [619] and is now Kate Sessions Park.

promoters advertised the advantages of the San Diego area in Eastern newspapers. Growing numbers of potential settlers, investors and speculators arrived in town and property values skyrocketed. By 1887 San Diego was in the midst of an unprecedented expansion known as the Great Boom. William Smythe in his 1908 *History of San Diego* described the real estate market during the boom years in metaphorical terms:

> If someone should suddenly discover the kingdom of heaven, of which the race has dreamed these thousands of years, and should then proceed to offer corner lots at the intersection of golden streets, there would naturally be a rush for eligible locations, and this sudden and enormous demand would create a tremendous boom. It happens that San Diego is the nearest thing on earth to the kingdom of heaven, so far as climate is concerned. This fact was suddenly discovered and men acted accordingly. The economy of heaven is a factor which has never been much dwelt upon, and economic considerations were sadly neglected by those who went wild over real estate in the height of the boom. It was forgotten, for the moment, that men cannot eat climate, nor weave it into cloth to cover their nakedness, nor erect it as a shelter against the storm and the night. Such a reminder would have seemed puerile at the time. The only vital question was: Can we find land enough between Los Angeles and Mexico to accommodate the people who are coming, and can we get it platted into additions fast enough to meet the demand? If this question could be answered affirmatively, it was enough. Obviously, the people would continue to come, prices would continue to soar, and everybody would get rich at the expense of his neighbor, living happy forever after [1].

1 The Pacific Beach Company

E. S. Babcock and H. L. Story had already found success platting land into additions when they developed Coronado in 1886 on previously empty beachfront land on the far side of San Diego Bay. Another group of San Diego developers was determined to replicate Babcock and Story's success with a different empty beachfront area, this time on the far side of False Bay. On July 28, 1887, the Pacific Beach Company was incorporated under the laws of the State of California to 'purchase, sell, lease, and mortgage lands and otherwise conduct a general business in real estate' as well as 'laying off town sites, laying out and improving streets and roads thereon, building, furnishing and conducting hotels and restaurants' and 'to aid and assist in the construction and maintenance of colleges, schools, railroads, wagon roads, telegraph and telephone lines' [2].

The initial directors and stockholders of the Pacific Beach Company were R. A., J. R. and W. W. Thomas, O. S. Hubbell, D. C. Reed, D. P. Hale, Thomas Metcalf, Charles Collins and George Hensley. Other local businessmen and land developers including Charles Pauly, A. G. Gassen and O. J. Stough became involved with the company in subsequent years. These men had already made fortunes in banking and real estate and were well established in San Diego business circles[3].

The July 31 *San Diego Union* announced the incorporation of the Pacific Beach Company under the headline 'A GREAT ENTERPRISE, A New City About to be Built at False Bay, BY A SYNDICATE OF MILLIONAIRES'. The *Union* article reported that the company was

---

[3] The Thomases were founders of the First National Bank of San Diego. Hubbell was a director of the First National Bank as well as the California Southern Railroad, and part owner of the San Diego Gas and Electric Light Company. Hensley was in the property abstract business and an owner of downtown property. Reed had also begun in the abstract business and had been a principal in other subdivisions in the San Diego area, including, with Hubbell, the Reed and Hubbell addition on the bay between San Diego and National City. Gassen, a San Diego pioneer and the colorful City Marshall from 1872 to 1875, was a major landowner in Pacific Beach, Rose Canyon and Mt. Soledad, and was involved with Hubbell, Hale and Hensley in the San Diego and Pacific Beach Railroad. Pauly was a real estate promoter who had subdivided Pauly's Addition in North Park. Gassen and Pauly jointly built the Gassen – Pauly Block, which still stands at the corner of Fourth and E Streets in San Diego's Gaslamp District (the bricks are said to have come from Gassen's brickyard in Rose Canyon [716]). Stough had been a founder of a village in the Chicago area (Hinsdale) before moving to San Diego in 1888 [731].

allied with the San Diego and Pacific Beach Railroad, incorporated a few days before, and that 'behind the two corporations, and going hand in hand, so to speak, is a College Company'. In addition to the information contained in the articles of incorporation, the *Union* claimed to have ascertained the magnitude of the undertaking by conversation with the incorporators. They learned from one of the gentlemen that the syndicate had obtained by purchase 1,665 acres of land fronting on False Bay for the purpose of laying out a town, and 'will christen the place Pacific Beach' [3].

In October 1887 H. K. Wheeler, City Engineer, drew up a subdivision map in which the entire area from the ocean to Rose Creek and from the southern tips of Crown Point and Mission Beach to the Mt. Soledad foothills was divided into rectangular blocks by a grid of north-south streets and east-west avenues. The streets and avenues were all 80 feet wide except for Broadway (now Ingraham Street), the main north-south street, which was 100 feet wide and Grand Avenue, the main east-west avenue, which was 125 feet wide. Each block was 270 feet north-to-south and 500 feet east-to-west and was further subdivided into 40 lots; 20 lots 25 feet wide and 125 feet deep lining the avenue on either side of the block with a 20-foot-wide alley behind each lot connecting the streets at each end.

The streets were numbered, beginning with First Street near the beach to Seventeenth Street near Rose Creek, plus Broadway, which was between Eighth and Ninth. North of Grand Avenue, the avenues were all named for states, with the exception of College (now Garnet) Avenue. South of Grand the avenues were named for officials or associates of the Pacific Beach Company; Thomas, Reed, Gassen, Hubbell, Hensley, Platt, Metcalf, Hale, Collins and Poiser (except at the tip of Crown Point, and Mission Beach, where the avenues were named for trees).

The Wheeler subdivision map of October 1887 included a few notable exceptions to the regular grid pattern created by the intersecting streets and avenues. A four-block area in the center of the subdivision, extending north from College to Vermont Avenue (now Emerald Street) and between Ninth and Eleventh (now Jewell and Lamont) Streets, was not subdivided and was designated as the College Campus. Grand Avenue was extraordinarily wide because it was meant to accommodate the right-of-way of a steam railway from San Diego to a depot at the beach near the foot of Grand, which itself was allocated several blocks of land. Grand Avenue (and the railroad right-of-way) followed the same east-west alignment as the other avenues between the beach and Eleventh Street but east of there it turned and sliced through several of the regular rectangular blocks to circle around north of the racetrack which had been laid out east of Rose Creek and north of the bay. Blocks on the western and southern edges of the subdivision were of irregular sizes and shapes to fit the shoreline of the ocean and bay.

At the end of 1887 none of the features described on the subdivision map actually existed on the ground in Pacific Beach. Nevertheless, daily notices began appearing in the *San Diego Union* on December 4, 1887, announcing that the Opening Sale of the Pacific Beach Company's property between False Bay and the Ocean would be advertised in a few days [4].

In a few days, on December 8, another ad appeared describing the Natural Advantages, The Soil, Climate, The Beach, Sports, and Improvements Under Way, including The College, The Hotel, Railroad Facilities, Water and A Boulevard, and announcing the Opening Sale on December 12, 1887 [5]. The following day, December 9, this ad was enhanced to feature a fanciful birds-eye view from a point over Pacific Beach looking south, with False Bay, Point Loma, San Diego Bay and the existing population centers of Old Town and San Diego in the background. In the foreground Pacific Beach was pictured as a checkerboard of streets with a college, railroad (including a train steaming toward the beach), railway station, hotel and racetrack. The advertisement included the advice that 'A large map showing Avenues, Streets, Location, Hotel Site, College, Race Track, &c., can be seen at the Company's Office, corner Fifth and E, opposite First National Bank' and again announcing that a limited number of lots would be placed on sale Monday, December 12, 1887 [6].

The opening sale did take place on Monday, and was described in a news article in the December 13 *Union*:

The Pacific Beach Sale
The Opening Sale Yesterday – A large Crowd of Purchasers

All things considered, yesterday's sale of Pacific Beach lots was the most successful in the history of San Diego real estate transactions. Realizing the value of their property, and having faith in its merits, the Pacific Beach Company did not resort to the usual methods of booming the sale. The property was sold in the same manner that all other business is transacted. No tickets for choice of lots were issued, but the sale was conducted on the recognized principle of "first come, first served." In consequence, eager purchasers were on hand many hours in advance of the sale to remain day and night in order to get choice lots. Many predicted that after the first rush of the morning there would be a lull in the sale, but it continued unabating during the day, notwithstanding the fact that no band was in attendance, no free carriages and no free lunch.

By evening over $200,000 worth of lots were disposed of. The buyers were all legitimate investors, and many of them signified an intention of improving their lots. The erection of five handsome residences will be begun immediately. The excavation for the college is finished and work on the brick work has been begun. College avenue was the favorite street with purchasers. The motor line runs along that avenue and there is no doubt that it will be the main business street. In the last few weeks many persons have been viewing the ground, and without doubt all purchasers bought intelligently. The property was made to stand on its merits and the immense success of the sale proves that it has the merit desired by purchasers. The company believe that they have a property that for beach and other advantages is not excelled by any other watering place on the coast. For this reason they are confident that Pacific Beach will be the most popular California pleasure resort. The sale will continue today [7].

The *Union* article noted that eager purchasers had remained day and night to obtain choice lots. First in line was presumably the representative of Bancroft & Company, who had advertised that they had taken their place at the door one minute after closing time Saturday night and had relays of men to hold the place until Monday morning. The Bancroft ad assured buyers that any lot in Pacific Beach could be secured by giving their order to Bancroft along with a check in favor of the Pacific Beach Company [8].

After the opening sale the Pacific Beach Company had followed up with an advertisement in the *Union* announcing 'A great many CHOICE LOTS still for sale, notwithstanding the immense sale of yesterday' [7]. On Saturday, December 17, a new ad informed buyers that as a result of the 'largest sale ever made in San Diego', the company had decided to 'advance prices' on January 1, but that sales would resume on Monday, December 19, and a comfortable conveyance would take buyers to visit the property if they wished to purchase at the original prices before that date [9].

The *San Diego Union* report had mentioned that over $200,000 worth of lots were disposed of on the day of the opening sale and claimed that all things considered it was the most successful sale in the history of San Diego real estate transactions. The *Union* even pointed out that this success was achieved without 'booming' the sale with the usual free transportation, free lunch and a band. The Pacific Beach Company's advertisement following the opening sale had also referred to the 'immense sale'.

In fact, the opening sale may not have been as successful as the initial reports suggested. The Pacific Beach Company's ad in the *Union* on the Saturday following the opening week repeated the claim that 'the last four days' was the largest sale ever made in San Diego, but also seemed to adopt at least some of the 'boomer' tactics that the *Union* had decried, urging prospective buyers to buy now before prices went up and offering a comfortable conveyance (free carriage?) to those who wanted to visit the property.

Within a few months, as the Great Boom collapsed and real estate prices plummeted, the Pacific Beach Company resorted to even more aggressive sales tactics. Their ad in the April 30, 1888, *Union* offered lots at one-half of February prices to insure buyers a good profit on their investments. Not only that, but previous buyers could select an equal number of lots to be included in their contract at no additional cost when making their second payment, presumably to encourage these buyers to make a second payment rather than walk away from rapidly-depreciating investments. The ad did threaten that prices would be advanced 10 per cent after 30 days, however [10].

There is a large (9- by 10-foot) copy of the Wheeler subdivision map of October 1887 in the San Diego History Center map library, possibly the actual 'large map showing Avenues, Streets, Location, Hotel Site, College, Race Track, &c' that potential buyers were invited to view at the Pacific Beach Company office in the days leading up to the sale. The map is very detailed, even including individual lots and lot numbers, and appears to have been used to keep track of lot sales. Some lots, groups of lots and even a few whole blocks are marked out, presumably indicating that they were sold and no longer available (and some marked-out lots have paper 'paste-overs' apparently indicating that the sales fell through and they were again available). This map thus provides a geographical representation of the extent and distribution of lot ownership in the first year or so of the Pacific Beach subdivision [11][4].

It is evident from the markings on this map that despite the enthusiasm generated by the opening sale, property ownership within Pacific Beach during the period this map was used to keep track was relatively thin and unevenly distributed. Of the nearly 400 blocks created by the grid of streets and avenues in Pacific Beach, counting Crown Point but not counting Mission Beach, only 78 blocks had even one lot marked out on the map. The largest concentration of marked-out lots was along the beach-front, particularly at the foot of Grand Avenue near the railway depot. Another concentration of sales took place near the center of the community, around the intersection of Grand and Broadway (Ingraham). Presumably these would have been

---

[4] Although the map was oriented so that the streets and avenues ran vertically and horizontally and appear to be aligned north and south, true north is actually offset 14 degrees 30 minutes clockwise and technically the streets run North 14 degrees 30 minutes West and the avenues North 75 degrees 30 minutes East. The streets and avenues of Pacific Beach aligned with the boundaries of the rectangular Pueblo Lots which were also offset 14 degrees 30 minutes from true north.

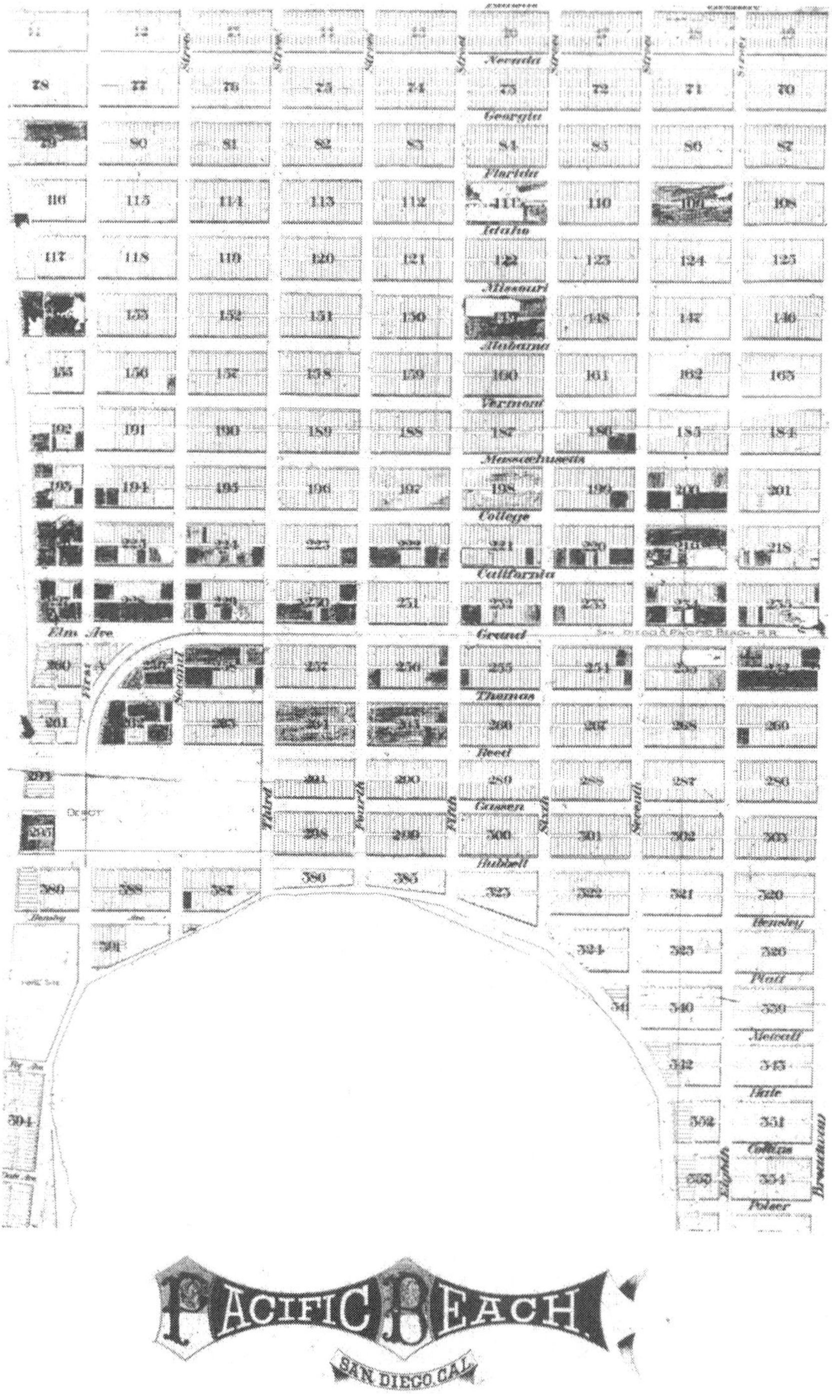
Nevada
Georgia
Florida
Idaho
Missouri
Alabama
Vermont
Massachusetts
College
California
Elm Ave
Grand
San Diego & Pacific Beach R.R.
Thomas
Reed
Garnet
Hubbell
First
Second
Third
Fourth
Fifth
Sixth
Seventh
Depot
Platt
Metcalf
Hale
Collins
Broadway
PACIFIC BEACH
SAN DIEGO, CAL.

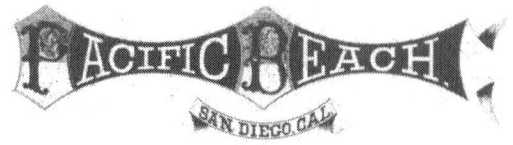

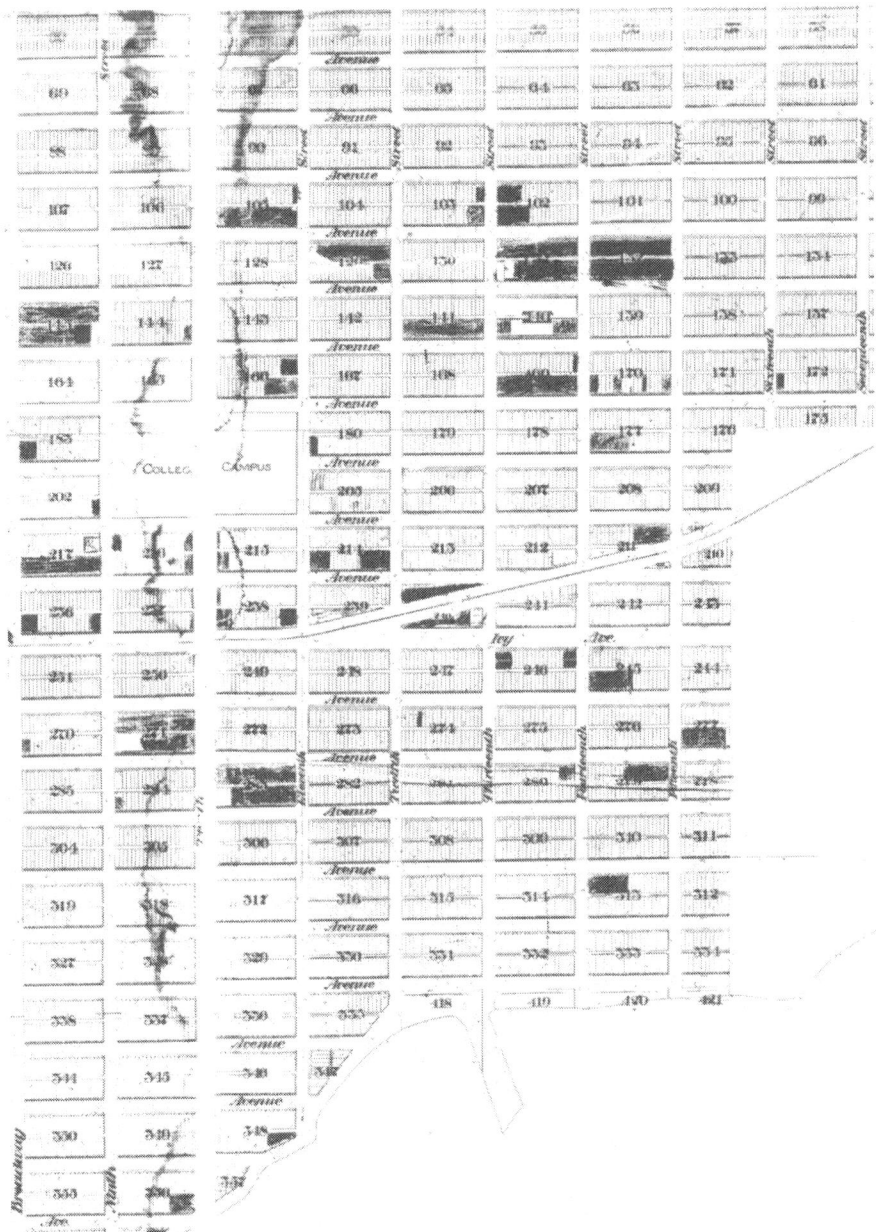

Subdivided for *The Pacific Beach Company* Oct. 1887.

by

H.K.WHEELER, C.E.

(SDHC #1669)

the locations of the 'choice lots' promoted by the company. Another area with a high volume of sales, as indicated by the markings on the map, was in the northeast of the subdivision, an area at a slight elevation overlooking the racetrack, bay and downtown San Diego area, which may have appealed to some as view lots.

While sales of lots by the Pacific Beach Company began on December 12, 1887, the Deed Books at the San Diego County Assessor's Office do not show any deeds granted by the Pacific Beach Company until late April 1888. Presumably the delay in recording the deeds resulted from a backlog of property sales accumulated during the boom. The county recorder would have been entering deeds not only from Pacific Beach but from other new subdivisions like Coronado, Ocean Beach and Oneonta, and of course from sales and resales in the downtown area of San Diego. Lots were sold on an installment basis and it is possible that deeds were not recorded until the final payment was made, months after the initial down payment. San Diego County was also much larger then and sales from far-flung areas in what are now Imperial and Riverside Counties would have been recorded in the San Diego County Deed Books.

Recording of deeds must also have been slowed by the fact that each deed was hand-written in cursive script which clarified every detail in the arcane legal terminology of the time; the grantor ('Pacific Beach Company, a corporation duly organized under the laws of the State of California, party of the first part'), the grantee (e.g., 'Madge Morris Wagner of San Diego, San Diego County, State of California the party of the second part'), the price (e.g., 'the said party of the first part for and in consideration of the sum of Two Hundred & Fifty Dollars Gold Coin of the United States of America, to them in hand paid by the said party of the second part, the receipt whereof is hereby acknowledged, and in consideration of the full performance of the covenants hereinafter contained, do by the presents grant, bargain and sell') and the description of the property (e.g., 'All the certain lots and parcels of land situate lying and being in Pacific Beach in the City of San Diego, County of San Diego, State of California and bounded and particularly described as follows, to wit: Lots Thirty Nine <39> and Forty <40> in Block One Hundred & Forty <140> Pacific Beach, as per Official maps'.

Each deed granted by the Pacific Beach Company also included the following covenant:

> It is provided and covenanted, with a covenant running with the lands, that if at any time said second party, her heirs, assigns or successors in interest or those holding or claiming thereunder, shall, with the knowledge or consent of the owner of said premises, use, or cause to be used, or shall allow or

authorize in any manner, directly or indirectly, said premises or any part thereof to be used for the purpose of vending intoxicating liquors for drinking purposes, whether said vending shall be directly or under some evasive guise, thereupon the title herby granted shall revert to and be vested in the Pacific Beach Company, a corporation, its successors and assigns, and it, or said successors or assigns, shall be entitled to the immediate possession thereof, provided that any bona fide mortgager of said premises, in case the foregoing covenant be broken, shall have the option to at once claim and enforce the foregoing reversion for himself and for his own use and benefit, subject, however, to the foregoing covenant running against any further violation thereof, otherwise the foregoing covenant shall have the same force and effect as if said proviso was not herein inserted. In the dedication of the streets and alleys in said town to public use, there is hereby reserved from such use the right to vend or otherwise dispose of intoxicating liquors for drinking purposes, and to that extent said streets are and hereby and forever shall remain the private property of said grantors and their assigns.

Altogether, a visual scan through the grantor index of the Deed Books found entries for 134 deeds covering 991 lots worth $138,000 granted by the Pacific Beach Company up to 1892; 61 deeds for 586 lots worth $80,631 recorded in 1888, 53 deeds for 284 lots worth $42,303 in 1889, 21 deeds and 121 lots worth $14,993 in 1890 and 1891[5]. The lot and block numbers recorded in these deeds generally match the marked-out lots on the Wheeler map at the History Center, supporting the theory that the map was used to keep track of sales.

A substantial amount of property was granted by the Pacific Beach Company at little or no cost, at least as recorded on the deeds. Three deeds for a total of 189 lots were granted to the San Diego College Company for $1 each, in addition to the grant of the entire four-block College Campus, also for a consideration of $1. The Board of Education was granted two deeds for 8 lots each, also for $1. The trustees of the Pacific Beach Presbyterian Church were granted 4 lots for $1. Another deed for 24 lots in Pacific Beach (and a tract of land beyond the eastern edge of the subdivision) was granted for no consideration other than the grantees were required to build and operate an asbestos manufacturing enterprise.

Many of the lots were sold to associates of the Pacific Beach Company or their families, including Charles Collins (40), D. C. Reed (18), J. R., R. A. and Mary A. Thomas (14), Thomas and G. B. Metcalf (8), Clifford and Kate G. Hubbell (6), and George Hensley (9). Frances A. Thomas, presumably a relative of company manager J. R. Thomas,

---

[5] Like the deeds themselves, index entries were entered in cursive script that was not always clear and are not in strict alphabetical order; Pacific Beach Company deeds appear along with other grantors beginning with 'Pa' in roughly the order they were recorded. Consequently some deeds may have been overlooked in this search.

and Alice Gassen, wife of A. G. Gassen, each bought two entire blocks. Other buyers, including Rev. L. Groh, Madge Morris Wagner and Rose Hartwick Thorpe, were associated with the college, which was under construction as lots were being sold. H. K. Wheeler, the City Engineer who had laid out the subdivision map of Pacific Beach, paid $750 for 3 of its lots. Lots even became wedding gifts; the February 19, 1888, *Union* carried a notice for the marriage of Frank Colwell and Carrie Lewis and noted that the bride received many valuable presents, 'among them a square of 10 lots in Pacific Beach' [12].

Assuming that the dollar amounts recorded in the grant deeds reflected the price paid by buyers, and not counting the lots transferred for token amounts, the average price per lot in Pacific Beach between 1888 and 1891 was about $180. Property near the beach and the railroad depot or near the center of the subdivision averaged $300 - $400. Lots on the fringes of the community were less, as little as $40 - $50. Corner lots were priced at a 25% premium to ordinary lots [13] and discounts were applied to purchases of multiple lots. Despite the threat to 'advance prices' starting January 1, 1888, the average price per lot recorded in deeds actually went down in the first years; $210 in 1888, $170 in 1889 and $125 in 1890-1891 (again not counting deeds granted for little or no consideration).

The total paid for all lots recorded in the Deed Books between 1888 and 1891, including lots purchased by company insiders, was far less than the $200,000 figure the *San Diego Union* claimed for the first day of sales alone. Actually the *Union's* report had stated that 'over $200,000 worth of lots had been disposed of'. It is possible that some buyers committed to purchase a lot during the opening sale and were counted toward the total worth of lots disposed of but then defaulted on subsequent payments and never received a deed. If so, and if the value of lots granted for token payments is included, the total worth of lots disposed of during this period could have approached $200,000, although over a period of 4 years and not after just the first day of sales.

San Diego's Great Boom came to an end in early 1888, just a few months after the Pacific Beach Company's lots had gone on sale, and with it the abrupt departure of a large percentage of the population and a sharp downturn in the real estate market. In Pacific Beach, the college had opened to great fanfare in time for the 1888 fall semester, but was unable to sustain the momentum and closed after the 1890-1891 academic year. The asbestos works apparently ceased operations in 1892 and had disappeared by 1894. Monteith's Directory of San Diego and Vicinity for 1889–1890 had listed a total of 37 residences in Pacific Beach along with the occupation of the resident [14]. Eleven of the 37 residents in 1889–1890 had been associated with the college, including the president and his extended family (a son was the financial agent, one daughter's husband was a professor and another daughter boarded at the college, possibly to care for the 80-year-old president), five other professors or teachers, E. C. Thorpe, whose wife Rose Hartwick Thorpe was an unofficial ambassador for the college (and whose daughter Lulo was a student), and E. N. Hoff, who had moved to Pacific Beach so his daughter Olive could attend the college [15] and whose son John D. Hoff was proprietor of the asbestos works. Four residents were involved with the asbestos works, including the proprietor, two salesmen and an engineer. Six other residents worked for the railroad, which carried day students, commuting faculty and staff, and visitors to and from the college, and transported raw material and finished goods for the asbestos works. The demise of the college and asbestos works and the prospect of reduced traffic on the railroad added to the general depression resulting from the collapse of the Great Boom and left Pacific Beach residents and the community itself with an uncertain future.

After having recorded 114 sales in 1888 and 1889, but only 16 in 1890 and 5 in 1891, the Pacific Beach Company apparently decided on a new development strategy. Map 697, filed with the recorder on January 2, 1892, significantly reduced and reconfigured the subdivided area shown on the Wheeler map of October 1887. Most of the area lying south of today's Pacific Beach Drive was eliminated from the grid entirely, including all of Pueblo Lots 1800, 1801, 1802 and most of 1803. Most of Pueblo Lot 1791, an area nearly half a mile square lying roughly between today's Everts and Ingraham Streets, and Loring and Emerald Streets, was also left blank (although Pueblo Lot 1784, to the north of 1791, remained) [16].

Map 697 left the central area of Pacific Beach mostly unchanged. In the area between Reed Avenue and Alabama Avenue (today's Diamond Street), the streets and avenues and the subdivided blocks in the original Wheeler map were retained (except for that portion of Pueblo Lot 1791 removed from the grid). South of Reed the avenues were eliminated and only three avenues were retained north of Alabama; Idaho Avenue (now Chalcedony Street), Georgia Avenue (Beryl Street) and a short stretch of Illinois Avenue (Agate Street). Most of the streets also terminated at Reed and Alabama. In place of residential blocks divided by streets and avenues, each with 40 25- by 125-foot lots, the areas south of Reed and north of Alabama were redrawn as agricultural lots averaging 8 to 10 acres, each essentially replacing a pair of the original blocks and the streets and avenue that ran between them.

Marketing Pacific Beach as an agricultural area did improve business for the company, at least at first. When sales based on Map 697 were initiated in 1892, 13 of the 19 sales recorded by the Pacific Beach Company were for these acreage or acre lots. The deeds recorded for these sales indicated that the lots were sold for $100 an acre, generally less than $1000 each, a fraction of what the 80 lots most of them replaced would have cost. J. R. Thomas wrote in February 1892 'The company made a very low rate on over two hundred acres in order to get people out there to improve. All are setting orchards, principally lemons' [17]. In the 1892 City Directory, only 4 residences

---

14   **Originally Pacific Beach**

Map 791

in Pacific Beach were associated with agricultural occupations, including a farmer, a dairyman, a horse trainer and a breeder of fancy chickens [18]. By 1895 17 of Pacific Beach's 34 residences were occupied by farmers, ranchers or dairymen [19].

However, even with the larger lots and lower prices the Pacific Beach Company's sales continued to decline. Only 7 sales were recorded in 1893 and 4 in 1894 (of which 2 were acre lots). In 1894 the company recorded another map, Map 791, superseding Map 697, adding a few acre lots in the southeast corner of the empty portion of Pueblo Lot 1791 [20]. Sales continued to slip however; only 1 deed was recorded in 1895 and 4 in 1896. In November 1896 the company's two remaining attractions, the beachfront hotel and pavilion, were sold to Sterling Honeycutt. The deed for this transaction also gave Honeycutt a half-block of property near the intersection of today's Lamont Street

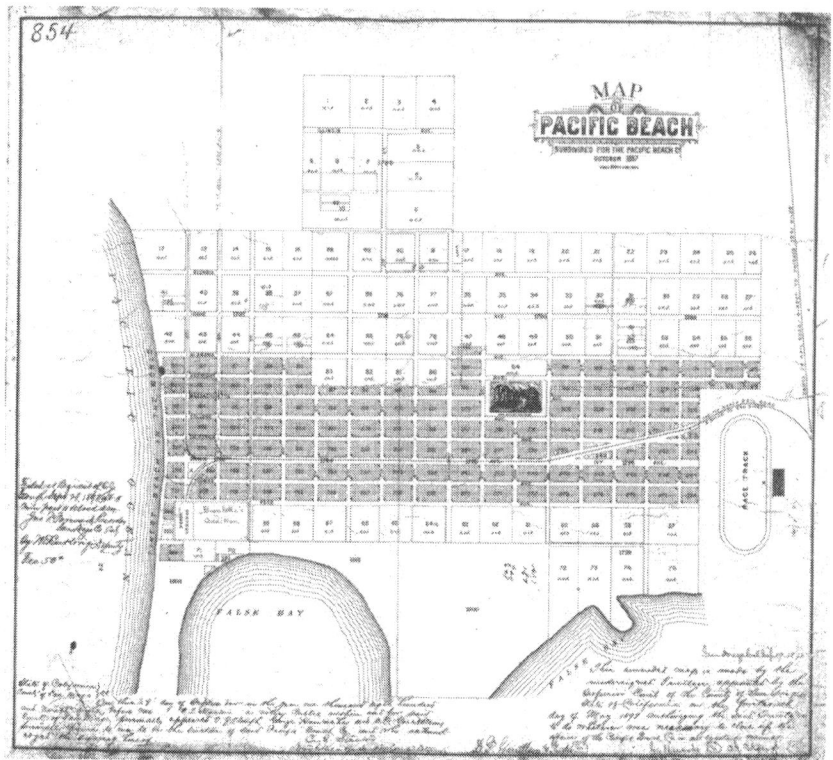

and Grand Avenue and required him to move the buildings from their original sites on the beach to this new, more central location [21].

In 1898 the Pacific Beach Company was dissolved. A final map, Map 854, was drawn up filling the remaining empty space in Pueblo Lot 1791 with additional acre lots [22]. On October 3, 1898, the Pacific Beach Company recorded its final deeds, making 'an equitable and fair division of the property' to the remaining stockholders, O. J. Stough, F. W. Garrettson, J. S. Akerman, and the First National Bank. Stough received the majority of the unsold inventory, amounting to about half of all the property in the subdivision [23]. The bank was awarded about a quarter of the total property [24], Garrettson received 51 lots in 4 blocks [25], and Akerman received a single acre lot [26].

Not only had property sales failed to meet expectations, but the actual settlement of Pacific Beach was slow to develop. The 1887 *San Diego Union* article reporting on the Pacific Beach Company's opening sale had noted that while all the buyers were 'legitimate investors', only 'many' of them intended to improve their lots, and only 'five handsome residences' were to be built immediately. In fact, most of the buyers of lots in Pacific Beach were speculators or investors who did not intend to become residents.

Olmsted and Bynon's Directory of San Diego City, published in 1892, included nearly 200 pages of listings with about 25 residences per page, a total of about 5000 residences. Only 20 of these residences were in Pacific Beach. The county Lot Book for 1893, which listed all property in the county for tax purposes, including the name of the owner and the value of any improvements, showed only 33 improved parcels in Pacific Beach, including the college campus, hotel, pavilion and a lumber company. The remaining 29 lots listed improvements of between $50 and $1000, averaging about $280, most of which were probably residences. The names of 9 of the owners of these improved lots were among the 20 residents of Pacific Beach listed in the 1892 City Directory while 6 other owners appeared in the City Directory with downtown addresses, presumably using their Pacific Beach properties as vacation homes or rentals. Half of these 33 improved lots, including the hotel and pavilion, were in the vicinity of the depot at the foot of Grand Avenue and several were actually beachfront property. The other improvements were located in other areas where lot sales had been concentrated, primarily in the corridor along Grand Avenue (and the railway line).

City Directories for later years indicated some growth in the residential population of Pacific Beach, primarily ranchers and farmers; 34 residences were listed in 1895 and 37 in 1897, of which 17 in each year listed agricultural occupations. The La Jolla Quadrangle of the U. S. Geological Survey topographic map series, surveyed in 1901–1902, which also covered the Pacific Beach area, showed the location of every building in the community, as well as those streets and avenues that actually existed at the time and other features such as the railroad and the racetrack. This map (Page 60) shows about 50 buildings of all kinds in Pacific Beach, including the former college buildings, churches, schools and businesses [27].

Despite promotion by the Pacific Beach Company and initial reports of record-breaking lot sales, the launch of Pacific Beach as a residential community got off to a slow start. The attractions intended to draw residents had not had the desired effect. The hotel and dance pavilion at the beach were relocated to the vicinity of the former college and repurposed as an office building and a fruit warehouse. The college buildings still stood but the students and faculty, who at one point had represented a sizable proportion of the residents of Pacific Beach, had gone. Although property sales had been revived by converting outlying areas into agricultural plots there were still only 30-40 residences in Pacific Beach ten years after lots had first been offered for sale. Most of the real estate remained unsold and was distributed to the remaining shareholders in 1898. Still, the company did succeed in putting Pacific Beach on the map and although it took much longer than expected the community eventually grew to look very much like what H. K. Wheeler mapped out in 1887. Most of the streets and avenues included in that map exist today, although most now have different names[6] and some, at the extremities of the community, have different alignments more suited to the topography.

---

[6] Renaming of streets was made necessary when San Diego adopted a policy in 1900 that required all street names within the city limits, including suburbs like Pacific Beach, to be unique. The numbered streets in Pacific Beach duplicated street names in the downtown area so all the streets in Pacific Beach, including Broadway, were renamed (in alphabetical order) after nineteenth-century statesmen (Bayard, Cass, Dawes, etc.). Broadway got its name back in 1907 but it was changed again, to Ingraham, when the former D Street downtown was made Broadway in 1913. Most of the avenues north of Alabama and south of Reed had already been eliminated when blocks in these areas were converted to acre lots on the subdivision maps. The surviving avenues named for states (north of Grand) duplicated state-themed streets in the University Heights area so these avenues (and College Avenue) were renamed for gemstones, also in alphabetic sequence (e.g., Beryl, Chalcedony, Diamond). Missouri Avenue had been eliminated beginning with map 697, but when Acre Lot 49 was re-subdivided into two standard blocks as Hauser's Subdivision in 1904 it was restored (as Missouri Street) since it did not then conflict with a street downtown. South of Grand only Thomas and Reed had survived among the avenues named for Pacific Beach Company officials, and they retain their original names to this day, as does Grand. Other avenues on the original Wheeler map but removed from later maps were also eventually recreated, but were given new names (e.g., Law Street, Oliver Street) [705].

2 The College

Harr Wagner was an 1881 graduate of Wittenberg College in Springfield, Ohio, who had been inspired by Joaquin Miller's 'Songs of the Sierras' to relocate to San Francisco [28]. In 1882 he purchased *The Golden Era*, a literary magazine that had been published in San Francisco since 1852 and in its early years had featured contributors such as Mark Twain and Bret Harte. In 1887 Wagner moved the magazine to San Diego, offering 'a rather abrupt notice to our subscribers' that San Diego was destined to become a great city and that *The Golden Era* was determined to contribute to the city's growth and earn a share of the benefits [29]. He credited A. H. Isham, then of the firm of Truman, Isham and Hooker, of San Francisco, for 'originating the idea and the plan' for the move, and thanked a long list of prominent San Diegans who had committed to subscriptions. Apparently Isham had also arranged a $5,000 payment to Wagner to settle his debts and cover moving expenses [30].

Wagner wrote an editorial in the May 1887 *Golden Era* outlining the benefits of an institution of learning to a town and suggesting that there was room for a college in San Diego, 'not a small insignificant institute, but an institution that will compare favorably with the noted colleges of America' and that the city was the right size to support such an institution [31]. The June issue referred to 'the new college, to be located in or near San Diego, with Dr. Samuel Sprecher as president' [32].

On August 16, 1887, Wagner, C. S. Sprecher, F. P. Davidson, O. S. Hubbell and T. S. Van Dyke incorporated The San Diego College Company in San Diego to 'erect and construct buildings to be used for colleges, universities, and in connection therewith; to carry on, control and maintain colleges and universities; to buy, sell, mortgage and lease lands'. Wagner, Sprecher and Davidson split 99.5% of the shares, while Hubbell and Van Dyke each owned 0.25% [33].

Rev. Cecil S. Sprecher was a graduate of Wittenberg and had been a Lutheran minister in Ohio, a Presbyterian minister in Stockton and pastor of the Second Presbyterian Church in Los Angeles [34]. He was the son of Samuel Sprecher, D.D., LL.D., who had served as the second president of Wittenberg College from 1849 to 1874 and played an important role in establishing it as a successful educational institution (Wittenberg University still exists in Springfield).

Frank P. Davidson was married to Samuel Sprecher's daughter (and C. S. Sprecher's sister) Eleanor or Ella. He had also attended Wittenberg College where he received an A.B. degree in 1875 and an A.M. in 1878. Davidson had been principal of a ward school in Springfield, an assistant instructor at the Wittenberg preparatory school and instructor of natural sciences at the Springfield high school before moving to San Diego in 1888 to play his part in establishing the San Diego College [35].

The three principal directors of the college were graduates of Wittenberg College and presumably saw Wittenberg as a model for the institution they hoped to create (although Wittenberg was and remains affiliated with the Lutheran Church while their college was to be non-sectarian). Sprecher and Davidson's family relationship with Samuel Sprecher undoubtedly inspired their plan to recruit him to lead their new college and repeat the success he had brought to their alma mater.

The college company's plan to 'buy, sell, mortgage and lease lands' would have sounded like a promising business model at the height of the Great Boom in San Diego, and was complemented by one of the Pacific Beach Company's stated purposes, 'to aid and assist in the construction and maintenance of colleges, schools, railroads, wagon roads, telegraph and telephone lines by the donation of lands, money or any other lawful means' [2]. An article in the November 1887 *Golden Era* explained that in the latter part of August the writer, presumably Harr Wagner, had been standing in the real estate office of A. W. Jewell looking for land suitable for the college when O. S. Hubbell happened by, was called in, and negotiations began which resulted in the location of the college in Pacific Beach (Hubbell was a founding director of the Pacific Beach Company and the San Diego and Pacific Beach Railway, both incorporated in July 1887, as well as the college company, incorporated in August) [36].

The September 4 *San Diego Union* reported that the enterprise was fostered by the originators of the Pacific Beach Company and was to be built at a beautiful site on the shores of False Bay, 'a picture that needs no colors to make it attractive'. Reid Bros., the architects of the Hotel Del Coronado, had completed the plans which consisted of a dormitory for gentlemen, one for ladies, a musical conservatory and a four-story central building containing the Lecture Hall, Museum, Art Hall, Laboratory, Literary Halls and Recitation Rooms. The buildings would form one of the most attractive places in San Diego and would be enclosed in a ten-acre park, and no college in the Pacific States and Territories would have the working facilities of the San Diego College.

Samuel Sprecher, D.D., LL.D. would be the head of the institution, Davidson would have charge of the department of natural sciences and

Rev. C. S. Sprecher would occupy the chair or moral and mental philosophy. There would be at least eight instructors the first year, two or three of whom would be men of national reputations, but whose names the *Union* were 'not yet at liberty to give'. The college would comprise at least seven different schools, including Language and Literature, Natural Science, Mental and Moral Philosophy, Music, Arts, Technical Arts and Agriculture, such as gardening, fruit-growing and silk culture in Southern California. An astronomical observatory would form an important feature and it would be the aim of the college company to obtain an astronomer, who would greatly aid the institution. The enterprise was 'now under full headway' and there was no reason any delays would be encountered [37].

The November issue of *The Golden Era* repeated the same general projections for the college, often in the same words, with additional details like the fact that the central building would be of brick with brown stone trimmings. On the subject of the astronomical observatory, *The Golden Era* even added the rumor that 'it is said that Richard A. Proctor, the celebrated astronomer, will have charge'. Proctor was indeed a celebrated astronomer, perhaps the best-known astronomer of his day, and according to some accounts he had been hired by the college before he died in 1888 [38].

The Pacific Beach Company's subdivision map of October 1887 had labeled a 4-block area in the heart of the proposed community as the College Campus and on October 9 the *San Diego Union* reported that President Sprecher[7] formally accepted the property from the Pacific Beach Company [39] (the deed, made for a consideration of $1, was recorded January 25, 1889 [40]).

An elaborate ceremony was planned for January 28, 1888, to lay the cornerstone of the college. The *San Diego Union* announced that the day would be a memorable one in the history of Pacific Beach and that trains to the event would leave the D-Street depot at 9 and 10 o'clock and return at 1 and 3 P. M. Fare for the round trip to the college campus and return would be 50 cents with children half price [41].

The following day's *Union* reported on the ceremony under the headline 'College Corner-stone, It is Laid at Pacific Beach With Imposing Ceremonies':

---

[7] Rev. C. S. Sprecher was president of the San Diego College Company. Rev. Sprecher's father, Samuel Sprecher, D.D., LL.D. would become president of the actual educational institution, the San Diego College of Letters. The president referred to here would have been the company president, C. S. Sprecher; Samuel Sprecher did not arrive in San Diego until October 18, 1888.

No one could have wished for a better January day then yesterday. In the morning the clouds were threatening rain, but before the second train-load of excursionists to attend the laying of the corner-stone of the San Diego College, had reached Pacific Beach, the sun had broken through the clouds, and it, with the green grass and the sublime scene from the college campus, made the occasion a most interesting one. The two trains that left this morning carried probably above 2,500 people to the Beach, among whom were a great portion of the representative citizens of San Diego.

College Vice President Davidson called the assemblage to order promptly at 11 o'clock, the City Guard Band played the overture to Barber of Seville, a prayer was offered, and Harr Wagner delineated the plans for the institution, which would afford facilities for the accommodation of 1,000 students. The City Guard Band followed with a medley of college songs, and a young lady read 'The Builders', a poem by Madge Morris, wife of Harr Wagner and a frequent contributor to *The Golden Era*.

Mrs. Wagner's poem was followed by an oration by the Rev. W. B. Noble, including thoughts such as:

How appropriate is this spot to the use to which we now consecrate it. This hilltop with its slopes stretching down to the placid bay and out to the roiling sea, while in the distance, but in full view, lies the busy city and the harbor filled with ships, and still beyond the majestic sweep of the mountains, some green with spring-like verdure, and others white with snow, the whole scene bathed in perennial sunshine; this is a spot which may well be chosen sacred to the attainment of all that is beautiful, and good and true.

When Joaquin Miller, the 'Poet of the Sierras' (and another *Golden Era* contributor) stepped to the front of the platform to read a poem he had composed for the occasion he was 'greeted with an ovation that could not but have gratified the gifted man of verse and sentiment'. When the applause had subsided, Mr. Miller read his poem, 'The Larger College', in a 'forcible manner', including such verses as:

We lift this lighthouse by the sea,
  The west-most sea, the west-most shore,
To guide man's ship of destiny
  When Scylla and Charybdis roar;
To teach him strength, to proudly teach
God's grandeur, by Pacific Beach [42].

After Mr. Miller's presentation, and another round of applause, Prof. Davidson introduced College President Rev. C. S. Sprecher, who delivered an address on 'The Influence of the College in opening up the Higher Avenues of Wealth and Happiness'. His address concluded with the promise that San Diego College would become a 'scientific and literary light-house, guiding the people of the city and the world into the golden harbor of wealth, culture, character and happiness'.

Laying the cornerstone of the San Diego College of Letters, January 28, 1888.

The cornerstone was then loaded with copies of the *Union, Bee, Sun, San Diegan, Mercury, Coronado, Pacific Beach* (the new college paper), and the *Golden Era*, copies of the poems and addresses delivered on the occasion, coins, a copy of the Bible, and a list of municipal officers and members of the Board of Education, and lowered into place while Rev. Sprecher declared that 'we lay the corner-stone of San Diego College – unsectarian but not un-Christian – her faith the faith of Christendom – her hope the hope of the civilized Christian world.' The band then played the national anthem and the ceremonies were concluded with a benediction [43].

The September/October 1888 edition of *The Golden Era* contained a First Annual Announcement from the San Diego College of Letters stating that the college would begin its educational work on September 20. The announcement declared that the college was undenominational and would admit both sexes to all the advantages of the curriculum, which included a thorough education in Science, Literature, Philosophy, Art, Music, Military Tactics, Voice Culture and Oratory, and Ancient and Modern Languages.

A Bachelor of Arts degree would be conferred on those who completed the Classical course. Applicants for the Classical course would have to be at least 14 years old and would be examined in Latin, Greek (or its equivalent), Mathematics, History, Geography, English and Physiology. The regular course of study would occupy four years. There were also to be Scientific and Literary courses for which 'degrees corresponding in character' would be given and for which Modern Languages could be substituted for Greek. Latin would be optional after the Sophomore year. Although the aim was to have a student enter one of these standard courses of study, those who chose to pursue a select course of special studies could receive a certificate of attendance. There would also be an Academic and Preparatory course for younger students, or students not meeting the requirements of admission, designed to prepare pupils to enter the Freshman class and also to provide a course of study that was complete and practical in itself.

The announcement went on to say that the faculty and corps of instructors would be guided by Samuel Sprecher, D.D., LL.D., ex-president of Wittenberg College, an educator with long years of successful experience. The chair of Philosophy and Political Science would be occupied by C. S. Sprecher, A.M., while Frank P. Davidson, A.M., would hold the chair of Natural Sciences and Harr Wagner, A.M., of Literature. The instructors and assistant instructors in Latin and Greek, Military Tactics, German, English branches, Elocution, Oratory and Reading and a matron were named. The directors were said to be in correspondence with well-known educators to fill the positions of professors of Mathematics, Latin and Greek, a principal of the Musical Department and the Academic Departments, and a teacher of painting and drawing. This faculty would represent the most approved methods of education and have supervision over the moral conduct and correct training of students.

The facilities would include the completed 126-by-50 foot East Building, the finest in Southern California, containing 'recitation rooms, a laboratory, reception rooms, a suite of rooms for a resident member of the faculty, and twenty rooms en suite for the accommodations of young lady students who wish to board and study at the College'. The young ladies' rooms included open fireplaces and large closets, and were said to be well lighted and ventilated with 'Sunlight in every room'. Boys and young men would be quartered in the college house and neighboring cottages. The students could also enjoy a superb view of San Diego, Mission Bay[8], the Pacific Ocean and the Cuyamaca Mountains. Students from abroad would be required to board at the college.

In keeping with the promise that both sexes would be admitted to all the advantages of the curriculum, one of which was the opportunity for out-door drill summer and winter due to the evenness of the

---

[8] This may have been the first-ever reference to the bay as Mission Bay; Rose Hartwick Thorpe had christened it in her poem *Mission Bay* ('now blue, now gray') in the previous month's issue of *The Golden Era*. The name was not officially changed from False Bay until 1915 [718].

climate, ladies would be allowed to form a military company 'as the exercise will be healthful and invigorating'. Other attractions were the location in Pacific Beach, 'the seaside suburb and college town', connected to San Diego by rail with 7 trains each way daily, with boating and fishing in Mission Bay, healthful amusement at the beach, extremely delightful surroundings and no saloons.

For all this, students would pay tuition in advance for each of three terms of 13 weeks. Tuition for Academic or Preparatory students was $16.50; for Classical, Scientific and Literary students tuition was $22.00. Board and room rent was $97.50. There were also Extras; $10.00 per month for Music, $3.00 for Voice Culture and Elocution, and $5.00 for Painting.

The announcement also noted that the college had 'several hundred thousand dollars worth of property' donated by the Pacific Beach Company and that a large amount of that had already been sold to persons interested in educational achievement and 'in the establishment of an institution that bids fair to do a great amount of public good' (and in making a profitable investment). Not only that, but the Pacific Beach Company had generously offered to increase their endowment by matching half of the price of every lot sold by the College Company [44].

The San Diego College of Letters did open on September 20 with 37 students [45]. A month later, on October 18, 1888, the *San Diego Union* reported that Samuel Sprecher, D.D., LL.D., the eminent educator, had arrived and taken up his residence at Pacific Beach. A man of scholarly appearance, with long white beard and hair, he would fill the position of counselor and President of the college [46]. A *Union* article on October 26 described the formal welcome to President Sprecher, a literary and musical treat featuring 'Margaret', a new poem by Rose Hartwick Thorpe. Seventy invited guests who left for Pacific Beach on a special train were pleasantly surprised to find the new college 'imposing in size, handsome in adornment, rich in material, thoroughly organized and manned, and having a student membership of fifty'.

Joined in the corridors of the college by the whole population of Pacific Beach, the San Diego contingent listened to a polonaise, a prayer and a welcome speech by the former mayor of Springfield, Ohio, the location of Wittenberg College, where Sprecher had been president from 1849 to 1874. Dr. Sprecher then made a lengthy reply, outlining his plans and the possibilities before San Diego, Pacific Beach and the College of Letters, followed by a piano recitation and Mrs. Thorpe's poem, 'read by that gifted lady'. 'The programme concluded with remarks by Rev. E. R. Wagner[9], the reading of "The Golden Gate", the famous poem by Madge Morris Wagner, of Pacific Beach, and presentation of a handsome field glass by Harr Wagner to Mrs. Davidson, daughter of President Sprecher'. After lunch in the dining-hall the San Diego visitors were soon on their way home [47].

The college opened for its second term on January 3, 1889. The *San Diego Union* reported that attendance was 104; 'This is considered an exceedingly large attendance, considering the fact that the college

The San Diego College of Letters in Pacific Beach, with the student body in formation in front and the faculty and administration on the porch behind them (the gentleman with the long white beard at the top of the stairs is presumably President Samuel Sprecher). The students appear to be organized by their 'military companies', the young ladies in uniforms with white stripes across the bottom and the young men with the stripes down their trousers and both wearing military-style caps (the young lady in the center of the first rank of the ladies' company, presumably their captain, also appears to be holding a sword - detail on opposite page). There are 37 students, 15 ladies and 22 men, matching the enrollment of the college's first term in the fall of 1888. (SDHC #9800)

[9] Harr Wagner's older brother, another Wittenberg graduate, and professor of German at the college.

has only been in working order about three months' [48] (and nearly three times the enrollment of the first term).

The San Diego History Center library owns a collection of documents from the early days of the San Diego College of Letters. One item in this collection is the First Annual Catalogue for the collegiate year 1888–1889 [49]. The catalogue includes a list of undergraduates with their names and home towns, and since it matches the total of 104 students reported by the *Union* was apparently produced some time after the second term had opened.

The catalogue began by describing the Object of the Institution:

> The idea of the founders was to establish an institution which would afford the highest and broadest intellectual and moral training, and by the dormitory and boarding system to establish a guardianship over students that gives in a large measure the protection of a Home.

The faculty and corps of instructors were listed. Samuel Sprecher was described as President and Counselor and also head of the department of Psychology and Ethics. In addition to his responsibilities for Natural Sciences, F. P. Davidson was listed as Superintendent of Instruction, but there was no longer a chair of Philosophy and Political Science and C. S. Sprecher was simply listed as Financial Agent. Harr Wagner (English language, literature and rhetoric), Rawlins Cadwallander (mathematics and civil engineering), E. H. Coffey (French and Spanish languages and literature), Lucia V. Woods (Latin and Greek), E. R. Wagner (German), Laura G. Riddell (elocution, oratory and reading) and Chas. L. Williams (tutor) were also named as faculty. The chair of military tactics and a music instructor were represented with an asterisk, indicating that professors in these

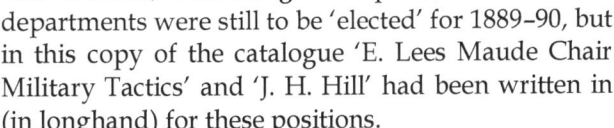

departments were still to be 'elected' for 1889–90, but in this copy of the catalogue 'E. Lees Maude Chair Military Tactics' and 'J. H. Hill' had been written in (in longhand) for these positions.

The catalogue also listed the requirements for admission. For admission to the freshman class applicants would be examined in arithmetic, algebra, plane geometry, English grammar and composition, English literature, history, physiology, and a language (Greek, German, French or Spanish; ability to translate readily at sight). An even more important prerequisite was Latin; students were expected to be able to translate at sight, both from

Latin into English and from English into Latin, and to be familiar with Caesar, Cicero and Virgil. The catalogue explained that it was the design of the founders that this should be a College of Letters, and therefore to give students not only a thorough knowledge of these classic languages but also a comprehensive view of Latin and Greek literature and history. They desired to give students a practical mastery of these languages, to show them the extent to which modern languages, especially English, are indebted to them, and that although the nations who spoke and wrote them are dead, Latin and Greek still live in their beauty and force:

> After entering the Freshman year, all students should be prepared to read the classics with literary pleasure, more interested in them as repositories of history and literature, and in the beauties and excellencies of their style, than in the mere mechanical formation of the languages.

In addition, students were required to furnish satisfactory testimonials of good moral character from reliable parties.

The catalogue went on to describe the curriculums for the Academical or Preparatory Department and for the Collegiate Department, which was divided into the Classical Course, the Scientific Course and the Literary Course. Students who took the full three-year preparatory course would take Latin in each term, progressing from grammar to Caesar, Virgil, and finally Cicero's Orations. The first year would also include arithmetic, reading, spelling and penmanship, the second would include German, Spanish or French, and the third year would include Greek (grammar and Anabasis) and mathematics (algebra and geometry). English grammar, history, geography and physiology would also be taught.

Within the Collegiate Department students taking the Classical Course would continue with Latin (Livy, Cicero, Horace, Tacitus) as well as Greek (Homer, Herodotus, historians, Crito and Apology, plays, orations) for their freshman, sophomore and junior years then concentrate on mental philosophy, logic, and political economy in their senior year. They would also take courses in classical literature, mathematics, physics, natural sciences, English, and history. Students in the Scientific Course would take the same course of Latin followed by mental philosophy, logic and political economy, but could substitute German, Spanish or French for Greek. They would also take literature, mathematics, physics, English, and history, but their natural science courses would be more extensive (inorganic and organic chemistry, crystallography, descriptive and determinative mineralogy, qualitative analysis, biology, paleontology, geology) and include laboratory work. The Scientific students would also take drawing courses (lead pencil sketching, instrumental; application of descriptive geometry and surveying, and mechanical). For Literary Course students Latin would be an elective and could be replaced by another language, but two languages must be taken. Literary students would take the same mental philosophy and political economy course as seniors. They would also take some mathematics and natural sciences but more English and literature courses.

Students were advised that they would be given the advantages of a good musical education under competent instructors, but that only those who gave evidence of being able to continue with profit to themselves would be encouraged to do so. Those who gave decided evidence to the contrary would be advised to save themselves from disappointment by devoting their energies to more profitable studies.

The list of 104 undergraduates did not differentiate between the preparatory and collegiate students, nor did it indicate which academic year the students had been admitted to. It was interesting that a number of the students appear to be related to faculty members (e.g., Charles and Eva Davidson, Frank and Harry Riddell, Samuel, James and Blanche Sprecher, Pearl Wagner and Eulalie Woods). Other students seem to be related to associates of the Pacific Beach Company, including Mabel Gassen, Della and Libba Hale, Nettie and James Pauley, Tillie and Sarah Poiser, and Oliver and Bert Reed. Altogether, 23 students were listed as residents of Pacific Beach, an additional 45 were from San Diego, 12 from Coronado and 10 from other areas of San Diego County, including El Cajon, Alpine, Oneonta, and Banner. Only 8 students were from out of state, including two from Lower California and Theodore and Edward Barnes, who were listed as coming from Madison, Nebraska, but whose family was establishing a residence across the street from the college campus. Judging by their names (Bessie, Jennie, Fannie, Mattie, Lottie, Nettie, Nellie, Tillie, Hattie, Mollie, Katie, Eulalie, along with Emma, Eva, Bertha, Rosella, Roberta, Della, Libba, Louisa, Venetia, etc.) 46 of the undergraduates were young ladies and 57 were young men (e.g., Hubert, Horace, Benjamin, Edgar, Oscar, Douglass, Oliver, Gabriel, Cyrus, Augustus, Herbert).

Although college regulations insisted that students from abroad would be required to board at the college, and there were 20 rooms for young lady students who wished to board and comfortable quarters for boys and young men in the college house and neighboring cottages, there is no indication of how many students actually were boarding students as opposed to day students. The railroad from San Diego stopped at the College Station (on Grand Avenue between today's Lamont and Kendall; two blocks from the campus) and the matron would accompany students from the San Diego station to the college station in the morning and back in the evening [50], so apparently some students did commute from San Diego. Students from Pacific Beach presumably lived at home.

The Pacific Beach Company's endowment to the college company had included not only the College Campus but also hundreds of residential lots [51] [52] [53] with the expectation that they would be sold to finance building and operations. The college company had also acquired portions of several blocks from O. J. Stough [54]. The *Union* reported on February 5, 1889, that to meet the requirements of finishing and completing payments upon the fine educational structure at Pacific Beach, the San Diego College of Letters had adopted a unique method of disposing of property; Prof. Sprecher would deliver an address and Harr Wagner would 'make his appearance for the first and last time as an auctioneer'. An advertisement for this 'Literature and Real Estate' event in the same issue indicated that the college would hold an 'Immolation Sale' of valuable real estate on Saturday, Feb. 9 [55]. On February 9, the *Union* added that lunch would be served at the college campus and all present should expect to have a good time. Special trains would be run hourly from D street station over the Pacific Beach railway [56].

The *Union* did not report on the results of this first sale but it must not have been an overwhelming success since an advertisement for 'Roasted Ox!' appeared in the February 15 *Union*. A fine young steer would be barbecued, carved and served to the Hungry Throng on Saturday, Feb. 16. Ladies would be served in the College Dining Hall and gentlemen under the shining canopy of heaven, followed by a

ROASTED OX!

Saturday, Feb. 16,

There will be

BARBECUED

A fine Young Steer on the Campus of

San Diego College of Letters

AT PACIFIC BEACH

He will be carved and served to the Hungry Throng at 12 o'clock. Ladies will be be served in the College Dining Hall, and the gentlemen under the shining canopy of heaven.

Upon the occasion there will be a continuation of the

IMMOLATION SALE

Of Real Estate by the San Diego College of Letters Company Choice Residence and Villa Sites

Will be sold to the highest bidder The sale does not affect the schedule price of this property, but is made at this time to meet the pressing needs of San Diego's Institution of Learning.

TERMS OF SALE-10 per cent cash; balance in 30 days. Title clear of mortagage and taxes.

SPECIAL EXCURSION!

Trains will leave D street Motor Depot at 9 and 10 a. m., 1:30 p. m. Fare for round trip, 25c.

continuation of the Immolation Sale. An accompanying article explained that the college had a heavy load to carry during the recent depression in business and the decline in real estate and other securities, and that its present necessities were not caused by any lack of financial management, but instead was due to the condition of affairs generally. Since the teachers gave their time for a very small remuneration, current expenses were met in full by income but there were bills payable on the building that must be met, so the college company had decided to sell a large portion of its villa sites, at a sacrifice, to the highest bidder. It was hoped that, for the sake of education in the West, there would be a large crowd at the sale and Harr Wagner had again volunteered his services as auctioneer. A fine ox had been donated and arrangements had been completed that would tend to make the day a successful one in the annals of the city [57][10]. The February 16 *Union* added that L. H. Warrington, an expert, had been secured to superintend the affair and the public would be sure of obtaining a juicy slice of well-roasted ox [58].

The barbecue did not take place on February 16 but was postponed and rescheduled for the following week, February 23, possibly because the weather report called for continued cool weather and local rain, not the promised 'shining canopy of heaven'. On February 23, the *Union* explained that while the cornerstone had been laid a year ago and $50,000 in improvements had been made and every room was occupied, the institution was in debt and there were bills

---

[10] A very different point of view was offered by Samuel Storey, a member of the British parliament and a newspaper publisher himself, who was visiting San Diego and happened to see the Roasted Ox! advertisement in the *Union*. Something about the ad so incensed him that he had it reproduced in its entirety in his book *To the Golden Land: Sketches of a Trip to Southern California* 'if not in letters quite as large as the original, still so that it may catch men's eye', and commented 'Ye gods! If a College of Letters must rear its front sacred to Truth and Learning by miserable lying tradepuffing like this, shall not Wisdom hide her head! I am thankful to say little land was sold, despite the Roasted Ox; perhaps because of him, for doubtless he was tough and burnt or underdone. I said – lying. Why, I visited (not on sale day) this "most lovely and classical suburb of San Diego." A bare, treeless slope of clay and sand, a wooden hotel untenanted, a few commonplace wooden dwellings scattered here and there; no avenues, no gardens, no cliff, no point or place of interest made by man or left by God save the yellow sea-sands and the rolling sea. Hear you, how it roars at your lies! Oh, Fathers of the College of Letters, Heaven forgive you! No one else can. A fine, truth-telling set of pupils you'll rear in your college if ever you get it. Hear a plain man: San Diego may get along without learning; it can't get along at all without men who speak the modest truth. Barbecue no more oxen, my friends; tell no more – tarradiddles.' (Storey represented Sunderland, a coal and shipbuilding center on the North Sea near Newcastle, presumably well-endowed with points and places of interest made by man or left by God) [717].

payable that must be met at once, so the Immolation Sale of property had been ordered. The cadets would be on parade on the campus, the buildings would be open to visitors, and ladies would be entertained at noon in the college dining room [59]. This time the *Union* did report the outcome in their February 24 issue. The well-advertised barbecue and immolation sale drew a large crowd; most people went out on the 9 and 10 o'clock trains, and those who went later swelled the throng to considerably over 800. They enjoyed themselves about the college buildings or at the beach until noon time, when they were all invited to partake of the roast ox, which had been cooked to a turn over the coals of an immense fire on the college campus. After lunch Harr Wagner conducted the auction which lasted about an hour, during which time 25 lots were disposed of at an average price of $100 [60].

Another continuation of the Immolation Sale was scheduled for March 9, this time headlined by a Fish Fry! [61], but apparently the auctions of lots did not raise sufficient capital and on April 9, 1889, the *San Diego Union* announced that the college company would issue first mortgage bonds covering campus improvements and other real estate to liquidate the present indebtedness and push improvements to completion before the opening of the fall term. The bonds would be placed by active personal canvass among people who are interested in Christian, yet non-sectarian, higher education for men and women on this coast. The purchasers of the bonds would derive a reasonable interest on the money and at the same time be instrumental in aiding a broad and liberal educational institution [62].

The 'present indebtedness' and 'bills payable that must be met at once' became more urgent on April 28, 1889, when the *Union* reported that James W. Reid had begun suit against the San Diego College Company for $3,721 claimed to be due for drawing plans for and superintending the construction of the buildings at Pacific Beach [63]. A few weeks later the college became involved in a different kind of difficulty when the *Union* cited a report in an out-of-town newspaper to the effect that Mrs. Sprecher, the 'somewhat younger' and 'very popular' wife of Prof. Sprecher[11], had left town as a result of 'undue familiarity with the youths of the college'. Major Birdsall, a drill instructor at the Pacific Beach college, was said to be her 'especial

---

[11] C. S. Sprecher, 43, whose first wife had died the previous year, had married Eunice Stacey, age 16, in December 1888. Miss Eunice Stacey had been pianist at the Pacific Beach Sunday School [616] and 'J. S., Estelle and Eunice Stacy' were among the nine original members of the Pacific Beach Presbyterian Church, founded by Rev. Sprecher in 1888 [721].

Originally Pacific Beach

favorite' and was charged with 'accompanying her a certain distance on her journey'. The *Union* assigned one of its representatives to inquire into the matter 'and the result is such as to contradict entirely that version of a very ordinary circumstance', which was that Mrs. Sprecher was on a visit to her parents in Stockton. 'Much sympathy is expressed in the community on behalf of Professor and Mrs. Sprecher, who have been so unjustly dragged into such unpleasant notoriety' [64].

Actually, whatever Major Birdsall's role may have been, Mrs. Sprecher's visit to Stockton turned out to be a one-way trip. On October 16, 1889, she wrote Sprecher from Stockton that he must certainly know by then that she would never live with him again and that when a woman cannot and will not live with a man he should 'release' her; apply for a divorce or 'I certainly shall'. This note became Exhibit A in his divorce complaint [65], which alleged that Mrs. Sprecher had willfully absented herself from his home with intent to desert and had refused and still refuses to return thereto. The evidence included testimony from Sprecher himself and from Thomas Woods, Harr Wagner, Frank Colwell and E. R. Wagner, colleagues, fellow church-goers and neighbors who had been in a position to witness his interactions with Mrs. Sprecher. These middle-aged men substantiated Sprecher's testimony that he had been a kind and considerate husband, had not ill-used Mrs. Sprecher and had given her no reason to leave him. E. R. Wagner, for example, testified that the couple lived in the suite adjoining his residence in sleeping room 22 at the College of Letters, that he had breakfast with them every morning and was with them frequently, that they had the best furnished suite of rooms of anyone at the college, that he never saw Mr. Sprecher treat Mrs. Sprecher in an unkind or harsh manner and knew of no reason why she should have left him [66]. There was no mention of Major Birdsall or of undue familiarity with youths of the college or that she was a teenage girl and he was nearly three times her age. Since there were no children or community property to be considered and Mrs. Sprecher did not appear to contest the allegations the marriage was dissolved in Superior Court on December 1, 1890; the December 3, 1890, *San Diego Union* reported that C. A. Sprecher [sic] had been granted a divorce from his wife, Eunice Sprecher, whom he married at Pacific Beach a short time ago, on the ground of desertion [67].

San Diego College of Letters students published a student newspaper, *The College Rambler*. The History Center collection includes the June 12, 1889, issue, the final issue of the college's first year. It includes an editorial: 'To you fellow students whose years work is so nearly ended, it extends congratulations if your record has been good, its sympathy, if ill. You, like it, have been making history. You as pioneer students have helped to found a College; to rear an institution of higher learning here in this bright Sunland' [50]. The History Center collection also has a blank report card showing the 'branches of study' offered at the college.

The First Annual Commencement Week began on June 18, 1889, with a 'contest for supremacy' between the two literary societies of the college, the Philomathean and the Palladian, before a standing-room-only audience at the Louis Opera House in San Diego. The *Union* reported that following the salutory a young lady from the Palladian Society read an essay on 'The Pleasures of Work' after which an essay on 'Oklahoma' read by her counterpart from the Philomathean Society 'divided the honors with her fair contestant'. An orator from the Palladian Society 'proved himself an eloquent advocate of the Nicaraguan Canal' while his Palladian Society opponent spoke eloquently upon 'Our Military Defenses', 'leaving the audience in doubt upon whom to bestow the honor of oratorical ability'. The principal event of the evening was a debate on the question 'War is Never Justifiable', with the Palladian representative taking the affirmative and the Philomathean 'striking out right and left to overcome his opponent's arguments'. After the valedictory and an address in Latin Dr. Sprecher conferred the college's first degree, a Master of Arts, as a special honor for attainments in scientific research to Rawlins Cadwallander, a former student of Williams University [68].

The ceremonies on June 19 were held at the College Assembly Hall where the Hon. J. F. Kinney, of Nebraska, spoke on the subject of The Benefits of Higher Collegiate Education. His remarks, reprinted in full in the *San Diego Union* [69] and *The Golden Era* [70], emphasized the importance of a liberal education to a career in the three leading professions (ministers, lawyers and physicians), and to 'active business pursuits'. Although his address seemed to be intended more for the 'young men' in his audience, he did advise them that:

> You have as competitors in your college course these young ladies, who, by reason of an enlightened and more liberal sentiment, are now permitted to enter college and contest for the honors of the class.

And, addressing the young ladies of the college:

> The door which was so long closed against college competition in the same classes with gentlemen has been thrown wide open. This examination has shown that in your class work you are the peers of the sterner sex. In some of the branches you have excelled the gentlemen,

and noted that women have been allowed to practice law and recently even the medical profession, 'peculiarly adapted to her tender susceptibilities and subtle perceptions'. He also touched on another feature connected with the student's life which should not be lost sight of:

> Young men are too often inclined to vice. How many have fallen into bad habits in our villages and cities, when, if they had been at college, would have been saved. This moral training at the most interesting, and I will add dangerous time of life, is quite as important as the knowledge obtained from books.

He concluded that:

> It does not task the imagination to predict that the time is not far distant when San Diego College of Letters will take rank among the leading institutions of learning in the country. It will become the fostering mother of many sons and daughters, whose education will add dignity to human nature, strength to the government, happiness to society, and Christianity to the world.

After a lunch served at the college the afternoon was devoted to an elocutionary contest, won by Miss Eula Woods who was awarded a handsome gold medal for her presentation of 'High Tide'. The second day's events were concluded with a lecture on education by Rev. McDaniel.

The final day of the commencement week on June 20 began with Class Day Exercises in which students presented a History of the School Year and Class Prophecy in addition to poems and essays. After a final address by President Sprecher and a few more words from Judge Kinney all were invited to the campus where they were amused by a foot race and a game of base ball between the college boys and the Clarkes of San Diego. The *Union* reported that the ball game was 'too one sided to be interesting' with the college boys winning 28 to 5 [71].

The September 1889 issue of *The Golden Era* announced that the second year's work had begun with many new patrons and a large number of the former students and additions to the faculty including Rev. L. Groh (a major benefactor) and Rawlins Cadwallander, A.M. (the recipient of the college's first degree in June)[12]. On the other hand, the article noted that while the founders had been given a land endowment that was supposed to be sufficient to erect the buildings, real estate activity had ceased and they were left with a building half finished, salaries unpaid and debts accruing through the greatest depression Southern California ever knew [72].

---

[12] One of the new students was Olive Hoff, sister of the J. D. Hoff Asbestos Company founder. The August 29, 1889, *Union* noted that Mr. Hoff of Elsinore, father of J. D. Hoff of the asbestos works, has taken his abode in one of the cottages just east of the college for the purpose of placing his daughter in school [15].

Early plans for the San Diego College of Letters had envisioned a complex of buildings filling the 16-acre campus. When the college first opened in 1888 only the East Building, or Girls' Hall, had been built on a gradual slope facing to the southeast and overlooking the southeast corner of the campus. On August 25, 1889, the *Union* reported arrangements for the erection of the Main Building, noting that the bills were to be sent to O. J. Stough who had generously come to the front in providing for the needs of the institution [73]. The September 13 *Union* reported that lumber would go out that day for the construction of the O. J. Stough Hall [74]. The new building would be situated to the west of the existing building in a more central location aligned with and overlooking College (now Garnet) Avenue.

The second term opened on January 2, 1890. An article in the *Union* on January 5 reported that Rev. L. Groh had recently been added to the board of directors and had brought financial aid in a most generous and philanthropic manner, and although the college was in a fairly prosperous condition the students needed a gymnasium, a laboratory and a boys' dormitory, and reference books [75].

Stough Hall was opened on January 9, 1890, with a program of music and speech making. The January 10 *Union* reported that a special train was run from the city with several carloads of people. The College buildings were brilliantly lighted and the avenue from the station to the buildings illuminated with rows of Chinese lanterns on either side. Stough Hall was a 'neat and substantial brick edifice' with a large audience room and several 'convenient and commodious' recitation and lecture rooms. Prof. Harr Wagner acknowledged the financial assistance of Stough, the Pacific Beach Company, Rev. Groh and others. The speeches focused on the value of small and private colleges and emphasized the importance of education; for individual happiness, as training for professions such as the law and journalism, for the greatness of the country [76].

Throughout the 1889–1890 academic year the public was entertained with a series of elocution contests and musical recitals featuring students at the college. The January 17, 1890, *Union* reviewed one exercise held in the chapel of the new Stough Hall which 'called out a large attendance from the city beside the residents of the suburb itself'. The three coach loads of people taking the 7:30 train enjoyed a 'really delectable treat' in which Miss Pearl Wagner won the first prize of $10 in gold for her elocutionary performance of 'A Scene from Leah', Miss Olive Hoff won second prize, Webster's unabridged dictionary, for reciting 'Count Canderpiro's Standard' and Miss Ida Lowe was third and received Plutarch's 'Lives' for a recitation of 'Miss Melissa on Boys' [77].

The 1890 commencement week began on June 17 with what the *Union* now called 'the annual elocution contest' at Louis' Opera house and which promised to be especially interesting in as much as the pupils had all been in previous contests. The committee of judges was late in arriving and was filled out by members of the audience. Miss Olive Hoff was first up with a most difficult part to portray in Act IV, Scene 1 of 'King John' but the *Union* reported that 'her dramatic fervor was admirable and the young contestant's personal attractions added greatly to the enjoyment of the selection'. Miss Venetia Lyons was also very winning in 'Mollie' and Miss Ida Lowe's elastic voice passed without a quaver between nasal twang and bass in 'Aunt Patience's Doughnuts' but the gold medal again went to 14-year-old Miss Pearl Wagner, beautiful in her classic drapery, her gestures intensely dramatic and her clear voice grandly strong in the final portion of her selection, 'Perdita'. Miss Wagner's cause may have been assisted by the fact that 'Perdita' had been 'adopted by Mrs. Harr Wagner (Madge Morris), who added the last portion' [78]. The *Union* did not need to add that Madge Morris Wagner, the then-famous writer, poet and wife of the college secretary, was Pearl's mother.

The closing exercises were held in Stough Hall on June 19 and the *Union* reported that about 100 persons took the Pacific Beach motor to the splendidly situated seaside suburb. The orator of the day was Judge Mossholder, who spoke on the theme of 'A college education is the best capital with which to begin life'. The speech, which was quoted at length in the *Union*, emphasized the unwritten knowledge which is acquired by observation, experience and the action of the mind, an 'intense, all pervading, diffusive intelligence which makes Americans stand pre-eminently above all other nations in all that goes to make up the civilization of the nineteenth century' [79].

Judge Mossholder's oration was followed by class day exercises which included Miss Lulo Thorpe reading 'The Springtime', 'her delicate beauty being suggestive of the outlines of her world famous mother, Rose Hartwick Thorpe'. Miss Laura Gearn claimed that the faculty 'were simply perfect' and then 'proceeded to touch up the vanities, shortcomings and preferences of her class-mates . . . Miss Gearn was a charming picture of dark-eyed roguishness as she made her shots tell'. There were college songs, an original poem by Miss Eula Woods, a gold medal to Miss Alice Heathe for the student making the most progress in Prof. Harr Wagner's literary class, a piano duo, a tour of the art department, and a musical contest in which Miss Olive Hoff took first gold medal for piano playing and Miss Jacqueline Oliver was awarded the gold medal in vocal music.

After lunch the boys adjourned to the campus for their games.

The rest of the company went to the beach to watch a game of ball between the college club and the Prentices of San Diego. The Prentices won 11 to 5 and the feature of the game was the excellent catching by Nass Corallis, pitching by Jack Edwards and the second base work by C. N. Louis of the Prentices.

During the summer of 1890 a number of changes were made in the administration and corporate structure of the college. The July issue of *The Golden Era* announced that Harr Wagner, C. S. Sprecher and F. P. Davidson, the principal stockholders of the college company, had 'transferred their interest to eastern parties', that Davidson would represent Rev. L. Groh (evidently he was the eastern party) at the college, and that Wagner and Sprecher had both resigned the faculty and would now devote their time to the magazine [80][13]. The July 13 *Union* reported 'arrangements which lift the burdensome debt from that young but vigorous institution' and 'still other changes which Prof. F. P. Davidson has in contemplation now that he has assumed supervision of affairs'. An eminent professor of mathematics would be engaged and other educators secured to fill the vacant chairs. Rev. L. Groh would make the college his home as soon as practicable. C. R. Orcutt's *West American Scientist* would be made a college paper. Samuel Sprecher would remain as president of the college [81]. The July 1890 issue of *The Great Southwest* added that it was understood the Rev. Groh would settle up the old debts of the college and 'hence the institution is now on a much better basis than heretofore and doubtless it will do still better work' [82].

Charles R. Orcutt was an eccentric young naturalist based in San Diego who spent much of his time on collecting expeditions in the region, particularly in Baja California. In 1884, when he was only 20 years old, Orcutt began publishing *The West American Scientist*, 'A popular monthly review and record for the Pacific Coast' as a way to present his discoveries. The August 1890 issue included 'The San Diego College of Letters, Pacific Beach, Calif.' on its masthead and an editorial announced that the journal was becoming 'in a measure' the representative of the scientific department of the San Diego College of

---

[13] C. S. Sprecher may actually have cut ties with the college earlier. In testimony for the 1890 divorce case against his wife Eunice, he indicated that after she left him she said she would come back if he would leave San Diego. Sprecher testified that he then 'made all arrangements, business arrangements, to change my location, selling out and everything of that sort, and went to Stockton to have her come with me and live elsewhere, and she had changed her mind.' Although Sprecher's testimony contained some obvious errors with dates, the sequence of events suggested that these actions must have taken place during the summer of 1889.

Letters. His large accumulation of specimens, which he referred to as the C. R. Orcutt Miscellaneous Collections, 'doubtless the most complete representation of the fauna and flora, the geology and the mineral wealth of Southern and Lower California that is in existence', were being arranged in Stough hall and would eventually be open to the public and students [83][14].

The editorial also announced that *The West American Scientist* would now include a supplement devoted to literary and educational matters, published in the interest of the students of the college in place of the usual college journal. *Literary and Educational Supplement, No. 1*, Edited by the Students and Faculty of the San Diego College of Letters, included a poem by Rose Hartwick Thorpe, two poems by Eulalie Powers Woods, one of the 'young ladies' of the college, 'Dawnings' and 'Pacific Beach', and a story by Lulo M. Thorpe called 'The Child of the Alamo'. A section called 'At Home, Locals and Personals', the student society column, included accounts of playing games and dancing on the green lawn in the moonlight at Miss Lulo Thorpe's home, Misses Mabel and Evangeline doing the honors at Mrs. Rowe's 'cottage by the sea', and the boys treating the girls to an ice cream social in Stough Hall ('well we are waiting for another').

These items underscore the extent to which the college and the community of Pacific Beach (and *The Golden Era*) were interconnected and even interrelated during these times. Lulo was the daughter of the 'famous authoress Rose Hartwick Thorpe' that the college was 'fortunate in having for a near neighbor' and who often published in *The Golden Era*. Eulalie was the daughter of Mrs. Woods 'our highly successful instructor in languages' who was 'resting at her home during the summer' (or at least trying to rest, since 'still another pleasant evening was later enjoyed at Miss Eulalie Woods's pulling taffy and having a good time generally'). Mr. T. E. Woods was *The Golden Era*'s solicitor and occasional contributor to its pages. Miss Mary Cogswell, who 'had a visitor', was the daughter of early Pacific Beach resident and dentist Thomas Cogswell. Mrs. Thresher and her bright daughter, Marian, were 'building them a cottage' near the college (Mrs. Isabella A. Thresher was a writer and contributor to *The Golden Era*). California's favorite Madge Morris, though frail in health

---

[14] In fact, the June 7, 1890, *Union* reported that after a musical soiree at the College of Letters the audience was invited on a tour of Stough Hall which included a room containing the Orcutt collection of ornithological and geological specimens, after which they did ample justice to a bountiful supply of substantial refreshments while being attended by the bright little lads and ladies of the school [697].

at times, never wearies with the pen. Miss Nettie Pauly is spending her vacation with her uncle in Los Angeles (Charles Pauly was president of the Pacific Beach Company). Mrs. Judge Kinney intends to send her young grand daughter to the college (Hon. J. F. Kinney was 1889 commencement speaker and now San Diego resident). Miss Ida Lowe was stenographer for the Pacific Beach Company.

The names of Wagner, Thorpe, Rowe, Groh, Thresher, Davidson, Sprecher, Cogswell, Woods, Barnes, Harr Wagner's sister Jennie Havice, and of course Stough are on the list of early purchasers of lots from the Pacific Beach Company. The Wagners, Thorpes, Rowes, Threshers, and Cogswells were among the few permanent residents of Pacific Beach in 1890.

The 'At Home' column also contained actual news items related to Pacific Beach. The Pacific Beach Hotel changed hands and Mr. McKay is the new proprietor. Harr Wagner and C. S. Sprecher would give their attention to the editing of the *Golden Era Magazine*, 'the oldest and most popular journal on the Coast'. Prof. Wagner was a candidate for County Superintendent of Public Schools and 'He would make an excellent officer' (he would, and did). Messrs. Frey, Sprecher and Barbours (students) under the direction of Mr. Thorpe, have erected commodious dressing rooms, wharf, etc., at the foot of Tenth street on the bay (the origin of the 'plunge' which stood for decades at the foot of what is now Kendall Street).

The *Literary and Educational Supplement No. 2* appeared in the September 1890 issue of *The West American Scientist*. The 'At Home, Locals and Personals' column included more student gossip. The boys had waxed the floors for dancing at Mr. Grolis' empty cottage where after a little dance they ate watermelon and played blindman's bluff. Miss Mary Cogswell, one of the resident students, gave a delightful ice cream party. Miss Laura Gearn couldn't wait for school to begin so she had been visiting Miss Pearl Wagner during vacation and enjoyed glorious fun, boating, swimming and driving 'in spite of the fact that she did get her nose freckled'. The 'Among the Wits, In Lighter Vein' section included the observations that 'The summer girl of southern California is perennial an all the year round girl' and 'Love making is a sigh-ence. (Not taught in this institution.)' [84].

The *Literary and Educational Supplement No. 3* in the December 1890 issue of *The West American Scientist* explained that *The West American Scientist* was published at San Diego College of Letters, Pacific Beach, California and was divided into two departments, a scientific, and a literary and miscellaneous. The 'At Home, Locals and Personals' column mentioned field trips to Old Town, and to the beach and the La Jolla Caves at low tide. A section titled 'College of Letters' provided a list of names of the current faculty and student body. The nine faculty members ranged from the president, Samuel Sprecher, to three assistant instructors. The other five faculty members and their academic departments were F. P. Davidson, Natural Sciences, Lucia Powers Woods, Languages – Ancient and Modern, Thomas Penfield, Mathematics, Mary Edith Gover, Art and English, and Carl Vandal, Music – Violin, Piano, Vocal.

The list of students included 52 names, 5 of whom were presumably related to faculty or officials of the college; Charles Davidson, James Sprecher, Pearl Wagner and Eulalie and Percival Woods. Three of the names in the list of students were also the assistant instructors included in the faculty list; E. N. Groh, Asst. Instructor of Latin, and Katie Woodford and Lita Kidwell, Asst. Insts. Preparatory. The student listing included their home towns and ten students were residents of Pacific Beach; Mary Cogswell, Charles Davidson, Evangeline and Mabel Rowe, Lulo May Thorpe, Marian Thresher, Pearl Wagner, Maud Wescott and the Woods. Twenty-three of the remaining students were residents of San Diego (including one from La Jolla), there were two each from Coronado and Valley Center, and one each from National City and El Cajon. Only seven students were from out of state, including two from Ireland and one from Lower California. The majority of the students, 28, were young ladies (e.g., Nellie, Addie, Bessie, Fannie, Nettie, Minnie, Eulalie), while 20 were young men (Theodore, Lewis, Horace, Oliver, Samuel, Vernon, Percival, etc.) [85].

The 1890-1891 academic year apparently began normally; the *San Diego Union* mentioned on October 31, 1890, that the fifty students were adding swimming to their accomplishments 'without distinctions of sex or class'. The college had furnished material for a six-room bath house and fifty-foot pier and the students had accomplished the building satisfactorily 'in a little sand beach cove on Mission Bay' and two afternoons a week pupils and faculty had their swimming lessons. They also had a sail boat and were learning to dive fearlessly [86].

On November 16 the *Union* reported that all but a few of the 53 students were regular boarders, and that four young women were preparing themselves to be teachers by taking the new Normal course [87]. On December 21 the news was that the term had closed and all but two or three students from the East had dispersed to their homes for the holidays [88]. On Sunday, January 4, 1891, the *Union* reported that when the college reopened on Monday there would be three new students from Lower California [89].

If the college did reopen in 1891 it is not clear whether or for how long it actually held classes. The January 1891 issue of *The West*

American Scientist no longer mentioned the San Diego College of Letters on its masthead and did not include a Literary and Educational Supplement; although Orcutt continued to publish the journal intermittently until 1919 the brief association with the college had ended. The March 5 *Union* reported that Captain and Mrs. Woods had moved into and taken charge of the College of Letters. There was no explanation for why this was necessary but the report explained that Mrs. Woods had been a teacher there for some time and was a lady of recognized ability and affairs at the college would be in good hands [90]. However, there was no further news about the college and no reports in the local media of elocution contests or commencement exercises for the remainder of the 1891 academic year.

The college campus did make news again when the Southwest Summer Training school was held in Pacific Beach from June 22 to July 17, 1891 [91]. Harr Wagner had won election as County Superintendent of Schools in 1890 and when his term began in 1891 he took the opportunity to introduce progressive methods into public school administration. One change Wagner hoped to make was to encourage school teachers to engage in continuing education rather than returning to their homes for a summer vacation. He arranged for the use of the San Diego College of Letters buildings (and many of the faculty, including Laura Riddell, F. P. Davidson, himself and his brother E. R. Wagner) and invited David Starr Jordan, a well-known marine scientist and president-elect of Stanford University (which was to open in the fall of 1891), to visit and present a lecture. Dr. Jordan did appear and spoke to the class after an exploring trip to La Jolla [92].

The *Union* again alluded to trouble at the college when it reported on July 23, 1891, that County Superintendent of Schools Harr Wagner had received a telegram from Vinton Busey stating that he would accept the presidency of the College of Letters to be opened at Pacific Beach. The *Union* article mentioned that Prof. Busey was an intimate friend of President Jordan of Leland Stanford University [93]. On August 18 the *Union* reported that Prof. Vinton Busby of the Indiana state university (presumably the same person) had actually arrived in the city the previous evening to make final arrangements to reopen the College of Letters at Pacific Beach [94].

However, these final arrangements apparently fell through and the college never reopened. The Pacific Beach Company had endowed the San Diego College Company with hundreds of residential lots throughout Pacific Beach that the college company had expected to sell to raise capital for development and operations but the end of the Great Boom and the ensuing depression in the real estate market had made this strategy untenable. The college company tried other ways to monetize the real estate endowment, including mortgaging lots to secure loans (from Rev. Groh) and placing other property, including the college campus itself, in trust to R. A. Thomas, J. E. Fishburn and William Collier of the First National Bank, as security for payment of bonds. Despite the capital raised by the sale of these bonds (the majority of which were purchased by O. J. Stough) the debts continued to be unpaid.

On March 28, 1891, architect James W. Reid's suit over the debt he was owed for design and construction of the first college building had been decided in Reid's favor. The sheriff was unable to recover sufficient personal property from the college to satisfy the judgment so the court directed the sheriff to seize the real estate and premises of the college company. The college campus was subsequently sold at auction at the court house door at 2 PM on October 19, 1891, to D. C. Reed, the highest bidder, for $3212.78. Reed assigned the Certificate of Sale to O. J. Stough and Stough received the deed for the college campus from the sheriff on July 23, 1892 [95].

On the same day that their campus was sold at the court house door, San Diego College Company directors Wagner, Sprecher and Davidson filed a petition authorizing proper insolvency proceedings, stating that the college had 'become involved in debts and liabilities to such an extent that under the present financial depression it is unable to meet its obligations'[15]. Their Voluntary Petition by Debtor listed debts and liabilities of $37,304.60, ranging from $10,379 cash owed Rev. L. Groh to $5.70 owed F. N. Hamilton on an open account for supplies (and a claim by the San Diego Union Company for $62.00 for advertising including "Auction Sale of Land", "Barbecue Ad", "Postponement of Barbecue", and "A Fish Fry"). As assets they listed real estate valued at $47,000, including the 'lands known as college campus with buildings thereon', although $32,500 of that had already been pledged to secure payment on loans and bonds. Three Bordman & Gray pianos valued at $1,200, less $800 balance due, were listed as personal property [96]. According to the *Union*, it was generally understood that O. J. Stough would 'buy up the claims and put the college on its feet' [97].

Although the funds recovered from the sale of the campus had apparently satisfied the debt to Reid, the campus property now owned

---

[15] Also on October 19, 1891, the *San Diego Union* reported that Harr Wagner had moved his family and household goods from Pacific Beach to the corner of Walnut and Albatross Streets in Florence Heights and that Mr. Havice (Wagner's brother-in-law) had moved into the house vacated by Mr. Wagner [727].

by Stough was still among the properties subject to the mortgage securing payment of bonds, the majority of which were owned by Stough himself. The mortgage was foreclosed on December 22, 1893, and all the mortgaged property except the campus was auctioned at the courthouse door on May 21, 1894. One bidder won 4 lots for a bid of $1.90 [98], another won 113 lots for $136.50 [99].

Since this first sale of lots did not realize enough to pay the interest on the bonds the campus property was again auctioned at the courthouse door on August 1, 1894. At this auction the attorneys for the trustees 'on their own responsibility and not for their clients' submitted the winning bid for $3000 but then refused to complete the sale, claiming a technicality. This led to further legal actions, complicated by the fact that Stough was both the owner of the foreclosed property and of the majority of the bonds the mortgage on the property was intended to secure, that were not resolved until a court affirmed the original order of sale on February 25, 1896 [100]. The campus property was then sold once more at the courthouse door to Thomas J. B. Rhoads, for $4,000 on April 28, 1896 [101].

In 1897 the college campus was mentioned as a possible site to attract a new State Normal School to San Diego. The December 23, 1896, *Evening Tribune* reported that an effort was being made to secure the Pacific Beach College property for the Normal School and that the people of Pacific Beach had subscribed liberally for this purpose [102]. A Normal School was established in San Diego in March 1897 but the Board of Trustees selected a site in University Heights (offered by the College Hill Land Association), even after being taken by a special train to look over the buildings in Pacific Beach [103][16].

On March 2, 1898, the *San Diego Union* reported that the residents of Pacific Beach had purchased the college buildings and would establish an institution of learning there. According to the *Union*, residents had organized the Pacific Beach College company and elected officers and a board of directors. The new college would have a full corps of teachers and 'it is intended to utilize the fine buildings to their full capacity' [104]. On March 15, 1898, Rhoads deeded the campus to 'William L. Johnston as trustee for Pacific Beach College' [105]. An article in the *San Diego Union* for July 10, 1898, reported that extensive alterations were being made to the college buildings by the company that had been formed to conduct a military school there. The

---

[16] The San Diego Normal School in University Heights opened in 1899. Upgraded to San Diego State College, the campus was moved to Montezuma Mesa in 1931 where it is now (2013) San Diego State University.

alterations included a tower on the south end of the building and a new front 200 feet long at the north end 'after the Spanish style of architecture' [106].

Although different authorities including the *San Diego Union*, the county recorder's office and the county Lot Books had described the Pacific Beach College company as owner of the college campus, the San Diego History Center does not have any record of such a company being incorporated and in subsequent transactions involving the college campus Rev. Johnston appears to be acting as an individual owner, not as a trustee. For example, on July 17, 1898, William L. Johnson [sic] was denied a reduction of assessments from $55 to $40 per acre and from $2,500 to $1,000 for improvements on the Pacific Beach college campus [107]. On October 21, 1898, the news in the *Union* was that Rev. Johnston had offered the Pacific Beach College as a home for 'superannuated members of the Presbyterian clergy' [108], although apparently nothing came of this offer[17]. When the College Campus property was eventually sold to the Folsom Bros. Co. in 1905 the deed specified the grantor as William L. Johnston and Ida F. Johnston, husband and wife; there was no mention of 'trustee' or 'Pacific Beach College' [109].

The May 14, 1899, *Union* reported that a stained glass window, eight feet in diameter, was being made in honor of Mrs. Catherine Spear, a former Pacific Beach resident who had recently died, and would be placed over the altar in the chapel of the college building in Pacific Beach [110]. On June 27, the *Union* reported that a handsome set of furniture for one of the rooms of the Pacific Beach college had been donated by D. F. Garrettson, cashier of the First National Bank, for and on behalf of that institution [111]. Meanwhile, Pacific Beach College was the site of the Y. M. C. A. Camp and Summer School, with the best of hotel and restaurant fare, rooms, cottages, sail and row boats, tennis and bathing accommodations, according to advertisements in the *San Diego Union* in August 1899 [112].

By 1901 the effort to re-introduce an educational mission to the former college had apparently failed and the buildings were being used as lodging and a community meeting place. The San Diego City Directory for 1901 had a listing for 'College Inn (The), Pacific Beach, W.

---

[17] Johnston was 'Stated Supply' or acting pastor of the Pacific Beach Presbyterian Church, located across the street from the College Campus. The church had been founded in 1888 by Rev. C. S. Sprecher who was also the first Stated Supply. The Presbyterian Ministerial Directory for 1898 included 'Pres. San Diego C. of Letters, Cal., 98 – ' among Rev. Johnston's titles [615].

Johnstone [sic], secy, and mgr' [113]. The local newspapers included weekly columns from suburban communities like Pacific Beach and between 1901 and 1904 the College Inn was a regular item in these reports, such as 'The College Inn has quite a number of eastern people enjoying its hospitality among them being . . .' [114] or 'Mr. and Mrs. Sewel of Los Angeles spent last week at the College Inn' [115]. According to the News and Notes in the March 14, 1903, *Tribune* the College Inn was to be moved to La Jolla in the near future [116] but the *Tribune* on March 16 reported that the deal for the purchase of the College Inn at Pacific Beach and its removal to La Jolla was 'based on slight foundation and the scheme, such as it was, has fallen through for lack of capital' [117].

Stough Hall was the site of dances and other celebrations. The January 9, 1904, *San Diego Union* reported that 'The first dance of the new year at Stough hall, under the auspices of the Pacific Beach club, eclipsed any of its predecessors in the number of the participants; in brilliance of costumes, and in the festive spirit shown by all' [118]. It also appears that the close relationship between the college and the Presbyterian Church had continued; the January 5, 1904, *Evening Tribune* reported that Mr. Clark, the new Presbyterian minister, was living with his family at the College Inn [119].

O. J. Stough had sold his extensive holdings in Pacific Beach to the Folsom Bros. Co. in November 1903 (the *Union* headline read 'Pacific Beach Has Changed Owners') [120]. On April 12, 1904, Folsom Bros. extended their control of Pacific Beach by agreeing with Rev. Johnston to rent the college campus, together with buildings and improvements, 'also the lower floor of the dormitory known as College Inn' [121]. As detailed in the *San Diego Union*, the rental was $50 a month, but the Folsoms were also required to spend a like amount in improving and repairing the grounds and buildings. The agreement included the option of a second year's rental at $100 a month, or the option to purchase the property for $15,000.

The Folsom Bros. Co. wasted little time making the former college campus a focus of their plans to revitalize the Pacific Beach real estate market. One idea was a contest to choose a new name for the building. The *Evening Tribune* reported on July 6, 1904, that 'After five days' careful consideration of over 1,200 names submitted for their new hotel at Pacific Beach, Folsom Bros. & Co. wish to announce that the name finally selected is "Hotel Balboa"' (the lucky winner, the first to suggest 'Balboa', received his choice of a $100 lot in Pacific Beach or $100 in gold; nine other contestants whose entries also included the word 'Balboa' were eligible to receive a $20 credit on any Pacific Beach lot providing the selection was made within thirty days) [122].

1906 Postcard of the Hotel Balboa in Pacific Beach. Stough Hall is at left and the original college building at right. In 1906, rows of lemon trees are still being cultivated in the foreground, in block 215.

When their lease expired in April 1905 the Folsom Bros. Co. did exercise their option to purchase the college campus and initiated a campaign to convert the premises into a first class resort. The May 4, 1905, *San Diego Union* noted that the old college building erected in 1887, which had been idle for a number of years, was being fitted up as a hotel and lodging house [123]. A year later, on May 4, 1906, the *Union* reported that the Hotel Balboa was again undergoing alterations and repairs that added greatly to its list of attractions; 'Larger palms in the ball room and ping-pong room, and several exterior cozy corners are among the latest features' [124]. In 1907 the hotel grounds were landscaped and the surrounding streets were graded and 'sidewalked' and lined with the palm trees which exist to this day [125].

Despite the efforts of the Folsom Bros. Co. the Hotel Balboa was not a success and within a few years the college campus was returned to its original educational purpose, this time as a military academy. On November 23, 1910, Col. Thomas A. Davis started the San Diego Army and Navy Academy in the Hotel Balboa buildings and in the early 1920s he purchased the College Campus property, most of Acre Lot 64, the former Barnes property north of the campus, and much of Blocks 183 and 202, across Jewell Street to the west. In the late 1920s the Army and Navy Academy added an auditorium building to the west of Stough Hall and rows of enormous reinforced concrete barracks along Lamont and Emerald Streets.

During the Great Depression in the 1930s the San Diego Army and Navy Academy faced the problem the college company had experienced nearly fifty years earlier; debts from building projects that could not be repaid. In 1936 lenders foreclosed on the campus property and Davis relocated to Carlsbad (where the Army and Navy Academy is still in operation today). The property was sold to Brown Military Academy, which extended the educational heritage of the site for another twenty-plus years before it also moved, in 1958. The buildings on the southern part of the former college campus, including the original college buildings, were then torn down to make room for a shopping center.

The August 20, 1958, *San Diego Union* reported that workmen razing buildings of the former Brown Military Academy found papers dating from 1887 in a tin baking soda can in the building's cornerstone. According to the *Union* the papers included the *Pacific Beach, San Diego Bee* and *San Diego Sun* as well as a subdivision map with a sketch of a large rambling hotel [126].

The original buildings of the Pacific Plaza shopping center that was built on the grounds of the former San Diego College in the early 1960s were themselves largely replaced when Pacific Plaza was remodeled in the 1980s. After standing vacant for years the concrete barracks were eventually demolished in 1965 and replaced by the Plaza apartment complex, which was later converted to condominiums. Like the college, the hotel, and the military academies in their time, the Pacific Plaza and the Plaza Condominiums are today a prominent presence in the heart of Pacific Beach.

The heritage of the San Diego College of Letters includes not only the old buildings and the property they occupied in Pacific Beach but also the lives of the many individuals; patrons, faculty and students, who had come together in this first effort to establish an institution of higher learning in San Diego.

Founders Harr Wagner and C. S. Sprecher resigned from the college faculty in 1890 in order to devote their full attention to *The Golden Era*, where Wagner was editor and Sprecher associate editor. When Wagner won election as Superintendent of Schools in 1891, his wife Madge Morris assumed the title of editor. Wagner served as Superintendent for 4 years, during which time he instituted a number of reforms and promoted the summer normal school which met for the first year in the empty college buildings in Pacific Beach. He also was involved, with O. J. Stough, F. P. Davidson and others, in the initial agitation for the establishment of a State Normal School in San Diego [1]. When he was defeated for re-election he resumed publication of *The Golden Era*, moving it back to San Francisco in 1895 where it was renamed the *Western Journal of Education* in 1898.

C. S. Sprecher moved back to Los Angeles in 1892, first as an agent for *The Golden Era*, then as an independent publisher and printer. His transition from the religious to the business world was completed when he 'demitted' (resigned from) the ministry in 1897 [127].

F. P. Davidson became principal of the Russ School in San Diego in 1890 and was principal during its transition to Russ High School (later San Diego High School). In 1897 he resigned to become San Diego County Superintendent of Schools, a position he held for another ten years [128].

Samuel Sprecher, president of the college and father of C. S. Sprecher and Eleanor Davidson, remained in San Diego where he lived with yet another daughter, Mrs. Laura Lewis, until his death in 1906 at the age of 95 [129].

Other former San Diego College of Letters faculty members also found positions in the San Diego area. The 1895 City Directory listed Lucia Powers Woods as a teacher at the Russ School; Lita Kidwell was teaching in Lemon Grove and Laura Riddell was a member of the County Board of Education.

Among the students, classmates Eulalie Woods and Edgar Miller (or Müller) were married in 1892. Mr. Miller/Muller became a teacher (at Roseville) and later principal (at Florence and Sherman Schools). Lulo Thorpe and Edward Barnes were also married, in 1895, and the couple moved into their new home next to the College Campus and only a block from both of their parents' homes [130][18]. Jacqueline Oliver continued her education, and her vocal performances, at St. Hilda's Hall in Glendale [131], away from her home on Punta Banda, across Todos Santos Bay from Ensenada in Baja California. She and her mother continued to live in Mexico after her father's death in 1896, traveling by steamship to San Diego to visit friends [132]. Pearl Wagner was married to Major B. Johnson in 1897, in Denver where she was studying for the stage.

---

[18] Their new home, 'El Nido', was at the southwest corner of Acre Lot 64, now the employee parking lot for Pacific Plaza at the northeast corner of Jewell and Emerald Streets. The Barnes family home was at the southeast corner of Acre Lot 64 (the northwest corner of Lamont and Emerald), and the Thorpe family home was across Lamont at the northeast corner of Lamont and Emerald. The Army and Navy Academy eventually acquired most of Acre Lot 64, extending the campus north to Diamond Street, and the former Barnes homes were used to house faculty and staff until they were demolished along with the rest of the campus in the 1950s and 1960s. The former Thorpe home became a Methodist parsonage and later the residence of academy founder Thomas Davis' mother. It burned down on the night of April 22, 1957 [728].

Theodore Barnes became famous as a sprinter and later manager of the track team at the University of California, and in 1897 was reported to have joined the Klondike gold rush [133]. Mary Cogswell was a San Diego schoolteacher, teaching third grade at Sherman School before opening La Jolla Elementary School with twelve students in 1896 [134]. She later continued her own education at Pomona College [135][19]. Ida Lowe also taught school [136] but the life of the young lady with the 'elastic voice' was cut short by consumption in 1894 [137]. Dr. Evangeline Rowe Caven graduated from University of Southern California Medical College in 1898 [138] and practiced medicine in Bisbee, Arizona, and San Diego, where the Evangeline Caven Bungalow built in 1915 is designated a Historical Landmark. She worked in Yugoslavia as part of the post-WWI Serbian Relief Commission in 1919 and visited her birthplace in India (where her father had been a missionary) before settling in Los Angeles where she once again shared a home with her sister Mabel Rowe Jowett.

Olive Hoff translated her success in college elocution contests into a career on the stage, including the 'racy role' of Cissy in 'What Happened to Jones' in West Coast theatres in 1898 [139] [140] and Lady

MISS OLIVE HOFF, THE NEW "CISSY."

Blanche Thistlewood in 'Becky Sharp' on Broadway in 1899 (with the celebrated Mrs. Fiske in her most famous role, Maurice Barrymore and Tyrone Power, Sr., father of the swashbuckling movie star) [141]. Venetia Lyons worked as a post office clerk before marrying fellow student Fred Thomas in 1901. Thomas had worked with Venetia's brother Daniel at Hawley Hardware and when Daniel Lyons took over and renamed the company Lyons Implement Company in 1902 Thomas was appointed secretary, a position he held until 1930[20]. Percival Woods

[19] Pomona College was opened in September 1888, the same month as the San Diego College of Letters and also in a suburban Southern California location, but Pomona's experience has been very different and it is now one of the highest-rated liberal arts colleges in the nation.

[20] The former Lyons Implement Company building at 4th and G downtown is now the Rock Bottom Brewery.

opened a business representing out-of-town newspapers and was elected to the San Diego City Council in 1908 before moving to Los Angeles about 1912. Laura Gearn also moved to Los Angeles where she published a book, *Many Mansions, A thesis of enlightenment pertaining to a larger conception of Life – Physical, Mental, Spiritual,* in 1931.

Next to the parking lot in front of the Great Plaza Buffet at the southeast corner of Pacific Plaza, not far from where the cornerstone for the San Diego College of Letters was laid in 1888, there is a small memorial dedicated by Brown Military Academy alumni to the 'West Point of the West'. The memorial includes a plaque and an aerial photo of the academy from 1938. The plaque notes the history of the military academy beginning with the Army and Navy Academy in 1910 and its transition to Brown Military Academy in 1936, its achievements in academic and military studies, and the tributes and distinctions bestowed on the academy. In the aerial photo, among the barracks, auditorium, parade grounds and other improvements added over the years, it is possible to identify the buildings that were once the original college building (Girls' Hall) and Stough Hall. This image is the only evidence of the former San Diego College of Letters on the site of the College Campus in what was supposed to be the college town of Pacific Beach.

3 The Railroad

Although in many ways Pacific Beach was an ideal location for a town it was also relatively remote and isolated from the commercial and population center that was growing in downtown San Diego. Development of Pacific Beach could not be contemplated without a transportation link to San Diego and in the 1880s that meant a railroad.

The first railroad line in San Diego was the California Southern Railroad, a subsidiary of the Atchison, Topeka and Santa Fe Railway, which built a line from National City to Colton via Temecula Gorge, passing through San Diego and Old Town, along the eastern shore of False Bay, as Mission Bay was then known, and through Rose Canyon. This line reached Colton in 1882, was extended to San Bernardino in 1883 and through the Cajon Pass to Barstow in 1885, where it linked up with the transcontinental Atlantic & Pacific Railroad, another Santa Fe subsidiary, and enabled the influx of population that fed the Great Boom.

With the growth of population, other rail transportation systems began growing up in and around San Diego. The San Diego Street Car Company laid tracks in city streets in the downtown area and began operating a horse car line in 1886. The development of Coronado in 1886 included construction of a rail line across the peninsula between the ferry landing on San Diego Bay and the site on the ocean where the Hotel del Coronado was being built, and the line was eventually extended along the Silver Strand and around the bay to provide direct rail service from San Diego.

In August 1886 the trustees of the City of San Diego granted a franchise for a railway connecting downtown San Diego and Old Town to James McCoy and George Neale. The San Diego and Old Town Street Railroad Company was incorporated on August 20, 1886, by McCoy, Neale, F. E. Bates, A. Hart, Amun Sevort and John R. Jones to construct and operate a street railroad under the terms of this franchise [142]. Rails were laid north along Arctic Street (now Kettner) from a station at D Street (now Broadway) to Bean Street where the line jogged west for a block then turned north again and continued along what are now California Street and San Diego Avenue to the Old Town Plaza. The line was originally constructed to be an electric railway, the first in San Diego and one of the first in the country, and a power station was constructed at Arctic and Kalmia Streets [143].

Construction of the Old Town line was completed in October 1887 and operations began using a steam 'dummy' acquired from the National Iron Works on October 9[21]. The electric 'motors' began running November 9, 1887 [144]. However, less than a month later, on December 3, 1887, the *San Diego Union* reported that the San Diego and Old Town Railroad would withdraw its electric equipment and transfer it to the Electric Rapid Transit Company for use on the Fourth Street Line. The Old Town line would install heavier rails and first-class rolling stock and steam power. 'The new motors will be capable of running thirty miles an hour, and the time between D street and Old Town will be reduced to ten minutes' [145].

With a railway from San Diego to Old Town already under construction in 1887 the 'syndicate of millionaires' planning the development of Pacific Beach took steps to extend this railway to Pacific Beach. The San Diego and Pacific Beach Railway Company was incorporated on July 18, 1887, with George Hensley, J. R. Thomas, D. C. Reed, Thomas Metcalf and O. S. Hubbell as the initial board of directors; R. A. Thomas and D. P. Hale were also listed as stockholders [146][22]. The San Diego Board of Trustees approved Ordinance No. 137 on September 26, 1887, granting the company the right to construct, operate and maintain a railroad commencing at the Old Town terminus of the San Diego and Old Town Street Railway on Washington Square and following a specified route to the ocean in Pacific Beach [147].

Although the October 1887 subdivision map of Pacific Beach had featured a railroad traversing the subdivision from the eastern shore of False Bay to the Pacific Ocean and the Pacific Beach Company had advertised a 'motor road now nearing completion' that would carry passengers to and from the Beach, trains were still not running by the time of the Pacific Beach Company's opening sale on December 12, 1887. A temporary interchange at Morena had been arranged with the California Southern and construction had begun from there through Pacific Beach to the ocean. From the interchange at Morena the route

---

[21]A steam dummy was a small steam locomotive entirely enclosed within an external superstructure so as to hide the boiler and other mechanical parts and give it the appearance of an ordinary coach or streetcar, supposedly making it quieter and less likely to frighten people or horses when operating on street railways.

[22] J. R. and R. A. Thomas, Hubbell, Reed, Hale, Metcalf and George Hensley, along with Charles Collins and W. W. Thomas were also the initial directors of the Pacific Beach Company when it was incorporated on July 28. By August 15, the Thomases, Hensley, Reed, Hubbell and Hale, plus Thomas Whaley, A. C. Platt, E. W. Morse and A. G. Gassen had also taken over the San Diego and Old Town Street Railroad.

---

passed around the north of the racetrack then followed the course of Grand Avenue to the beach[23]. The December 11, 1887, *Union* reported that ties had been strung along the line of the San Diego and Pacific Beach railroad from Morena to the beach, that grading on the line was progressing rapidly and that the 'Santa Fe people', presumably the California Southern Railroad, had agreed to run excursion trains from San Diego to Pacific Beach as soon as the new road was completed [148].

On January 8, 1888, the *Union* reported that arrangements had been nearly perfected for an excursion to run to the College Campus on or about the '20th inst' (i.e., the 20th of this month). The article said that the excursion would go over the California Southern to Morena and then on to the campus over the line of the Pacific Beach Railway Company, which will be completed in less than ten days [149]. Apparently this was done since on January 29 the *Union* reported that the laying of the cornerstone for the San Diego College of Letters was attended by about 2500 people, most of whom had come on two trains (or two trips by the same train?) of 8 coaches [42]. By February 19, 1888, the *Union* reported that track laying on the Pacific Beach Railway had been completed to within a quarter-mile of the ocean [150].

Completion of the line had evidently been delayed by a shortage of rails, but the March 3, 1888, *Union* reported that the Pacific Beach Railway Company received two miles of railroad iron by the ship George W. Elder which had arrived on Thursday morning, and another mile of the steel would be on the Queen of the Pacific this evening. That would be enough steel to finish laying the track to the ocean from the present terminus in Pacific Beach and to fill in the gap between Old Town and Morena, which would complete the line from D street through to the beach:

> It is graded and the ties are placed throughout the entire length and nothing now remains to be done but the laying of the rails, which will be done within ten days, while trains will be running into Pacific Beach over the new line within two weeks [151].

The April 6, 1888, *Union* admitted that owing to unlooked for delays 'through trains' would not be run for about 10 days but that the road was now 'completed through to the ocean at Pacific Beach and trains are running regularly on it from the foot of D street to Old Town' [152]. The unlooked for delay was in the arrival of a 'crossing' required

---

[23] Grand Avenue then ran from the beach to what is now Lamont Street, then followed what is now Balboa Avenue to Garnet Avenue and continued east on Garnet. What is now Grand Avenue east of Lamont was then Ivy Avenue.

for the intersection of the Pacific Beach and the California Southern tracks at Old Town, without which trains could not cross the line and continue 'through' to Pacific Beach. The April 17, 1888, *Union* reported that the crossing and a motor (locomotive) had arrived [153]; the April 19 *Union* reported that the motor had been set up and run up to Old Town and back and gave the best satisfaction and that the crossing would be laid today and doubtless the first through trains would be run tomorrow [154].

It may have taken a few more days, but by April 24 the line was complete. The April 25, 1888, *Union* reported:

PACIFIC BEACH
A Delightful Trip Over a Well Constructed Road
IMPORTANT IMPROVEMENTS UNDER WAY
A Ride Around the Bay and Through a Beautiful
Country – A Charming Sea View – The Site of
the College

An excursion was run over the San Diego, Old Town and Pacific Beach railroad yesterday, the train leaving the foot of D street at 10 o'clock. The party comprised the officers of the road and prominent citizens and their wives, two car loads in all [155].

An advertisement appeared in the April 29, 1888, *Union* in which A. G. Gassen announced that on and after Sunday April 29, 1888, trains would run to Pacific Beach every hour during the day, commencing at 7 o'clock in the morning. The round trip fare would be 25 cents until further notice [156].

The trains which ran over the newly constructed railroad consisted of closed and open coach cars pulled by coal-burning steam locomotives. The first locomotive was the dummy that the Old Town line had acquired in October 1887 but the Pacific Beach railroad obtained two additional, somewhat larger steam dummies from the Baldwin Locomotive Works as the new line went into service, one in April and one in May, 1888. The railway also apparently owned four closed and two open coaches, one combination closed/open coach and two combination baggage/closed coach cars [157]. The small locomotives could not pull many cars; contemporary photos show trains consisting of two cars, a closed coach and a combination baggage/coach car. Sometimes another closed, or open/closed combination coach, was added. The power of the engines also limited speed; timetables indicate that the under-10-mile trip required over thirty minutes (including stops), an average of less than 20 miles per hour.

A trip from San Diego began at the depot at the 'foot of D' (now

Broadway)[24]. From the D Street depot trains headed north over the former San Diego and Old Town Street Railway to the Old Town station. From Old Town trains crossed the Santa Fe tracks near where the Old Town transit station is located today, then turned north to cross the San Diego River on a newly-constructed bridge and continued parallel and west of the Santa Fe right-of-way, where Interstate 5 runs today. Beyond the Morena station, located near where the Clairemont Drive off-ramp from northbound I-5 begins, the Pacific Beach railway diverged from the Santa Fe, skirting the edge of Mission Bay along the approximate route of today's Mission Bay Drive to a station at the racetrack, near what is now Magnolia Avenue. From the racetrack station trains continued north then west around the racetrack, turning from Mission Bay Drive onto today's Garnet Avenue and continuing west across Rose Creek to where Garnet now joins Balboa Avenue. The route then followed Balboa to a point just west of its intersection with Grand Avenue where the College station stood on the north side of Grand between Tenth and Eleventh Streets (todays Kendall and Lamont Streets). From the College station trains continued west on Grand to Second Street (now Bayard Street), two blocks from the beach.

The streets over which the right-of-way passed between the beach and the racetrack (now Grand, Balboa and the eastern extension of Garnet) were then all called Grand Avenue, which was laid out to be wider than other streets in Pacific Beach to accommodate the railroad right-of-way. On the portion of Grand between Second and Eleventh Streets (Bayard and Lamont) the tracks were laid in the center of the street, today's median strip, while on the portion between Eleventh and the racetrack, now Balboa and Garnet, the tracks ran along the northern edge of the street.

At Grand and Second (Bayard) the tracks made a sharp turn toward the south cutting through residential blocks to enter the Depot Grounds, a 10-acre property centered on today's Mission Boulevard

---

[24] In 1888 D Street, now Broadway, ended at Atlantic Street, now Pacific Highway and at the time the shoreline of San Diego Bay. The Santa Fe tracks ran over California Street, a block east of Atlantic and the Pacific Beach tracks ran over Arctic (now Kettner) Street, a block east of California. The depots for both railways were originally located in the block between California and Arctic and north of D, the Santa Fe depot on the west side of the block and the Pacific Beach depot at the southeast corner, and both were described as being at the 'foot of D'. Broadway was extended to what is now Harbor Drive after dredging and filling of the bay in 1914 and the 'foot' of Broadway is now nearly a quarter-mile further west. The 'new' (1914) Santa Fe depot and platforms now occupy the entire block.

between Reed Avenue and Pacific Beach Drive, where there was a platform for passengers and an 'engine house' for the locomotives. The Hotel del Pacific and the dance pavilion were built to the west of the curve between Grand and Second and the Depot Grounds[25].

With trains now operating between San Diego and Pacific Beach over the San Diego and Old Town Street Railway and the San Diego and Pacific Beach Railroad, steps were taken to consolidate the two lines into one. The San Diego, Old Town and Pacific Beach Railway Company was incorporated on April 20, 1888, with A. G. Gassen, R. A. Thomas, E. W. Morse, Thomas E. Metcalf and J. R. Thomas as the initial directors [158]. An ordinance merging the franchises of the two existing railroads into one franchise was granted in the Council meeting on June 12, 1888, and went into effect two weeks later, despite opposition from 10 of the leading residents of Old Town. Councilman Marston voted against the ordinance since he believed the road should not run through the Old Town Plaza and a better route would be west of the Plaza [159]. The ordinance made the road a standard railway and took from the city council the right to prohibit the use of steam power.

San Diego, Old Town & Pacific Beach RR.

THE SEA SERPENT!

IS DUE AT

PACIFIC BEACH

On Sunday, July 15.

THE RED HUSSAR BAND

Will endeavor to charm it. Trains every hour from 8 a. m. to 7 p. m., from corner D and Arctic streets. Last train from Beach at 6 p. m. 25c for Round Trip.

However, the council reserved the right to fix the rates of fare, the placing of stations along the road, and the times at which trains would be run.

With construction and corporate reorganization complete the railroad company began an advertising campaign to attract riders. A series of ads for Sunday band concerts at Pacific Beach featuring the Red Hussar Band began appearing in the *Union* in June 1888. Trains would leave the corner of D and Arctic Streets every hour from 8 a. m.

---

[25] Actually, Grand Avenue also followed the railroad right-of-way south into the Depot Grounds. The continuation of Grand Avenue between Bayard Street and the beach was then called Elm Avenue.

to 5 p. m. and the last train back from the beach would leave at 6 p. m. The fare was 25c for a round trip. The ad for the Sunday, June 24 concert noted that 'Surf Bathing at Pacific Beach is at the Finest' [160] and the July 8 ad announced that 'Clams are Ripe!' [161]. The ad campaign reached a climax the following week with the claim that 'The Sea Serpent! Is due at Pacific Beach on Sunday, July 15. The Red Hussar Band will endeavor to charm it. [162]'

Although President Gassen had announced when opening the line on April 29, 1888, that trains to Pacific Beach would run every hour, and trains did run every hour on summer Sundays when the Red Hussar Band was entertaining at the beach, the hourly departures were apparently just an introductory offer. The May 6 *Union* announced that commencing Monday, May 7, trains to Pacific Beach would leave the D Street Station at 7 and 10 a. m. and 1 and 4 p. m. although trains to Old Town would continue to leave hourly and there would still be hourly departures to Pacific Beach on Sundays [163]. On July 14 another timetable was announced with departures to Pacific Beach and way points at 7 and 9:30 a. m. and 1:30, 3:30, 6:30 and 8:30 p. m. and a special to Old Town only at 11:45 a. m. This timetable also listed the departure times from Pacific Beach; 6, 8:15 and 10:30 a. m. and 2:30, 5:15 and 7:15 p. m. [164] The fact that the first train of the day departed from Pacific Beach and the last train ended its run there indicates that the trains and presumably the crew were based in Pacific Beach[26].

Schedules (and way points) continued to evolve as Pacific Beach underwent changes in its first years, including the opening of the asbestos works in 1889 and the closing of the college in 1891. A timetable from the September 27, 1891, *Union* showed that trains would leave San Diego from D and Arctic streets for Old Town, Moreno, Driving Park, Rose Canyon, Asbestos Works, College and Pacific Beach daily at 9:00 a. m., 1:30 p. m. and 5:30 p. m. and would leave Pacific Beach for San Diego and way points at 7:30 a. m., 12:00 a. m., and 4:20 p. m. (the daily stage from Pacific Beach to La Jolla connected with the 9:00 a. m. train from San Diego and returned from La Jolla in time to connect with the train leaving Pacific Beach at 4:20 p. m.) [165]. Again it would appear that the train and crew spent the night in Pacific Beach.

The railroad to Pacific Beach had been created to serve the interests of the Pacific Beach Company and the shareholders, directors

---

[26] The 1889 Monteith City Directory lists 6 (of 37) Pacific Beach residents as railroad workers. Three of them, Thomas Fitzgerald, F. H. Woodworth and E. C. Doyle owned property in Block 262 adjacent to the Depot Grounds. The home now at 854 Reed, Doyle's lot, may date from that time.

---

and officers of the two companies were mostly the same men. On July 17, 1892, however, the *Union* reported that the San Diego, Old Town and Pacific Beach road had been sold to a wealthy eastern resident [166]. The July 19 *Union* added that the deal was closed, the stock transferred and the entire amount paid over in cash, but 'The stockholders are in ignorance as to the identity of the purchaser' and 'It seems to be the general sentiment that there is more behind the transaction than appears on the face of it and that it means great good to the city' [167].

The mystery continued the next day; according to the July 20 *Union* the old board of directors and officers resigned and a new board was elected; Capt. J. H. Barbour, Roscoe Howard, W. R. Rogers and H. N. Matthews. Capt. Barbour was elected president, W. R. Rogers secretary and Herbert Dabney general manager. The selection of Dabney as general manager particularly interested the *Union*:

THEIR IDENTITY CONCEALED
Who Purchased the Pacific Beach Road? Officers Elected

Considerable speculation is being indulged in as to the identity of the purchaser. The election of Mr. Dabney caused several persons to fix on J. Malcolm Forbes as the new owner of the road, but there is no positive proof of this [168][27].

Railway service to Pacific Beach was apparently enough of a success that residents of La Jolla also wanted a railroad and 'expected to have it too'. According to the February 16, 1889, *Union*, a representative from La Jolla stated that there was a probability that the San Diego, Old Town and Pacific Beach road would be extended and that if so it would receive material encouragement in regard to right-of-way and money or land subscribers [169].

However, it wasn't until September 1893 that Superintendent Boyd of the San Diego, Old Town and Pacific Beach Railroad applied for a franchise to extend the railway from Grand Avenue in Pacific Beach to La Jolla. The application was approved on October 3 and Boyd announced that work would probably begin between the 10th and 15th of November [170]. Work did not begin in November 1893, but the December 14 *Union* reported that Superintendent Boyd had succeeded in securing right of way from the property owners for extension of the road to La Jolla; 'This gratifying information removes all doubt about

---

[27] John Malcolm Forbes, in addition to owning railroads, was a noted horseman and yachtsman who built and skippered the Americas Cup winner Puritan in 1885. Dabney caused people to 'fix on' Forbes because they were brothers-in-law; Forbes' wife Rose Dabney Forbes was Herbert Dabney's sister.

the Pacific Beach road being built on to La Jolla and beyond' [171]. Not only was there no opposition by the land owners but the plan met with such hearty approval that they made up the necessary subsidy of $2,500 required by the owners of the road. Ties and rails were ordered and the company intended to have the road completed by January 10, 1894 [172].

The January 10 date came and went but on March 8, 1894, the *Union* reported that an agreement was finally reached by which the San Diego, Old Town and Pacific Beach railroad would be extended from its current terminus in Pacific Beach to La Jolla within three months. The agreement would require the railroad to run at least three passenger trains daily each way and at least two excursion trains on separate days each week, and also to build a suitable depot in La Jolla. In exchange, the railroad would receive title to several parcels of La Jolla real estate two years after the road's completion [173].

With an agreement in place construction of the extension to La Jolla actually began, with the *San Diego Union* reporting from the front lines on an almost daily basis. The March 13 *Union* detailed the bids received for construction of the four-mile extension (e.g., Goodbody & Sons, 8¾ cents per cubic yard for grading, 1 cent for overhaul, and $195 per mile for track-laying). Goodbody was the lowest bid and secured the contract, by the terms of which work would at once begin. 'Construction camps will be established today, and dirt will fly tomorrow. The road must be finished and trains in operation by May 1' [174].

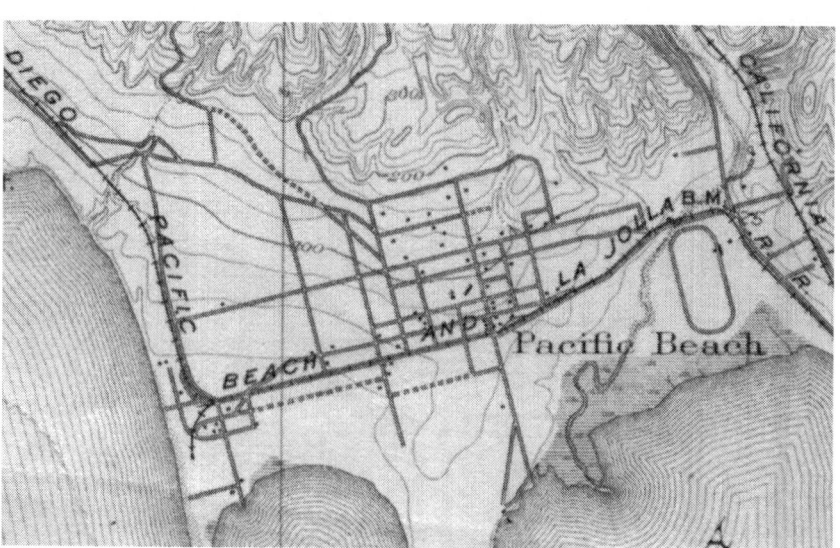

The March 22 *Union* reported that the Pacific Beach Railroad's extension to La Jolla had been graded about a mile. The work began near La Jolla canyon and 60 men were working toward Pacific Beach [175]. According to the March 27 *Union*, steel rails for the Pacific Beach extension had been shipped from Belleville, Ill. and would arrive the following Monday and track-laying would begin as soon as they arrived [176]. By April 2 grading had been completed for about two miles, almost half the distance, and the steel rails were expected to arrive from Belleville Ill. on Thursday and track-laying would begin immediately thereafter [177]. Although the schedule for the arrival of the rails from Belleville continued to slip they finally did arrive on April 12 and two miles of rails were laid by April 25. The line was finally completed and the first train made a trial run from San Diego to La Jolla on May 13, 1894 [178].

An elaborate ceremony to commemorate the completion of the railway was arranged for May 15 in La Jolla. Fifty members of the Lodge of Elks, accompanied by the City Guard band, took an excursion train from San Diego to La Jolla where the Grand Exalted Ruler commanded an Esteemed Knight to pick up a silver sledge and drive in the golden spike. After one swing at the golden spike, the Esteemed Knight surrendered the silver sledge to a lady, Mrs. Emma Harris, a guest at the La Jolla Hotel, 'in honor of womankind generally, as befitting the gallantry of the Order'. The *San Diego Union* reported that 'contrary to tradition she did not miss the mark. With great vigor she drove the spike to its last resting place, while the assembly cheered and the band played' [179].

While construction was still underway, in April 1894, Harry Titus, Ralph Dabney, Herbert Dabney, C. D. Boyd and R. Gail Nichols had incorporated the San Diego, Pacific Beach and La Jolla Railway Company to control the extension to La Jolla and the rights granted by its franchise [180]. Although the entire line from San Diego to La Jolla was generally known thereafter as the San Diego, Pacific Beach and La Jolla Railway, tickets and timetables were printed with the new company's name and locomotives and rolling stock lettered with its initials, this company and the San Diego, Old Town and Pacific Beach Railroad were never actually merged until both were taken over by the Los Angeles and San Diego Beach Railway Company in 1906.

From the point at Grand and Second (Bayard) where the original Pacific Beach railway turned south into the depot grounds, the new line turned north onto First Street, Mission Boulevard today, and continued along First to a point near today's Loring Street, where it turned toward the west along the route of today's La Jolla Boulevard, crossed Tourmaline Canyon and continued along what is now La Jolla

Hermosa Avenue toward La Jolla. The original timetable, effective May 16, 1894, listed three trains daily, leaving La Jolla at 7:00 A. M., 12:35 P. M. and 4:00 P. M. and returning from San Diego at 9:10 A. M., 2:00 P. M. and 5:30 P. M. with stops at Pacific Beach, College, Race Track, Moreno, Hardy's, Old Town and Middletown. One-way times were one hour from end to end; 20 minutes between La Jolla and Pacific Beach and 40 minutes between Pacific Beach and San Diego [181]. The increase in traffic led to other improvements along the line; the College station in Pacific Beach, for example, was 'very much enlarged and beautified' in 1897 [182]. By the end of 1898 there were still three trains a day, leaving La Jolla at 7:15 A. M., 12:00 A. M. and 3:45 P. M. and leaving San Diego at 9:10 A. M., 1:25 P. M. and 5:00 P. M. Times had improved to as little as 45 minutes from end to end [183][28].

In 1899 the two railroad companies, the San Diego, Old Town and Pacific Beach and the San Diego, Pacific Beach and La Jolla, were sold by J. Malcolm Forbes (who indeed had been the mystery buyer) to Charles T. Hinde and E. S. Babcock, who also owned the Coronado Railroad. In 1905 Babcock was behind construction of an electric street railway in San Diego which connected the La Jolla depot on Arctic (Kettner) Street to the National City and Otay depot at the foot of Fifth and the San Diego, Cuyamaca and Eastern depot at the foot of Tenth Street (Babcock also owned the Cuyamaca railroad). This line ran on C Street between Arctic and Sixth, down Sixth past the National City depot to the Santa Fe tracks, then along the Santa Fe to the Cuyamaca depot. The electric cars met trains of each line at their respective depots and transferred passengers to the other depots or to other destinations downtown [184].

In March 1906 Babcock led a group that incorporated the Los Angeles & San Diego Beach Railway Company, which then absorbed the Pacific Beach line, the La Jolla line and the C Street line. The railroad's new name seemed to suggest an extension north of La Jolla but the March 30 *Union* reported that officers of the company refused to state the significance of the transfer or whether there was any significance to it [185].

The route followed by the San Diego and Pacific Beach Railway from its earliest days had circled around the northeast corner of the Pacific Beach Driving Park, the racetrack located east of Rose Creek and north of Mission Bay. The racetrack had also once been an

---

[28] The October 20, 1898, timetable also changed the name of the College station on Grand between Tenth and Eleventh (Kendall and Lamont) from College to Pacific Beach, and the station formerly known as Pacific Beach, at the foot of Grand, to Ocean Front.

important stop for the railway, at least when races or other events were being held, but by 1906 racing had been discontinued, the track had been abandoned, and the entire property was sold and subdivided into residential lots. With the racetrack no longer an obstacle and no need for a station to service it, the railway proposed a realignment of its route to cut across the former racetrack site and shorten the route to the beach. Starting at the point near Grand and what had become Lamont Street, where the original line turned toward the northeast on what is now Balboa Avenue, the new line would continue in a straight line on what was then called Ivy Avenue (now the continuation of Grand Avenue east of Lamont) before curving southeast along the current alignment of Grand to connect with the existing track near where Grand currently meets Mission Bay Drive.

The realignment was approved and construction began in January 1907. Improvements to the Los Angeles and San Diego Beach Railway, which also included heavier rails and lowered grades, led to speculation that the railway was laying the groundwork for an electric railway to Los Angeles, perhaps in league with the Pacific Electric, a Los Angeles-based interurban line. The *San Diego Union* reported that 'rumors of an electric line north are filling the air':

> Word has also reached this city that in the shops of the Pacific Electric company at Los Angeles are two immense trolley cars, bigger by fifteen feet in length than any now operated by the Pacific Electric system. The information received states that these cars are brand new and that they bear the words "Los Angeles & San Diego Beach Railway company." [186]

Although a franchise had been approved to extend the line from La Jolla to Del Mar, the line was never extended beyond La Jolla and never linked up with the Pacific Electric. The immense trolley cars were never seen in Pacific Beach.

The improvements to the railroad line created a different kind of interest in Pacific Beach. An ad by the Folsom Bros. Co. in the January 13, 1907, *Union* announced that contracts were being let and 'dirt is flying on the new Short-line to Pacific Beach' [187]. The ad claimed that the 'Babcock interests' had been quietly acquiring property and rights-of-way, shortening the line and straightening the curves preparatory to installing a new rapid transit electric system. Property prices would be 'doubled and over' on the day the first electric car passes through, so 'The time to buy Lots at Pacific Beach is NOW Not after the Line is Completed[29].

---

[29] The Folsom Bros. Co. followed the Pacific Beach Company and O. J. Stough as owner and developer of most of the unsold property in Pacific Beach.

Los Angeles and San Diego Beach Railway train steaming westward on the realigned section of the line, what would now be Grand Avenue in front of Mission Bay High School, in this 1914 panorama of Pacific Beach and Mission Bay with San Diego in the background. (The house on the hill at lower left is the residence of former fire chief A. B. Cairnes.) (SDHC #91:18564-1666)

The line was completed a few months later but the first electric car did not pass through Pacific Beach until 1924 and when it did it was operated by a different company on a mostly different route. By that time the old steam railroad was history, its rails and equipment dismantled and sold for scrap, a victim of changes in transportation patterns brought about by the introduction of the automobile in the first decades of the twentieth century. As residents of Pacific Beach and La Jolla began to drive and road systems were improved, fewer depended on the train for the short trip to San Diego. For those without their own cars, the La Jolla Scenic Stage Line began service between San Diego and La Jolla (in an open touring car) in 1916.

In March 1917, the Los Angeles and San Diego Beach Railway applied to the Public Utilities Commission for permission to reduce service and increase rates. That application was dismissed, but on January 10, 1919, the commission considered the railway's application to discontinue its service, dismantle the railroad and dispose of its property. The commission granted the application to discontinue service, but dismissed the portions of the applications dealing with dismantling and disposition of property on the grounds that they were not within their jurisdiction. Within a year, the rails had been torn up and loaded on a freighter bound for Japan [188]. The abandoned right-of-way along Mission Boulevard and into Bird Rock were later reused by the interurban line between San Diego and La Jolla via Mission Beach which brought the hoped-for electric rapid transit to at least a part of Pacific Beach between 1924 to 1940.

Much of the equipment and rolling stock with which the Pacific

Beach railway line began operations in 1887 and 1888 continued to be used throughout its 30-year lifetime. The steam dummy that pulled the first train to Old Town in 1887 operated on the Pacific Beach line until 1897, at which point it was relegated to the engine house as a backup. One of the pair of Baldwin steam dummies purchased when the Pacific Beach line opened in 1888 remained in service until 1917. The other was sold to the Coronado Railroad in 1894 but returned in 1906 and finished its career with the Pacific Beach line in 1918. Both had been rebuilt and had much of the dummy superstructure removed. A steam locomotive built for the New York elevated railway and received from the Coronado Railroad in exchange for the Baldwin dummy served from 1894 to 1906 and three other second-hand steam locomotives, acquired in 1906, 1912 and 1915 were used before 1918. Of the six coaches and 2 combination baggage/coaches that entered service in 1888, one combination baggage/coach was destroyed and one coach damaged in an accident at the Old Town crossover in June 1917 and the others scrapped in 1918 [157].

In 1908 the railroad acquired a pair of McKeen gasoline powered rail cars. They were painted red and came to be known as 'Red Devils' or 'submarines', due to their circular 'porthole' windows. Since they were not steam-powered the ordinances restricting steam operations over city streets did not apply and they could operate over the street railways as well as the main line. The McKeen cars alternated with steam trains in the schedule and began their run from Fourth and C Street downtown, allowing passengers to travel directly to or from downtown and Pacific Beach or La Jolla without changing trains. However, the McKeen cars were underpowered and unreliable and were phased out by 1916.

The railroad carried freight as well as passengers between San Diego, Pacific Beach, and La Jolla. One major commercial customer was the John D. Hoff Asbestos Company works on the line just west of Rose Creek, which opened in 1889. This plant received carloads of asbestos from mines at Elsinore, as well as shipments of other materials and equipment, and shipped finished products like asbestos paint, roofing and boiler coatings before it closed in 1892. Another customer was the West Coast Lumber Company on the line just east of today's Lamont Street. The railroad carried lumber and other building materials to this site from which they were distributed to construction projects in Pacific Beach such as the San Diego College of Letters. A siding built at that location also served a hay and grain company and later a lemon packing plant.

The route from downtown San Diego east and north of Mission Bay crossed the San Diego River, just north of Old Town, and Rose

Creek, just west of the racetrack in Pacific Beach. In California's dry summers the flows of these streams is minimal, but winter storms can cause sudden flooding. A storm on December 16, 1889, the most serious in years according to the *San Diego Union*, produced a flood in 'Rose's canyon' that demolished the racetrack as well as about 300 feet of the Pacific Beach Railroad's track at the trestle bridge [189], and resulted in the drowning death of Master Mechanic W. O. Wilson [190]. Another storm later in the month resulted in further damage and caused the Pacific Beach line to suspend operations. The December 25, 1889, *Union* reported that:

> The heavy washout at the mouth of Rose Canyon, which caused the former delay, was repaired and trains were running regularly until a part of the same track went out with the recent flood. Since then repairs have not been undertaken, and will not be until the rains cease and the waters subside [191].

Storms in February 1891 washed out the line in two places between Old Town and Morena. The *Union* reported breaks 100 and 175 feet long near Harvey's slaughter house[30], but said they would be easy to repair [192]. Two days later, service had been partially restored; the February 26 *Union* reported that the trains would come into town by switching over to the Santa Fe track at Morena and would make two trips daily until the line was repaired, which was expected to be in two days [193].

Additional rounds of storms caused flooding in March 1893 and January 1895. The January 17, 1895, *Union* reported that the creek running into False Bay from Rose Canyon was a roaring river, the country around the Pacific Beach race track was a vast lake, and the tracks of the Pacific Beach railroad were nowhere to be seen and in many places were wiped out of existence. The *Union* added that it would be some days before the railway was in running order [194].

The low speeds maintained by trains over the Pacific Beach railroads meant that most mishaps were minor, but the line did experience two serious train wrecks, both during its Los Angeles and San Diego Beach Railway phase. On January 16, 1908, the 1:45 P. M. northbound train had just left the downtown depot and was approaching Winder Street where there was a slight curve toward the west, just south of where Interstate 5 now crosses over Washington

---

[30] Hardy's (not Harvey's) was a slaughter house on the north side of the San Diego River just east of the Pacific Beach and the Santa Fe tracks, later taken over by the Cudahy Meat Packing Company. The site is now marked by Cudahy Place near West Morena Boulevard.

Street. Apparently the inside or 'low' rail on this curve came loose and the rails spread, causing the locomotive to run 300 feet along the ties before rolling over and coming to a stop. Although the passengers were uninjured, the engineer was trapped under the wreckage and killed and the fireman burned so severely that he died 10 days later. According to the headline in the January 17 *Union*:

ENGINEER OF LA JOLLA TRAIN LOSES LIFE WHEN LOCOMOTIVE TURNS OVER
SPREADING RAILS, CAUSE
STEAM SCALDS HIM TO DEATH
Thomas Robertson, Pinned Under Wreckage, is Literally Cooked Alive
THIRTY OCCUPANTS OF CARS ESCAPE UNINJURED
Girl in Fright Jumps Through Window of Car

The girl was Miss Zoe Overshiner, 16, a Pacific Beach resident, who was on a front seat of the first coach and therefore among the 'most badly shaken up and scared'. She told a 'graphic story':

> I was talking with friend of mine about something. I've forgotten what it was now, when all of a sudden the engine began to act funny and our car began bumping heavily. This was due, as we afterwards found out to the fact that it had left the rails. The first shock was not so bad as might have been expected and we were not frightened until we saw the engine plunge over the bank and turn over on its side. Then the steam hid the engine and I climbed through the window of the car and jumped to the ground. I didn't want to get hurt and the door wouldn't open, or at least at first sight it wouldn't. I don't remember whether I screamed. Maybe I did. It was enough to make any one scream when the engine reared up in the air and turned over on its side. It's no joke to be in a railroad wreck.

(to which the *Union* writer added 'it is probable that she is right') [195].

Another passenger, Andrew McKnight, also in a front seat of the first coach, got his wife out of the car and then tried to calm the remaining passengers; 'They were making a grand break to get out of the cars and I did the best I could to stop the rush' the *Union* reported. He then attempted to rescue the engineer amid the clouds of steam from the cab of the locomotive but although he and the conductor were eventually able to shut off the steam and loosen a bolt and work loose the lever that was pinning him down it was too late.

The fireman, Thomas F. Fitzgerald, was 'hurled headlong into a clump of cactus and in addition was badly burned by the escaping steam'. He was taken to the Hearne sanitarium for treatment but died there of his injuries. Fitzgerald was an original Pacific Beach resident, one of the contingent of railroad employees who lived near the railroad's base at the Depot Grounds when Pacific Beach was the terminus of the line. When La Jolla became the terminus and base of operations after the 1894 extension the employees, including Fitzgerald and Robertson, also relocated to La Jolla.

As for the other passengers, women screamed and men broke for the doors but 'Not a passenger was even as much as scratched or was there a window in either of the three cars broken. The fright incident to the cars bumping along over the ties and a severe shaking up which lasted only a minute or two sums up the damage to the passengers'.

The general manager of the line explained that workers had been replacing the light 35-pound rails with 60 pound rails as part of the general upgrade of the line, but that the upgrade project had not reached the point where the wreck occurred and that the track had been in good shape two or three days before. He also noted that trains ordinarily place greater stress on the outside or 'high' rail in a curve, but in this case the low rail had given way.

The Pacific Beach line ran from a downtown depot on the east side of the Santa Fe tracks and crossed the Santa Fe mainline just to the north of Old Town before continuing toward Morena and Pacific Beach on the west side of the Santa Fe tracks. The crossing at Old Town was at grade and the Santa Fe had the right of way. Apparently the normal protocol was for the Pacific Beach train to stop short of the crossing where the fireman/brakeman would jump off and flag the engineer when it was clear to proceed.

On June 30, 1917, the southbound 10:05 A. M. train from La Jolla approached the crossing but failed to come to a complete stop and drifted into the path of a southbound Santa Fe freight train. The Santa Fe train, travelling at an estimated speed of 35 miles per hour, hit and demolished the baggage car, which also contained a smoking compartment, and badly damaged the second coach. A 14-year-old girl, Nethemia Rodriguez, who was getting off at the nearby Old Town station and had been standing on the platform at the front of the coach, suffered serious injuries and eventually had to have a leg amputated. Several other passengers were less seriously injured. According to the *San Diego Union*, when the fireman of the Pacific Beach train realized that his train was not stopping at the crossing and saw the Santa Fe train approaching he signaled the engineer to go ahead so that the approaching train would hit the baggage car and do little damage. Whether he acted on this advice or on his own instincts, the *Union* credited the engineer with saving the lives of all the passengers by clearing the engine from the track. The Santa Fe train included a carload of dynamite, and the police had to keep the crowd of several hundred spectators at a distance while the wreckage was being cleared [196].

There are few signs in Pacific Beach today of the railroad line that was once the community's principal transportation link. The unusual width of Grand Avenue and the portions of Balboa and Garnet that were originally Grand, and the median strips in these streets, are vestiges of the railroad right-of-way that once shared the same streets. The diagonal alignment of those portions of Balboa and Garnet, compared to the rectangular grid of most other Pacific Beach streets, traces the circuitous route the railway originally took to avoid the racetrack east of Rose Creek. La Jolla Boulevard between Loring and Turquoise Streets is also built over the right-of-way of the San Diego, Pacific Beach and La Jolla Railway, and north of Turquoise, in Bird Rock, 'Electric Ave' is still stamped in the concrete curbs of what is now called La Jolla Hermosa Avenue, also unusually wide because the La Jolla railroad and later the San Diego Electric Railroad line to La Jolla once ran down the center of the street.

4 The Racetrack

On July 6, 1887, a few weeks before the founding of the Pacific Beach Company, the San Diego & Pacific Beach Railroad and the San Diego College Company, the Southern California Breeders' Association was incorporated by Ben P. Hill, A. G. Gassen, W. G. Rifenberg, J. A. Roark and W. W. Stewart [197]. The *San Diego Union* reported on July 20 that the Southern California Breeders' Association had purchased Pueblo Lot 1797[31] and that they would build a racing track on it [198].

On July 31 the *Union* announced that a contract had been let for grading of the 'race track at False bay' and that ground would be broken within a few days. There would be a mile track, a half-mile course and a grand stand. Wells would be sunk and a high board fence placed around the grounds [199]. By August 4, the *Union* was reporting that forty men were at work on the new race track at False Bay and that it should be ready for the County Fair races in October [200]. According to the September 11, 1887, *Union*:

> The Southern California Breeders' Association are now pushing along operations lively in the construction of their race track and buildings at False Bay. Bordwell, Kooken & Co. are the architects of the grand stand, club house and stables. The grand stand has a frontage of 150 feet and a depth of 32 feet. The judges' stand will be three stories high. The club house will be a very fine and convenient structure. It will be 45 X 32 feet in size, with an attic. Two towers and two large bay windows will give the front a very showy appearance. Near the clubroom there will be a shed 100 feet long for the accommodation of teams. There will also be fifty stables, and each will be 14 X 14 in size. A tight board fence, eight feet high, will surround the track. A pole fence will run around the inside of the track, while a fence 2,350 feet long and four feet high will separate the outside of the track from the main fence.
>
> Inside of the main track there is also a track for exercising horses.
>
> Abundant water will be secured and the grounds will be beautified with shrubbery, etc.

---

[31] Pueblo Lot 1797 is the pueblo lot immediately east of Pueblo Lot 1796 and south of Pueblo Lot 1789, the easternmost pueblo lots included on the Pacific Beach Company's subdivision maps; not part of the Pacific Beach subdivision but a natural extension of Pacific Beach to the east. Like other pueblo lots in the Pacific Beach area Pueblo Lot 1797 is 160 acres, a half-mile square, and its boundaries are aligned with the grid of streets and avenues in Pacific Beach. These boundaries today include the western and southern sides of Mission Bay High School at the southwest corner and the intersection of Garnet Avenue and Mission Bay Drive at the northeast. Then and now Rose Creek flowed from north to south through Pueblo Lot 1797.

The Association expects to have the track and buildings ready in time to hold a race meeting sometime late this Fall [201].

A month later, on October 16, 1887, the *Union* was still reporting that 'work is being pushed on the race track of the Southern California Breeders' Association, located at the head of False Bay'. The grading of the track and the fence were almost completed, 30 stables had been finished, the grand stand was ready for painting and work would begin next week on the club house [202].

Whether or not the clubhouse had been completed, the grandstand was apparently ready for fans on November 15 when the opening of the 'Pacific Beach Driving Park' featured a game of 'base ball' between Philadelphia and San Diego. The *San Diego Union* had advertised on November 10 that round trip train tickets and admission to the grandstand, with special accommodations for ladies, would be 75 cents. Trains would leave from the California Southern depot at 1 P. M [203][32].

The visiting team was the actual Philadelphia franchise of the National League, then formally named the Quakers but more commonly known as the 'Philadelphias' or 'Phillies', as they are still called today. The November 15 edition of the *San Diego Union* enthused at the arrival of the 'Famous Philadelphia Baseball Club' at the Horton House the day before:

> BASE BALL.
>
> Philadelphia vs. San Diego.
>
> Opening of the Pacific Beach Driving Park,
>
> Tuesday & Wednesday
>
> November 15th and 16th.
>
> Train leaves California Southern depot 1 P. M. each day. Special accommodations for ladies. Ample transportation or all.
> Round trip tickets and admission to grand stand 75 cents. Tickets for sale by the members and at the stores.

> The Horton house was the center of attraction last evening to the lovers of baseball, and the local followers of the national game crowded its corridors and clustered round a number of ordinary but athletic looking young men who stood about in various attitudes of ease and received the homage of the throng. From a position of vantage outside the window a small boy voiced bulletins to a crowd of urchins: "I sees de batt'ry, boys; der's Ferge and Maguire, an' Jack Stafford is talking to 'em. I know 'em, you

---

[32] In November 1887 the Old Town railroad had only been in operation about a month and its extension to Pacific Beach was many months from completion. An interim solution was to run trains over the California Southern tracks from the downtown San Diego depot to an interchange at Morena, where they were switched over to a segment of the Pacific Beach tracks which were to be completed from there to the College of Letters (passing the racetrack) in time for the cornerstone ceremony in January 1888. Apparently the interchange was already in existence and the tracks ran some distance toward the racetrack by November 1887.

bet; didn't I use ter see 'em play in 'Delphy." And the brat left his perch to recount wonderful baseball games he had seen in the East.

The athletic young men spoken of represent the famous Philadelphia Baseball Club, and their names as shown by the hotel register are Wood, J. Fogarty, Mulvey, Irwin, Ferguson, Maguire, Foster, Vian, Fogarty.

The boys arrived on the evening train and the San Diego club will cross bats with them today at the Pacific Beach race track. The home team has been in training for several days and the game promises to be an interesting one. A special train will leave the D street station at 1 o'clock for the park [204].

The actual game on November 15, 1887, apparently the first public event held at the Pacific Beach racetrack, was pretty much what one would expect for an exhibition between a major league team and a group of local amateurs. As the *Union* described the game on November 16:

THE VISITING BALL-PLAYERS

They defeat the Home Nine by a Score of Thirty-one to Seven

The Philadelphia and the San Diego Baseball Clubs crossed bats yesterday afternoon and the home team was most woefully beaten. The game had been extensively advertised and the local nine were up in high feather at the prospect of a contest with the celebrated League club, who gave the Detroits such a hard tussel for the pennant last season. That the boys were defeated by a score of 31 to 7 is not so much owing to their being poor players, but to the magnificent work of the visitors. They are a thoroughly drilled club, composed of athletes who make a profession of playing ball, while the San Diego club is a new organization only lately put in the field and the members have practiced together but once. It was but natural to suppose that the game would be rather one-sided, still the more sanguine members of the club did not think they would be so easily defeated. The game was played at the new driving park at Pacific Beach and about 300 lovers of the National game witnessed the exhibition, among the spectators being a number of ladies. The game was advertised for 2 o'clock and a few minutes after the appointed time game was called, the San Diegos going to the bat.

Osburn led off for the San Diegos and struck out, followed in quick succession by West and Mertzman. The visitors then took a turn at knocking the sphere about and succeeded in getting in two runs before they were retired. In the second and third innings the San Diegos retired with two more goose-eggs, while

The score is as follows:

PHILADELPHIA

	A.B.	R.	1B.	P.O.	A.	E.
Wood, 1b	7	5	3	2	0	0
J. Fogarty, lf	6	4	1	2	0	0
Mulvey, 3b	6	3	2	2	2	1
Irwin, ss	7	2	2	3	1	2
Ferson, p	8	0	1	8	0	0
Maguire, c	7	5	1	2	0	0
Foster, 2b	7	6	1	0	1	2
Vian, rf	6	4	2	2	0	2
Fogarty, cf	6	2	1	3	0	0
Total	60	31	14	24	4	7

SAN DIEGOS

	A.B.	R.	1B.	P.O.	A.	E.
Osburn, p	5	0	0	4	1	0
West, 1b	4	1	1	3	0	1
Mertzman, c	5	1	1	2	0	5
Eagan, 2b	4	2	2	2	1	4
Gilmore, ss	5	1	1	3	2	2
Stafford, 3b	4	1	1	2	1	2
Hult, rf	4	1	1	3	0	1
Rose, lf	4	1	1	3	0	0
Shuldt, cf	5	0	0	5	0	1
Total	40	7	8	27	5	17

Score by innings:

	1	2	3	4	5	6	7	8	9	
Philadelphia	2	1	1	2	8	4	5	8		31
San Diegos	0	0	0	2	0	0	0	0	5	7

Base on balls-Philadelphia, 3; San Diego, 1. Two-base hits-Philadelphia, 7. Home run-San Diego, 1. Double play-Irwin, Foster and Vian. Left on bases-Philadelphia, 4; San Diego, 3. Passed balls-Mertzman,6; Foster, 1. Struck out-By Schmidt, 1; by Osburn, 4. Umpire-M.Bernard. Scorer-Bert Taylor. Time of game-2 hours, 5 minutes.

The Philadelphia nine will make their last appearance to-day, playing the San Diegos again.

Philadelphia scored two runs.

In the fourth inning the home club picked up a little and managed by heavy batting to get in two runs before they were sent out to the field to chase the ball for the Phillies. Two more scores were piled up the visitors in this inning, and the home club began to lose their grip. During the following four innings San Diego's score remained unchanged, while each time they came in from the diamond the Phillies added 4 to 8 to their string. It was not until the beginning of the ninth inning that the San Diegos pulled themselves together and began playing ball. It was too late for them to hope to do anything, but they added 5 more runs. This closed the game, which was interesting only from the fact that the spectators had an opportunity to see a first-class club play on a San Diego ball field [205].

Opening day for racing at the new track was scheduled for May 1, 1888. The *San Diego Union* reported on April 3 that the Pacific Beach Driving Park was being put into condition for the spring meeting. The track, built entirely of 'made ground', had been pronounced a good track by no less a horseman that Budd Doble[33]. The clubhouse, a three-story building of 22 rooms, was just about finished [206]. On April 11 the *Union* added that about twenty horses were already in the stalls and were being trained on the new track. J. I. Case, a well-known breeder of harness horses, had inspected the track and pronounced it to be, in his opinion, the finest track on the coast [207]. An advertisement in the *Union* on April 22 announced the Grand Opening of the Pacific Beach Driving Park under the auspices of the Breeders' Association of Southern California, A. G. Gassen, President and W. W. Stewart, Sec'y. There were to be three days of racing, May 1, 2 and 3, and $1,250 in purses [208].

The May 2 *San Diego Union* carried an extensive account of opening day at the new racetrack:

The sun did not shine too brightly yesterday, and the wind blew a cloud of dust in the streets, but it was a good day for horses, and by noon a large crowd was "off for the races." The procession which passed through the gates at Pacific Beach Driving Park was a jolly and good-natured, and expectant throng of well-dressed admirers of horse-flesh – and the pools. They were there, all of them. Gentlemen of leisure and gentlemen of business. Ladies too, in their brightest array of spring colors sat in their carriages, and the throng which filled the grand stand was a lively and interested one. The broad track over which the racers were to fly was smooth as a floor, firm, fast and in fine condition as any race-course could be [209].

---

[33] Budd Doble was a celebrated trainer and driver of harness horses who was considered one of the greatest of his time and perhaps of all time. He set a world record of 2:14 for a mile driving Goldsmith Maid in 1874 and in 1892 set another world record of 2:04 with the 'trotting queen' Nancy Hanks, owned by J. Malcolm Forbes.

(Even though this was opening day, the ladies' hats did not merit special mention in 1888.)

There were actually only two events; a half-mile 'running' race and a mile trotting race, or 'gentlemen's driving race', and only five horses were entered, three runners (Kangaroo, Triumph and Gladstone) and two trotters (Ed Sykes and Josephine). The running race consisted of three heats and the trotting race was best three of five heats. The day began with the first two heats of the running race followed by the first heat of the trotting race, then the final heat of the running race and the final heats of the trotting race. Buyers rushed to the 'pool-seller' between each heat.

Triumph was the favorite for the running event and the race became a duel between that 'handsome gray' in colors of red and orange and Gladstone, a sorrel ridden by a 'colored boy' wearing a jacket and cap of green. The black jockey became the story of the day; 'he rode not in the best style, but he rode hard, to win, and he did win the first heat' with Triumph coming in second. Triumph won the second heat, beating Gladstone by a short length, and after the first heat of the trotting race, and another rush to the pool-seller, the third and final heat of the running race was held.

Kangaroo had been 'distanced', so the third heat of the running race was between Triumph and Gladstone. The *Union* reported that 'Triumph took the pole, but there was a dangerous light in the eyes of the black boy who mounted the sorrel'. Triumph jumped out to a lead, but down the stretch 'the black boy on the sorrel plied the whip and came in under the wire with Gladstone winner by a neck'. The 'insiders' who had backed the favorite Triumph had thought they had a sure thing, 'but the black boy who rode Gladstone had a quiet business transaction of his own – and "he fooled 'em"'.

> Great was the disgust of the 'insiders' and the chagrin of Triumph's trainer, the latter even so losing his temper as to make a brutal attack on the colored rider of Gladstone. He was placed under arrest and steps will be taken by the Association which will probably result in his expulsion from the race course.

The trotting race was much less interesting. Ed Sykes won the first three heats handily, and therefore the best three-of-five race.

The excitement generated by the victory of the long shot Gladstone and his African-American jockey in the running race apparently carried over to the second day of the meeting. According to the *Union's* report on the following morning, May 3:

> Yesterday's bright sunshine, blue sky and refreshing breezes made it a perfect race day. From early morning until afternoon the motor trains bore out their loads of merry freight, and the road to the north along the bay, was

lined with carriages laden with business men, beaux and beauty, bound for the races at Pacific Park. Every man who could get away from the busy duties of city life and evade the rules of domestic remonstrances against the seductive attractions of the uncertain pool box, donned his brightest plaid, and with dustproof hat, departed for the track. Many there were who pleased their wives and at the same time avoided all danger of a cross-examination by taking with them the fair members of the family to enjoy the pleasures of the day. Long before the bell had sounded the summons for the contending steeds, the carriage space of the Driving Park was well filled with a variety of gay equipages, a happy throng of pedestrian spectators moved to and fro and the grand stand presented a picture of fashion and feminine beauty. In fact, if not in name, it was "Ladies' Day" at the races, and the fairest of San Diego's fair were out in all their style and bright colors of spring costumes [210].

The actual races may have seemed like an anticlimax. There were two races on the programme, a trotting race with horses in the 2:40 class and a 'free-for-all' pacing race. Both events covered a mile and were decided by the best three of five heats. In the trotting race, Scott won the first three heats, and the race, with Phoenix coming in second and Top third, except that Top was 'drawn' from the third heat on account of lameness. The pacing race provided the excitement of the day, with Lawyer winning the first two heats, but losing the next three, and therefore the race, to Barbara.

The May 4, 1888, the *Union* summarized the third and final day of the race meeting at Pacific Beach Driving Park:

Yesterday's attractions proved irresistible, and the third day of the races found the largest crowd of the season at the Pacific Beach Driving Park. Everybody was there that could get there, and they went without much regard to the manner of their going. They came in the closed coaches, and in the open cars of the motor, and even crowded upon the flat-cars and came out with the band. Vehicles of all descriptions were brought into use, and a constant stream of carriages poured through the gates of the Park. There were buggies, phaetons, tandams and more than one four-in-hand in the procession, and even the "one-horse shay" was not missing, while manly equestrians and lovely equestriennes added their skillful grace to the scene of motion. It was a great day and all had come prepared to enjoy it, so that not a cloud arose to cast its shadow over the field of pleasure – at least not until the unforeseen contingencies of the race course began to drop like a moist blanket upon the spirits of the heavy losers.

There were two trotting races, one for 3:00 class horses and one free-for-all, with best three-of-five mile heats. There were only two horses in each race; the 3:00 class race was a rematch between Scott and Phoenix and the free-for-all matched Len Hayden against Jim Blaine. Although Scott had swept the race in three heats against Phoenix the previous day, on the final day the two horses alternated wins and Phoenix beat Scott in the final and deciding heat, although there was some controversy about the judging. In the second race, Jim Blaine won the first two heats, lost the third, then won the fourth heat and the race. At half-past 5 o'clock the third day's sport was finished and the first season of the Pacific Beach Driving Park had closed. Everybody who enjoyed it pronounced it a complete success, and hoped for other seasons in the future [211].

With the spring race meeting over, the racetrack once again became the venue for a base ball game, this time between Los Angeles and San Diego. The July 1 *Union* advertised that round trip train fare, including admission to the game, would be 50 cents and that the grand stand would be free [212]. On September 9, 1888, Admission Day[34], horses and men again raced at the track but the participants belonged to the San Diego Fire Department. There was a hook and ladder competition, a hose team race, and a man and horse race [213].

Despite the base ball games and exhibitions by the fire department, the track had been built for horse racing and on July 30, 1888, the *Union* had announced the October meeting to take place October 23 to 27 at Pacific Beach driving park, 'a noted Pacific coast watering-place, and where racing is certain to be received with hearty support'. There were to be nineteen races over five days, and the event, distance, class of the horses, entrance fee, forfeit, purse and other dollar amounts to be won by coming in second or third, or by coming in under a certain time were described in detail [214].

Pacific Beach Driving Park --- Two Great Extra Days.
"LADIES' DAY," Saturday, Oct. 27.
"PEOPLE'S DAY." Sunday, Oct. 28.
SWORD COMBAT ON HORSEBACK—Jaguarina vs. Capt. Wiedemann

As the October meeting approached, an advertisement appeared in the *Union* on October 7 promoting not only the Fall Race Program!, Four Days of First-Class Racing! Including running races, trotting and pacing, but also Two Extraordinary Special Days!, a Ladies' Day and the People's Day, with the 'Greatest, Most Diversified and Most Novel Series of Popular and Exciting Out-door Sports ever presented to the public', including 'special arrangements for the safety and comfort of Ladies and Children' [215]. On October 21, the *Union* followed up with a detailed schedule for the four days of racing, including a list of

---

[34] The date on which California was admitted to the Union in 1850.

the horses entered for each race and more details of the Ladies' and People's days, which promised to be 'the two greatest days in the annals of sport on the Pacific slope' [216].

The *Union* provided the usual detailed reports of the four days of racing and on October 27, after the close of the 'first fall meeting' added the observation that since the meeting was not 'classed in the regular circuit' many a good horse which would have been entered were too far north to warrant the trip, a condition which they said would be avoided hereafter and 'much of the best blood in the state will be stretched over the magnificent course at Pacific Beach' [217].

As the *San Diego Union* had promised, People's Day on Sunday, October 28, 1888, was a great day in the annals of sport, at least for Pacific Beach. According to the *Union* report on October 30, nearly 7,000 people were in attendance (out of a total San Diego population of perhaps 25,000 in late 1888, after the sudden collapse of the Great Boom). The *Union* credited Fred Engelhardt for 'securing the attendance', railroad president Gassen and superintendent Connors for attending to the comfort of the excursionists, and even conductors Hixon, Bogan and Seigler, and engineers Wilson and Doyle for carrying so many passengers without mishap.

The crowd first watched a series of footraces and a blindfold wheelbarrow race before a recess was taken at noon for luncheon, 'served in excellent style in the clubhouse'. After lunch there were a couple of quarter-mile horse-races before the 'event of the day', the mounted sword combat between Captain Wiedemann and the woman who called herself Jaguarina[35]. 'A rush was made to every vantage point, and crowds of the spectators swarmed upon the track, in order that a good view of the combat could be obtained'.

Captain Wiedemann was from Germany and a leader of the local Turnverein (or Turn Verein), a gymnastic movement popular among the German immigrant population in the nineteenth century. According to the *Union* he weighed 185 pounds with a chest measurement of 43 inches and biceps measuring 15 inches, and had received a thorough training in fencing. Jaguarina was described as a famous swordswoman now at Ensenada who had participated in (and

---

[35] Jaguarina was actually Ella Hattan, who had been an actress in Ohio before studying fencing in Chicago in the early 1880s. In 1886 she appeared in San Francisco and, managed by Frederick Engelhardt, engaged in contests with various weapons, on foot and on horseback, generally beating her male opponents and culminating in a victory over Sgt. Owen Davis of the U. S. Cavalry in 1887. She and Engelhardt then moved to Ensenada, from where they returned for her contest at the Pacific Beach Driving Park in 1888.

generally won) similar battles in the past (her fine French military cuirasse [breastplate], of brass and copper, 'still bears deep indentations, as marks of respect from Captains Davis, Jennings and Marshal, received in former contests')[36].

The contest was to consist of eleven rounds, called 'attacks', of three minutes each unless a point was scored first ('A point is a fair cut on head or body above the waist'), with a one-minute rest between attacks [218]. The contestants each had a second, also mounted, who apparently were supposed to claim a point when their principal landed a blow on their opponent. The referee would then decide whether to allow the point.

Wiedemann rode into the arena first wearing blue military trousers, steel breast and back plates, and a 'regulation' broadsword mask, and armed with a German rapier. Jaguarina followed a few minutes later dressed in fawn-colored knee breeches, top boots and a white flannel shirt. The *Union* reported that she was cheered heartily as she rode bareheaded in front of the grand stand, the picture of health and wearing an air of supreme confidence. She donned her cuirasse and the combatants made their customary salutations to each other, the judges, the referee and the audience, before retiring to their respective corners.

> The vast crowd was now on the tiptoe of expectation, and, without delay, the tones of the trumpet sounded the signal to the first attack. Both plied their spurs and met in the center of the field at a gallop and lost no time in crossing arms, Jaguarina taking the initiative with a high carte cut, which was skillfully parried by her opponent, who attempted a return, which was again neatly stopped by a return parry and quickly followed by a prime cut, which was effective and brought home a resounding whack. This, the first point, was claimed and allowed for Jaguarina.

The *Union* continued with a blow-by-blow account of the battle. The second attack involved considerable fencing before Jaguarina 'essayed to force the fighting' and reached short, leaving herself unprotected. Before she could return on guard, the Captain availed himself of the advantage and scored a point, which was allowed. In the third attack, both horses acted badly but Wiedemann's recovered more promptly allowing him to deal a succession of rapid cuts.

---

[36] The *Union* did not provide Jaguarina's measurements but she may have actually outweighed Wiedemann. In a *New York Times* interview from 1897 'the Champion Swordwoman of the World' described herself as weighing 197 pounds and 'round as a ball all over', meaning that her muscles were 'evenly developed all over the body'. The interviewer reported that she was 'large, as women average' with a 'solid, muscular covering of her body' [633].

Jaguarina's friends claimed these were all parried but the Captain's judge claimed a point, which the referee allowed. In the fourth attack, there was considerable fencing, much bad behavior on the part of the horses, and much excitement amongst the spectators, but no point was scored. No point was scored in the fifth attack either, despite 'some animated discussion between the judges and the referee, in which the multitude commenced to participate'.

The *Union* report continued:

> When the charge was made in the sixth attack it was evident that Jaguarina's blood was up, and that she was determined to force the fighting. She circled around her opponent rapidly and attacked him fiercely front and rear. Jaguarina drove her opponent to his corner, his horse backing, rearing and plunging. Jaguarina now made a hot assault and scored a point which was allowed.
>
> During the seventh attack the excitement commenced to run high. The vast multitude being on their feet, and it was no longer possible to exercise any control over those who found points of vantage from which to obtain a full view of the contest. There was good, sharp, quick fighting on both sides, well-meant cuts and skillful parries. There was the ring of the clash of weapons on the armor, and the contestants parted to their respective corners.

Both seconds claimed a point, but the referee 'not being in a position nor sharp enough to see the point' awarded it to the Captain.

> This raised a howl of indignation on the part of the throng, and Sergeant Roos [Wiedemann's second], evidently fearing some danger to himself, ungracefully slid off his steed and "was hustled back among the populace."

A replacement was found for Wiedemann's second and the contest continued. The eighth attack was 'short, sharp and decisive' and the point was awarded to Jaguarina, but the ninth attack was 'long and hot, the blood of the Teuton was up, and so was that of Jaguarina'. The contestants forced each other all over the field and 'points were clamorously claimed on both sides', but the referee was unable to give a decision and ordered the attack to be renewed. Jaguarina drove the Captain to his corner and 'after much clashing of steel, the combatants were seen to come apart and Jaguarina and her second galloped gaily to her corner'. When the referee awarded the point to Wiedemann the cheering by his partisans was 'drowned in a general outburst on the part of the adherents of the fair mistress of the sword'. In response to the vigorous protest, the referee was removed and replaced by a graduate of West Point.

With the score standing at Wiedemann 4, Jaguarina 3, the judges decided that the two attacks in which no points had been scored would not count, and the contest would be extended to thirteen attacks. Wiedemann was awarded the point at the end of a melee of the tenth attack and in the eleventh Jaguarina 'went in with a headlong rush and forced him back until his horse went on his haunches, and scored a "palpable hit."' During the twelfth attack 'a blade was seen to flash through the air and Jaguarina threw the fragments of a broken sword from her to the ground'. Another sword was put into her hand and she went on to take another point.

When on the thirteenth and last time the trumpet called the contestants to the charge, to say that there was excitement among the respective participants of the combatants would be feebly express the temper of the multitude, as the score at this time stood five to five.

This final attack ended with Wiedemann aiming a cut at Jaguarina in high carte, which she parried and, before he could protect himself, 'the sound of Jaguarina's blade was heard on his cuirasse from a vigorous and unmistakable cut in carte' which ended the contest with a score of six to five in favor of Jaguarina.

The victor at once doffed her helmet and cuirasse and received round after round of applause from those present, many of her more enthusiastic friends throwing their caps high in the air. After a gallop round the track with her second, Jaguarina returned to her dressing room receiving the congratulations of her friends en route.

(The day ended with a vaquero tournament, what today would be called a rodeo, and prizes were awarded for 'catching, throwing and tieing a steer', a 'picking up' contest which consisted of picking up a handkerchief from the ground while riding at full gallop, and a contest of ring tilting.) [219]

Two weeks after the mounted exhibition in Pacific Beach, Jaguarina and Wiedemann met for a rematch at the D Street Theater in which they fenced on foot 'unhampered by refractory and unwilling horses' [220]. The event, on Monday, November 12, 1888, was again staged by Engelhardt and began with a 'flag march' by the juvenile pupils of Captain Wiedemann, a vocal solo by Jaguarina ('The Gems of Tyrol'), which showed that she had an excellent voice, and a gymnastic exhibition in which the Turn Verein showed muscle and skill on the parallel bars. Jaguarina again appeared in what were called classic art pictures, or tableaux vivantes, living representations of classical works of art, closing with a representation of 'Diana in the Chase' presumably featuring Jaguarina herself. The main event of the evening was a 'salle d'armes scene', the sword contest between Jaguarina and Captain Wiedemann, which was exciting and realistic and again won by Jaguarina by 6 points to 4 and 'showed that the famous swordwoman was altogether too quick for the redoubtable Captain, able though he is' [221][37].

Back at the track, the news was that the owner and trainer of the Bell Boy, at the time the most valuable trotting horse alive and the first to be sold for $50,000, had visited from Los Angeles and 'spoke in high terms of the Pacific Beach track and the park as a place for wintering valuable stock' [222]. Apparently Bell Boy and other valuable stock did winter at the track since on December 20, 1888, the *Union* advertised that he would trot against time to beat the world record and Irma, the fastest pacing mare in the world, would also attempt to lower the world record for her class, on Christmas Day at the Pacific Beach Driving Park. Bell Boy would trot promptly at 3:00, Irma would start at 3:15 and people could eat Christmas Dinner at home at 4:30 (less than two months after nearly 7000 people were reported to have watched the epic mounted sword contest featuring Jaguarina, the solo runs of these two horses against a clock to break their own records was billed as 'The Greatest Attraction ever Brought Before the San Diego Public') [223].

That attraction never was brought before the public; the December 25 Brief Mention section in the *Union* simply announced that 'There will be no entertainment at the Pacific Beach Driving Park to-day' [224] and the December 27 *Union* reported that Bell Boy's owner said he was not trying to break the 3-year-old record but was simply trotting against his own time (but that it was expected he would beat his previous record while in San Diego) [225]. The December 29 *Union* did advertise that Miss Myrtie Peek would put on an exhibition at the Pacific Beach Driving Park featuring Lady Riders and Drivers and also her great Roman Standing Exhibition in which she stood on the backs of two running horses. There was also to be a Five Miles Running Race against a 'well-known young lady from Los Angeles' in which the riders changed horses at the end of each mile without touching the ground [226].

Baseball returned to the Driving Park grounds at Pacific Beach on March 3, 1889, with a championship series between the Colton Base Ball Club and the Schiller & Murthas, a San Diego team [227]. On April 14 another Great Out-Door Event at the track was advertised, including

---

[37] Jaguarina continued to frequent San Diego and Ensenada and Engelhardt attempted to stage more mounted sword contests for her around Southern California but with limited success, possibly because there were few opponents willing to risk combat with her. She moved east a few years later and retired from fencing a few years after that. There is speculation that some or all of the sword combats were 'fixed', but there is no doubt Jaguarina, or Ella Hattan, was an expert swordswoman and athlete. She is on the Roll of Honor in the Fencing Hall of Fame [700].

a grand international cowboy contest and fiesta de vaqueros featuring genuine wild bulls and untamed broncos, dare-devil riding, startling feats of horsemanship and a great round-up and starring the "Arizona Queen" Carrie Beasley, Champion Cowgirl of the World, and Charley Meadows, Champion Cowboy of Arizona [228]. A program of races for the Fourth of July was advertised on June 20 [229].

Like the Pacific Beach railway, the racetrack's location at the mouth of Rose Creek made it vulnerable to winter storms. The storm on December 16, 1889, which washed out the railroad bridge, also wreaked havoc on the track. According to the December 17 *Union*:

> The Pacific Beach race track was demolished by a stream that came down Rose's Canyon and was deflected across the north side of the grounds across the track, in the neighborhood of the Judges' stand. It is estimated that fully one-fourth of a mile of the track has been washed away on the east side, and several hundred feet more on the west side at the grand stand. The water at one time was five feet deep and backed up the hill to the Pavillion. Several of the lower sheds, down near the private gates, were also washed down.
>
> A. G. Gassen and G. W. Rifenberg left for the track early yesterday morning, and before leaving announced their intention of making arrangements for the repair of the track at once [230].

Gassen and Rifenberg may not have followed through on their intentions, since there don't seem to have been any races or other events at the track during most of 1890. On October 25, 1890, the *Union* reported that Ben Hill of El Cajon had taken charge of the Pacific Beach Driving Park Company's grounds and clubhouse and would put on a two-day race meeting as soon as the track could be put in order. The *Union* added that there were six horses then at the track, one runner, two pacers and three trotters. Mr. Hill would move into the clubhouse [231]. A few days later, on October 30, the *Union* announced that the racing season at Pacific Beach would open November 1 and that there were nine horses in training and another nine expected in a few days [232].

If races did take place over the next year they were not advertised or reported in the *San Diego Union*. However, the *Union* did report on other forms of entertainment staged at the track. On November 27, 1891, the *Union* reported that fully 1,000 people visited Pacific Beach to watch as a great balloon flew skyward about 2,000 feet and 'from that giddy height a woman and monkey descended by means of parachutes' [233]. A few weeks later, on December 17, the *Union* announced a triple parachute jump at the Pacific Beach race track for Christmas Day (and also some good races) [234]. The December 20 *Union* added that the balloon would be 'monstrous'; 75 feet high and 41 feet in diameter, and that the triple parachute drop would involve a man, a woman and a monkey [235]. The 'daring young monkey', Yan Yan, had been separated from his 'paternal group' for several months but the December 23 *Union* reported a family reunification 'of a very touching character' in which the mother clasped her arms around her long-lost son while chattering 'what seemed to be words of endearing welcome and love' to which Yan Yan reciprocated 'in a most affectionate and human-like manner' [236].

While there was little subsequent news of racing or other entertainment at the track, there was considerable activity involving the racetrack in court and in the county recorder's office. In 1890, Kate T. Cobb, administratrix of the estate of Edward A. Bliven, deceased, filed suit against the Southern California Breeders' Association, the San Diego, Old Town and Pacific Beach Railroad and several individuals claiming that Mr. Bliven's estate was the actual owner of the property by virtue of his 1859 purchase of Lot B Rincon Valley, and that a deed which purported to show his sale of the property to T. J. Daley and A. G. Gassen, who then deeded it to the Breeders' Association, was 'false, fraudulent and forged . . . and was made and recorded for the purpose of cheating and defrauding the said heirs of Edward A. Bliven'. The original trial ended in favor of the Breeders' Association at the end of December 1890 when no official map showing Rincon Valley could be produced and expert witnesses were unable to satisfy the court that Lot B Rincon Valley and Pueblo Lot 1797 were one and the same [237]. Mrs. Cobb filed a motion for a retrial which was granted in 1893, but by that time, according to E. W. Britt, an attorney for the Breeders' Association, the company had become insolvent, or at least very heavily indebted, and did not seem to have any further interest in the property and declined to maintain the defense any further [238].

Frederick Schulenburg, a retired lumber magnate from St. Louis, had apparently lent the company $6000 and held an interest in the property as security (Frederick Schulenburg's son, A. R. Schulenburg, had been Secretary of the Breeders' Association in 1889). In a series of events that Britt found 'somewhat mysterious', Mrs. Cobb transferred the property to another of Frederick Schulenburg's sons, Otto Schulenburg, who then became the plaintiff in the case. When the case went to trial the defendants declined to appear and in October 1893 the court declared the plaintiff, Otto Schulenburg, to be the owner of Pueblo Lot 1797, also known and described as Lot B Rincon Valley. In December 1893 Otto deeded the property to Frederick Schulenburg.

Frederick Schulenburg died on May 30, 1894, and A. R. Schulenburg was appointed administrator of his estate on July 4. In his role of administrator, Schulenburg sued the San Diego, Old Town and Pacific Beach Railway on March 14, 1895, for $8,000 in damages allegedly sustained by the Pacific Beach racetrack property as 'a result of the careless manner in which the defendant constructed a bridge across Rose Creek canyon'. The damages related to flooding during winter storms in March 1893 and January 1895 which Schulenburg claimed was due to the obstruction of Rose Creek by the railroad bridge, causing the waters which 'customarily and usually' flowed through the channel to be 'backed up and impounded' and to flow over the racetrack. The railroad argued that the floods were 'an unusual and extraordinary and rapid accumulation of water' caused by a heavy storm and 'entirely beyond the defendant's control' [239].

Two weeks later Schulenburg filed another suit against the railway claiming that the outcome of the case over the ownership of Pueblo Lot 1797 entitled him to possession of the railroad right-of-way, which ran through the property, and asking $1,500 in damages because the defendant 'entered upon said land and ousted and ejected plaintiff therefrom' and a further $1,000 for building an embankment and railroad track on the property. The railroad countered that it had a franchise granted by city ordinance to build and operate a railway over Grand Avenue where it ran through the property [240]. Both of these suits were eventually dismissed in December 1898.

A. R. Schulenburg resigned as administrator of the estate on October 29, 1896, and Nat Titus was appointed in his place [241]. In May 1897, apparently in response to unpaid debts, the estate was ordered by the court to sell real estate [242], and the January 29, 1898, *Evening Tribune* noted what it called 'A Rare Opportunity':

> Attention is called to the legal notice in this paper offering for sale the 160-acre tract known as the "Race Track" in this city. The sale, by the administrator of the Schulenburg estate, affords the opportunity of securing a fine acreage adjoining the elegant suburban ranch homes and lemon orchards of Pacific Beach. This land is capable of producing as equally fine orchards, and a portion has been pronounced the best of alfalfa land. The improvements alone cost more than is asked for the place [243].

The rare opportunity apparently did not envision a revival of racing; the September 18, 1898, *Union* reported that Titus had sold 160 acres of land belonging to the estate to a Los Angeles man, Dr. J. Mills Boal, who intended to 'plow up the race track and set out the property to trees and otherwise improve the same' [244]. On November 22 the *Union* added that he would set up a meteorological observatory on his place as soon as the necessary instruments arrived from the east [245].

A few days later, however, on November 26, 1898, the *San Diego Union* reported that A. G. Gassen had outbid Dr. Boal and became the owner of the Pacific Beach racetrack (again). The *Union* article added that the racetrack and neighboring property consisted of about 360 acres and that Col. Gassen would spend about $2,500 for improvements intended to make it a pleasure resort and summer home for himself and his family. He was expected to set out about 2,500 eucalyptus trees to afford a place for picnics and other forms of recreation, build a five-board fence around the track, clear willows and other unnecessary trees and bushes from the creek bed and put part of the land into grain and alfalfa. Water would be piped from Col. Gassen's tract of 4,000 acres immediately north of his new property [246]. Gassen's initial plan apparently did not see a future for the racetrack either, since he offered to donate a right-of-way for a road across the Pacific Beach racetrack in 1899 [247] [248].

On May 10, 1903, the *San Diego Union* reported a rumor that Col. Gassen had sold the track to A. G. Spalding, the sporting goods magnate then living in Point Loma[38], although neither Gassen nor Spalding could be reached for confirmation. The *Union* noted that the track had at one time been one of the finest speedways on the Pacific coast but had fallen into disrepair and would have to be wholly rehabilitated to become what it once was [249].

Spalding's interest apparently caused Gassen to reconsider his indifferent attitude to the track and just over a month later, on June 19, the *Union* reported that he was having the track thoroughly overhauled and more stalls built in anticipation of reopening in the fall and winter. The *Union* article said that fifty or sixty fine animals from Kentucky and Illinois would winter there, with the possibility of many more joining them during the cold season. According to the *Union* Gassen said it was 'not improbable' that there would be a number of meets involving the eastern and local horses. It was not expected that the track would require a great deal of work to put it in proper shape, and the fence, which had been out of repair for some time had been

---

[38] Albert Goodwill Spalding was a former professional baseball player who played for the Boston Red Stockings and Chicago White Stockings in the 1870s and as a pitcher with a win-loss record of 253 – 65 still holds the major league record for winning percentage at .796. He was instrumental in founding the National League in 1876 and was elected to the Baseball Hall of Fame in 1939. Also in 1876 he founded the A. G. Spalding & Bros. sporting goods company which made baseballs and, in 1877, the first baseball gloves, which he was one of the first players to wear. The Spalding company also published the first Official Rulebook for baseball, which required the use of the Spalding baseball, the official ball of the National League until 1976. Spalding and his second wife, an ardent Theosophist, moved to Point Loma in 1903 to participate in Katherine Tingley's Lomaland Theosophical community. Their home, designed by Madame Tingley and featuring an amethyst dome, is now Mieras Hall, the familiar landmark on the campus of Point Loma Nazarene University. The Spalding company, now a division of Russell Corporation, a unit of Berkshire-Hathaway, still sells baseballs, gloves and other sporting goods.

repaired and painted and the grandstand and judges stand had also been fixed up [250].

Gassen also fixed up the organization of the track, incorporating the Belmont Breeders Association with himself, D. C. Reed, L. P. Swayne, J. P. Burt and A. S. Fleming as directors on June 30, 1903 [251], and he tried to convince the Santa Fe Railroad to build a siding to the track so that horses could be unloaded at the stables [252]. An article in the July 23, 1903, *Union* again referred obliquely to the poor condition of the track, claiming that the 'foundation of the fine track still remains', which would make it easier to repair [253].

The first shipment of the eastern horses arrived on September 1, 1903 [254], but the big news, a few weeks later, was that Spalding had taken over the Belmont Breeders' Association and its 250 acres of land where the track and stables of the Pacific Beach racetrack were located. The *Evening Tribune* reported on September 18 that the board of directors had resigned that day and Spalding, his son Keith and Charles T. Hewitt, a horseman that Mr. Spalding had known in the east and in whom he had every confidence, had been elected in their places. The name was to be changed to the American Saddle-Horse Breeding Farm and the track to be hereafter known as American Park. The article explained that Mr. Spalding had always been an admirer of the American or Kentucky type of combination gaited saddle and driving animals and 'the breeding of this high class of horses will be the special purpose of the establishment' [255]. The following morning the *Union* linked the takeover to their previous rumor:

> It will be recalled that several months ago it was stated that Mr. Spalding was considering the proposition of purchasing, but at that time the report was denied, though not strenuously. It seems that Mr. Spalding became interested at the time, but for business reasons did not want to be known in the deal until he had succeeded in purchasing a number of horses in the east that he wanted [256].

A few days later, on September 21, 1903, the American Saddle-Horse Breeding Farm was incorporated. A. G. and Keith Spalding were the principal shareholders, with Hewitt, D. C. Reed, and L. P. Swayne holding the balance of the shares [257]. Spalding was president, his son secretary and treasurer, and Hewitt was named manager. Reed and Swayne had been directors of the Belmont association and were retained on the board of the new company.

In the summer of 1904 Hewitt and some 'splendid representatives' of their stock went to San Francisco to show the San Francisco Riding Club. According to the *San Francisco Daily Call* on June 4, 1904, frequenters of the bridle paths of Golden Gate Park noticed a new type of saddle horse, a 'peacocky high stepper from the blue grass country, which has all the airs and graces of a ballet dancer'. The story included photographs of Hewitt mounted on Grace Boyd, Artistic and Chief, 'showing off the airs and graces of some of the Spalding high steppers'. The article explained that the Spaldings had a 'country place at Pacific Beach, near San Diego, where they had established the American Saddle-horse Breeding Farm' [258].

The saddle-horse breeding venture apparently was less than successful and was abandoned later the same year, perhaps due in part to what the *Daily Call* article had called 'the advance in public favor of the automobile as a vehicle of pleasure and of utility'. Although the newspapers had referred to Spalding's take-over of Gassen's Belmont Breeders' Association as a purchase or buy-out, the transaction apparently did not include the racetrack property itself and there is no record of any actual transfer at the San Diego County Recorder's office. Gassen retained ownership, and in a deed dated November 2, 1904, granted the racetrack and other property[39] at the mouth of Rose Canyon to U. S. Grant, Jr., son of the Civil War general and former president [259].

Another real estate deal occurred on June 17, 1905, when the *Union* reported an 'Important Sale'; the Union Brick Co. had purchased these properties from U. S. Grant, Jr. for $25,000 [260]. A few weeks later, on July 29, Union Brick deeded the southern portion of the property, including the racetrack property at the mouth of Rose Creek, back to Grant while retaining the properties in Rose Canyon where the deposits of clay necessary for their brick enterprise were located [261].

On March 10, 1906, the *Union* reported that the Pacific Beach racetrack had been sold by U. S. Grant Jr. to John Burgess, a well-known business man of El Cajon. The track was known as one of the best in Southern California 'in years past' and was popular with horsemen.

> Meets were held frequently and there was hardly a time during the entire year when a number of the best racers in the west could not be found there. In winter time especially it was the custom of race horse owners to ship their horses to Pacific Beach for winter training. As a result there was always plenty doing there and it was a favorite gathering place for horsemen who happened to be in this section of the country.

---

[39] The deed included Pueblo Lot 1787, the northern half of Pueblo Lot 1788 (except the right-of-way of the California Southern Railway and the city wagon road up Rose Canyon and 10.66 acres in the northeast part previously deeded to James R. Wade), 'all of that certain property known as the Pacific Beach Race Track' (Pueblo Lot 1797 or Lot 'B' Rincon Valley, except the right-of-way of the Pacific Beach railway), Pueblo Lot 1798, and those parts of Pueblo Lot 1208 lying west and south of the Pacific Beach railway.

Pacific Beach Racetrack about 1906. The grandstand is on the left and club house on the right with the judges' stand and flagpole barely visible behind (above and below) the roof on the left side of the grandstand. The mile-long oval racecourse itself is not visible but would have run between the grandstand and the judges' stand with the backstretch on the near side of Rose Creek, the area of slightly darker vegetation beyond the grandstand. Grand (now Balboa) Avenue and the railroad line cuts across the center of the photo with central Pacific Beach, including Stough Hall and the College of Letters building, then Hotel Balboa (top left), in the background. (SDHC #344)

> Of late years not much has been done with the track, although it is still in good condition. There is a club house and grand stand on the grounds, the latter having a good seating capacity. The accommodations at the track are first class in every respect.

This *Union* report concluded with the customary statement that although Mr. Burgess had gone away and it was accordingly impossible to learn from him what he contemplated doing with the track it was understood that a number of improvements would be made to the grounds and buildings though the nature of these improvements would not be announced until later [262].

Again the newspaper report was not substantiated by a deed at the Recorder's office and on October 10, 1906, another *Union* headline announced that the 'Pacific Beach Track Is Sold For $75,000.00'; this time U. S. Grant, Jr. had sold Pueblo Lot 1797, popularly known as the Pacific Beach race track, and other adjoining property to Archibald Hart, who intended to divide the property into villa lots and city lots [263]. On November 8, 1906, Hart, Burgess, S. H. Kroff, and Otho B. Wetzell incorporated the Mission Bay Park Company 'to lay out, improve and beautify any part of the land now owned or hereafter acquired by this corporation and particularly, that part to be acquired known as the Pacific Beach Race Track' [264].

The *San Diego Union* reported on November 22, 1906, that officers of the company and an engineer planned to visit the property with a view of laying off the grounds suitable for suburban homesites and improvements of the park. 'A unique feature of the park improvement will be a canal from the bay, which will encircle the race track, in the center of which will be the lands set aside for recreation purposes of all kinds, such as one sees in the parks of the larger cities of the east'. One attractive feature of these lands was the presence of Mission Bay 'for aquatic entertainments can be carried on in the most gigantic and gorgeous manner'. Other features of high class amusement would be

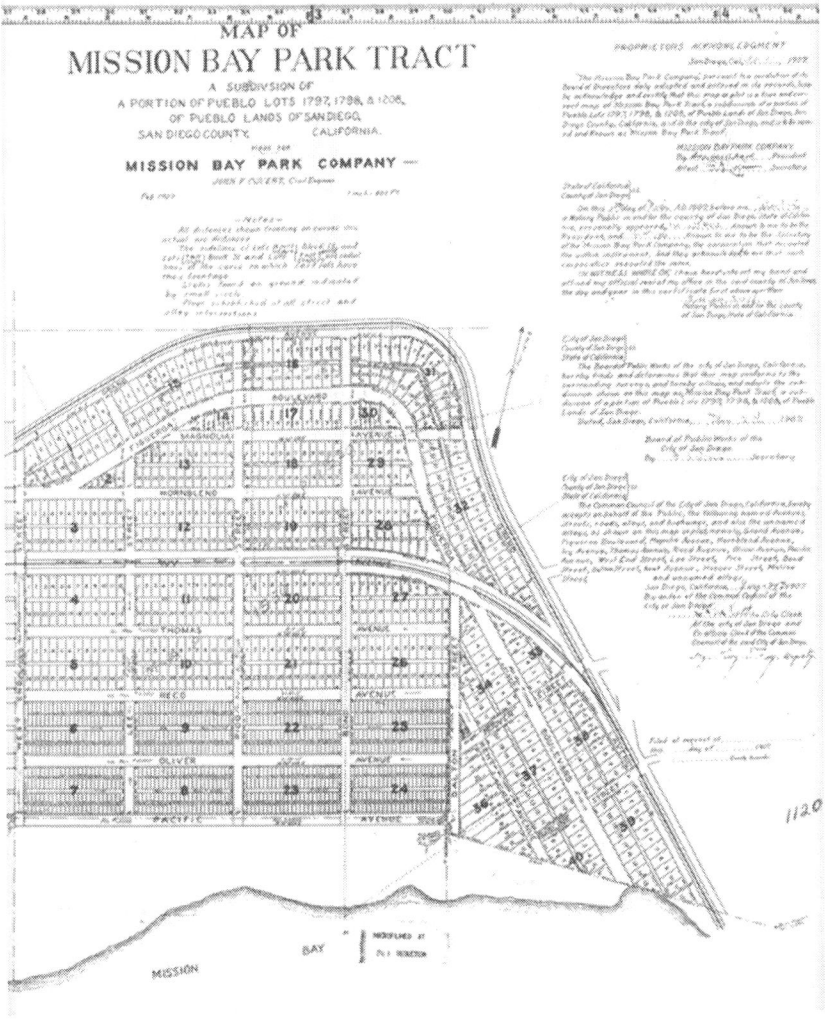

had there, but the officers of the company were not at liberty to state the nature of them [265].

One feature of high class amusement that would not be there was a racetrack. The map of the Mission Bay Park tract filed in February 1907 subdivided the property acquired by the company in much the same grid pattern as that of the Pacific Beach subdivision to the west, including extensions of Hornblend, Ivy (now Grand), Thomas, Reed, Oliver and Pacific Avenues (now Pacific Beach Drive)[40]. The subdivision map showed the Los Angeles and San Diego Beach Railway in both its original alignment, circling the perimeter of the tract along what are now Mission Bay Drive and Garnet Avenue (both then called Grand Avenue) and in the realignment then under construction on Ivy (today's Grand) Avenue. Construction of this railroad bypass across what had formerly been the infield and straightaways in early 1907 put a definite end to the existence of the Pacific Beach racetrack.

Despite their efforts in subdividing the racetrack property, the Mission Bay Park Company failed to effectively develop or market their tract and the only property sale they recorded was for lots 6, 7 and 8 of block 29 and lots 1, 2, 3 and 30 to 33 of block 32, Mission Bay Park [266]. These lots, on each side of Figueroa Boulevard between Magnolia and Hornblend and the southwest corner of Magnolia and Mission Bay Drive (then Grand) were the locations of the actual structures remaining from the former racetrack; the judges' stand, club house and grandstand. This parcel was sold on March 14, 1907, to Ye Olde Mission Inn Company, a corporation set up in February 1907 by James H. Babcock, J. R. Richards, L. E. McHenry, A. E. Morgan and J. G. Anderson to 'hold, own and operate hotels, clubs, café, real estate, theaters, amusement grounds, yachts, steamboats, stocks, bonds, mines, mortgage, merchandise properties and interests and rights in any and all such properties' [267].

Ye Olde Mission Inn Company apparently did proceed with the 'hold, own and operate hotels' part of its charter. Under the headline 'Fire Threatens Pretty Hostlery', the February 3, 1908, San Diego Union reported that 'The Mission Inn, a picturesque country resort located about a mile south of Pacific Beach' had narrowly escaped destruction by fire. Although a shed was a total loss, volunteers using a garden hose and bucket brigade prevented the fire from spreading to the

---

[40] The Mission Bay Park tract map of 1907 does not appear to acknowledge the existence of Rose Creek, a stream which flows through the center of the tract and during wet winters in the recent past had inundated much of it.

nearby hotel 'formerly used by the racetrack people as a club house'. Former San Diego fire department chief A. B. Cairnes 'rendered yeoman service in staying the progress of the fire'[41] [268].

However, even Chief Cairnes was unable to save Ye Olde Mission Inn when it caught fire again later in the same year. The November 27, 1908, *Evening Tribune* reported the 'Mission Inn Completely Destroyed by Fire Early Today' and that there was 'only a heap of smouldering ruins where last night there was a pretty and substantial structure' [269]. The *Union* report on the following day (barely twenty years after the original construction of the track) noted that with the destruction of the inn 'there is little left to remind one of the old days' [270].

Apparently unable to interest prospective buyers in their tract, the Mission Bay Park Company transferred it back to U. S. Grant, Jr. on November 30, 1908, (except for the 1.25-acre Mission Inn property) [271]. Grant gave C. F. Willard, President of the Mission Bay Park Company, an option to buy 450 acres between Pacific Beach and Morena, including Pueblo Lot 1797 but excluding the property containing the former racetrack buildings [272], but Willard apparently did not exercise this option.

In July 1910 James H. Babcock, a founder and president of Ye Olde Mission Inn Company, proposed building a new club house to occupy the site of the structure that had burned down in 1908. According to the *Evening Tribune*, the handsome club house to be built at Mission Bay Park would have 15 sleeping rooms, a large dining hall and grill, and would be for the use of members of the Pacific Coast Automobile & Driving Club, an organization 'perfected' by Babcock, 'the leading spirit in the movement'[42]. Club membership would be limited and a

---

[41] Chief Cairnes was a neighbor; he owned property in Pueblo Lot 1788 and 1789 north of and adjacent to Pueblo Lot 1797 and had lived there since shortly after his retirement from the Fire Department in 1905. His home on a prominent rise at what is now the northwest corner of Soledad Mountain Road and Felspar Street overlooked the racetrack property and the former fireman undoubtedly responded instinctively to the sight of smoke and flames.

[42] James H. Babcock had been proprietor of Babs, a 'Bohemian' café or restaurant in San Francisco which featured 'little rooms made to represent prison cells, undertaking establishments, mausoleums and similar weird places. Coffins were used for tables and skulls for drinking cups'. In the aftermath of the San Francisco earthquake and fire in 1906 he had disappeared and been mourned as dead by his family before reappearing in San Diego [617]. After the failure of the Mission Inn venture he operated the grill at the Cecil Hotel and the adjoining Bab's German Garden Restaurant on Sixth Street downtown before their licenses were revoked on New Year's Eve 1912 for violating liquor laws (and because 'morals were not all that could be desired') [618].

---

membership certificate would cost $25. Every courtesy would be extended to women members of the families of male members. Each woman of a member's family would be issued a ticket which would give her the privileges of the club at all times, including the right to invite their women friends as their guests. The club house was to be located on both the Los Angeles & San Diego Beach and the Santa Fe railways and the automobile boulevard connecting Los Angeles and San Diego passed the grounds [273].

The new club house was never built but the October 18, 1910, *San Diego Union* carried a story that a Sperry biplane built in San Diego had been moved to Pacific Beach where it was being put into flying condition at a shop near the 'old race track', where it would be given the first trial. The article noted that 'the old race track, which is owned by I. H. Babcock' (presumably J. H. Babcock) is to be improved for an 'automobile and areoplane course [sic]' [274].

This improvement also never happened and the Mission Inn property was auctioned at the courthouse door on February 17, 1912, for $3,862.76 [275]. In 1931 a story in the *San Diego Sun* reported that the ruins of the grandstand and the stables were still to be found 'almost hidden by the rank vegetation of two score years' [276]. Aerial photos of the area from 1941 show the outlines of some of the streets laid out in the Mission Bay Park subdivision map but little actual development and no trace of anything resembling the former mile-long oval race course.

The Federal Public Housing Authority took over much of the property of the Mission Bay Park tract in 1940 and parts of the Bayview Terrace Project for wartime defense workers and Bayview Terrace Elementary School were built on the western portions. The southern portion of Pueblo Lot 1797 eventually became Mission Bay High School, the Mission Bay Athletic Fields and the back nine of the Mission Bay Golf Course. One structure from the track itself, a three-story wooden judges' stand, remained standing and was incorporated into the Rancho 101 Motel on Pacific Highway (Mission Bay Drive) in 1947. The motel (and judges' stand) was finally demolished in 1968, eliminating the last remaining trace of the former racetrack in Pacific Beach. The block west of Mission Bay Drive between Magnolia Avenue and Hornblend Street where the club house, grandstand and judges' stand once stood and where thousands of nineteenth century San Diego sports fans once gathered to enjoy races, baseball games, mounted sword combat and parachute drops is now (2013) occupied by an automobile dealership.

Rancho 101 Motel

6596 Pacific Highway
(U. S. 101) San Diego 9, Cal.

5 The Asbestos Works

When the Pacific Beach Company sold lots to the public beginning in 1887 the typical deed specified that the property was granted for and in consideration of a sum of money and other valuable considerations (the deeds also included a prohibition against 'vending intoxicating liquors . . . directly or under some evasive guise'). However, the Pacific Beach Company's deed to John D. Hoff and George W. Hazzard on September 24, 1888, was a little different. Hoff and Hazzard received Fractional Blocks 173 and 174 in the Pacific Beach subdivision and a parcel of land extending 400 feet east of and adjoining these blocks 'upon the Express condition and for no other consideration than the herein shall construct a corrugated Iron Building to be located on the lands herein described and to provide the necessary machinery to carry on the manufacture of Asbestos goods and wares':

> Said building and machinery contained therein to Cost not less than "Four thousand Dollars" $4000.00 and the construction of the same to be commenced within thirty <30> days from this date and to be completed and in full operation within three <3> months from date and to maintain and operate the same as such manufactory for a period of three <3> years' [277].

The property in question was west of Rose Creek and immediately north of the San Diego, Old Town and Pacific Beach Railroad which at that time ran along the north side of Grand Avenue (later Balboa, now Garnet) after swinging around the racetrack which was south of Grand/Balboa/Garnet and on the east side of Rose Creek. Pacific Beach Blocks 173 and 174 were in Pueblo Lot 1789, on the eastern edge of the Pacific Beach subdivision. The additional parcel extended 400 feet east of these lots, in Pueblo Lot 1788 and outside the Pacific Beach subdivision (although apparently owned by the Pacific Beach Company). Today the land granted in this deed extends about a block west and a block east of Soledad Mountain Road and about two blocks north from its intersection with Garnet Avenue.

Asbestos is a naturally occurring fibrous mineral with physical and chemical properties that give it a number of potential commercial applications. It is non-flammable and possesses high thermal resistance, making it an ideal insulator in high-temperature environments such as furnaces and boilers. It is insoluble and chemically inert, which makes it a desirable addition to coatings of all kinds, particularly, in view of its fire-resistance, to paints intended for wooden buildings. Asbestos mining on a commercial scale had only begun in the second half of the nineteenth century and the development of products incorporating this miracle ingredient was in the early stages in the 1880s. Of course, we now know that as production and use of asbestos increased in the twentieth century, particularly as insulation and boiler coatings in shipbuilding, asbestos miners and shipyard workers began suffering lung ailments, including fatal cases of asbestosis and mesothelioma, which was eventually traced to their exposure to asbestos dust. By the end of the twentieth century, asbestos had been banned from most products and interest in asbestos has turned to removal and disposal, and of course, litigation.

John D. Hoff was 30 years old in 1888 and had been active in acquiring and developing asbestos mining properties in the Elsinore area. At various times in his career he was described as a chemist (or even an alchemist) and he apparently hoped to use the Pacific Beach plant to develop products such as paints and insulating coatings enhanced by the asbestos from his mines. George W. Hazzard was a San Diego pioneer, arriving in a city of a few hundred residents in 1868. He became a prominent businessman and property owner and two-time president of the San Diego Chamber of Commerce, with real estate holdings from downtown to the rural areas of the county. He had a particular interest in mining and minerals, and owned mining claims in the Julian-Banner district. His interests in real estate and minerals would have coincided in the Pacific Beach asbestos manufacturing project.

Less than a week after the deed to this property was recorded, the September 29, 1888, edition of the *San Diego Union* ran a story under the headline 'A New Industry, An Important Manufacturing Establishment Located at Pacific Beach':

> It is stated that an asbestos manufactory will soon be in operation near the driving park at Pacific Beach. Asbestos is a mineral found in large quantities near Elsinore, and constitutes the base material for manufacturing boiler covering, fire-proof cement and roof-paint. The San Diego Asbestos Mining and Manufacturing Company will put in an establishment capable of crushing 8,000 pounds of this mineral per day. A number of men are now at work upon the necessary buildings, and the enterprise will be pushed forward with all rapidity possible. A spur will be extended from the San Diego and Pacific Beach road to the building to facilitate shipments. George W. Hazzard, of this city, is one of the prime movers of the new industry, and John D. Hoff, of Elsinore, is manager [278].

A few weeks later, but well within the three month deadline to have operations up and running, the 'Brief Mention' column in the October 17, 1888, *Union* reported that the Pacific Beach asbestos works would soon be in operation:

The boiler, engine and pumps were tested Monday, the steam whistle sounded first, and all worked satisfactory. It is expected that the machinery ordered from San Francisco will arrive in a few days, and once on the ground no time will be lost in placing it in position [279].

Apparently no time was lost, and by January 19, 1889, the *Union* reported the manufacture of paint was to be undertaken on a large scale:

> The success which has attended the manufacture of asbestos roof paint at this factory has decided the proprietors to embark in the manufacture of various colored house paints, and in this connection they yesterday let the contract for several thousand cans of different dimensions, in which the famous boiled oil and lead product will be put up [280].

Hoff also continued to experiment with other uses for asbestos. An April 18, 1889, *San Diego Union* article headlined 'Making Fire Brick' claimed that Hoff had mixed asbestos with local clay to produce a brick that could withstand the heat of cupola furnaces in iron works and 'not only equals but excels that shipped from England' [281]. The *Union* reported on July 20 that the asbestos works at Pacific Beach had a contract for covering the steampipes and boilers of three plants owned by the Los Angeles Cable Car Company and that it had received its first carload of long-fiber asbestos from the desert mines [282].

By the end of 1889 the plant had overcome a slow startup to become among one of San Diego's most valuable industries. The *San Diego Union* on January 5, 1890, called the asbestos industry one of San Diego's principal enterprises:

> Among the manufacturing industries of San Diego which is specially entitled to the notice of the public is that known as the John D. Hoff Asbestos Company. Although it is but little more than a year ago since the plant was put in, at which time the result of the company's efforts may be said to have been very problematical, the operations of the institution have now become so well established and so widely appreciated that it has become to be regarded as one of the most valuable permanent industries of this section. No better illustration of its value to the county could be supplied than the work that is now being done by the company at Governor Waterman's mines at Julian. In the first place the raw material was taken from its natural location, near Elsinore, was brought to the works of the company at Pacific Beach, and having been converted into the manufactured article, is now being applied to its various uses at the mines mentioned, in each instance giving employment to many men, and keeping the money within the county. The huge boilers and steam pipes are being made for that purpose, every building is being painted with the asbestos paint, and, indeed, wherever an opportunity offers itself to utilize the products of the company, no matter in what form it may be, advantage is taken of it. The principal uses to which the asbestos is put are in the manufacture of house and roof paints, boiler and steam pipe covering, fire proof roofing and asbestos stone lining cement [283].

Governor Waterman's mine at Julian was the Stonewall Mine, the largest gold mine in San Diego County, which was at the peak of its production in 1890. Robert W. Waterman, who served as Governor of California from 1887 to 1891, had purchased the Stonewall in 1886 and invested heavily in improvements, including new shafts and hoists, and an expanded stamp mill, all powered by steam engines and boilers which were apparently insulated with asbestos from the Pacific Beach plant[43]. San Diego County at the time also included Imperial County and much of what is now Riverside County, including the asbestos mines in the Elsinore district and the Colorado desert that supplied the manufacturing plant in Pacific Beach, so in this illustration every stage of the process, from mining to manufacture to application, was conducted locally, 'keeping the money within the county' in the words of the *San Diego Union*.

Although floods in December 1889 washed out the bridge over Rose Creek, isolating the asbestos works from its transportation links, it apparently continued to thrive. The May 28, 1890, *Union* reported that another large shipment of asbestos goods had been sent down from Pacific Beach and forwarded by steamer to San Francisco and an order had been received from Denver for about two tons of asbestos roofing and asbestos paint [284]. On May 30 the *Union* noted that the John D. Hoff Asbestos Company was the only manufacturer to have succeeded in amalgamating asbestos, white lead, zinc and linseed oil for house paint, and had also applied for patents for their asbestos fire-proof whitewash coatings [285].

The success of the asbestos plant in Pacific Beach called for further capital improvements, as the *Union* noted on June 18, 1890, in an article titled 'A Paint Machine Arrives at the Asbestos Works and Is a Corker':

> A large combination paint mill weighing three thousand pounds arrived yesterday at the asbestos works. It consists of a combination of three machines of large capacity, producing the paint ground, colored and canned, ready for the market. It mixes the paint thoroughly and evenly and grinds finer than can be done by any other process [286].

On July 6 the *Union* added that the Hoff Asbestos Paint Company was enlarging its works at Pacific Beach to accommodate new and improved machinery, a crusher and grinder to 'work up the asbestos to be mixed in the paint'. Two new engines had replaced the one formerly used [287].

---

[43] The value of the ore declined abruptly after 1890, Waterman died in 1891, and the mine was shut down in 1893.

The *San Diego Union* had been referring to the asbestos works in Pacific Beach under a variety of names including the San Diego Asbestos Mining and Manufacturing Company, the Pacific Beach Asbestos Company, the John D. Hoff Asbestos Company and the Hoff Asbestos Paint Company, perhaps because in its first two years the business had no formal corporate structure. The land had been granted to John D. Hoff and George W. Hazzard as individuals under the condition that they provide a building and machinery for the manufacture of asbestos goods.

It wasn't until September 11, 1890, that The John D. Hoff Asbestos Company was incorporated under the laws of the State of California for the purposes of acquiring and owning mines, owning and constructing works, and the manufacture and sale of asbestos goods of all kinds. Although George Hazzard continued to own a half-interest in the property, he was not listed as a director or stockholder in the Articles of Incorporation. The individuals who were listed were Hoff himself (140 shares), his wife Minnie D. (10 shares), Amos J. King (100 shares), A. H. Isham (125 shares), Edwin A. Wells (124 shares), and H. L. Story (1 share) [288]. Amos King, like Hoff, had a background in mining and minerals and also owned asbestos mines in the Elsinore area. Presumably Hoff and King provided the overall direction and technical expertise for the mining and manufacturing side of the company. Isham, Story and Wells, who were also principals in the Story & Isham Commercial Company, evidently directed the marketing and logistics side.

Alfred H. Isham had been a wagon salesman in San Francisco before moving to the San Diego area in 1885 and allying himself with Frank A. Kimball, founder of National City, and J. S. Gordon, another San Diego pioneer and former president of the Chamber of Commerce, in Isham, Gordon and Company, dealers in wagons, carriages and agricultural implements. Earlier in 1890 H. L. Story had bought out Gordon's interest and the company was reorganized as Story & Isham Commercial Company with Story as president, Isham as vice president and Wells as secretary. H. L. Story was already a legendary figure in San Diego; Story and Elisha S. Babcock had bought and developed the Coronado peninsula in 1886 and were the builders and owners of the Hotel Del Coronado, among other major commercial enterprises.

The *San Diego Union* wasn't the only periodical following the story of the asbestos works in Pacific Beach. *The Golden Era* had begun as a weekly newspaper in San Francisco in 1852, moved to San Diego in 1887, and in 1890 was a literary journal publishing monthly issues dedicated to the 'artistic and industrial progress of the West.' The

April and May 1890 issue featured a pull-out panorama of San Diego and Coronado, engraved from a photograph, which appears to be from an elevated vantage point in the vicinity of Cortez Hill ('Showing only that portion of the City that Borders on the Bay'). One panel of the panorama shows the Los Coronados Islands in the distance, Coronado across the bay, downtown San Diego with four-story buildings and church steeples, and in the foreground, a two-story building with 'Hoff's Asbestos Paint' lettered across it, the only sign visible in the entire city [289] (the actual photo appears in Smythe's *History of San Diego* and shows the same building with 'San Diego Daily Bee' written on it [1]).

A. H. Isham was vice president of Story & Isham and a director of the Hoff asbestos company but he also had an agenda of his own. Mary Proctor, daughter of the world's most prominent astronomer, had expressed an interest in building an observatory in her father's memory after his death in 1888. Isham had the idea of promoting Mt. Miguel, a 2500–foot peak overlooking Sweetwater Reservoir, as the site of the observatory. He invited Miss Proctor and other dignitaries, including 'father of San Diego' Alonzo Horton, to an Independence Day celebration at the summit, complete with a 40-foot tall flagpole and fireworks after dark.

The June 1890 issue of *The Golden Era* contained a cartoon spoofing the procession of these dignitaries to the top of Mt. Miguel. 'The First Liberty Pole Ever Erected on San Miguel July 4, 1890' showed an enormous flagpole being carried over a canyon on the backs of four mules, two on each end of the pole on either side of the canyon, while three other mules dangle over the canyon from the middle section of

THE FIRST LIBERTY POLE EVER ERECTED ON SAN MIGUEL, JULY 4, 1890.

Made by the Silver Gate Manufacturing Company.
Painted by the Hoff Asbestos Company.
Varnished by the Murphy Varnish Company.
Flag by the Old Reliable Tent Company.
Erected by the Story & Isham Commercial Company.

the pole (a rider in the background carrying a parasol and riding sidesaddle presumably represents Miss Procter). 'Painted with Hoff's Asbestos Paint' is prominently written on the pole [290] (77-year-old Alonzo Horton fell off his mount at 'Horton's slide' on the trail to the summit, the fireworks were invisible to observers on the flatlands below because of low clouds - although they did start a fire on the mountain - and Miss Proctor ultimately decided to establish her observatory elsewhere)[44].

These nineteenth century examples of product placement were supplemented by full-page advertisements for Story & Isham Commercial Company featuring John D. Hoff Asbestos Goods which appeared in *The Golden Era* in 1890 (also drawn by John C. Hill).

The November and December 1890 *Golden Era* included an article about Manufacturing in the San Diego Bay Region (with actual portraits of H. L. Story, A. H. Isham, J. D. Hoff and E. A. Wells):

---

[44] The *San Diego Union* also carried this cartoon, which they credited to John C. Hill, the advertising artist for 'Hoff's asbestos department' of Isham & Story. 'He made the city laugh on Sunday last at his caricature in The Union of the Proctor party climbing San Miguel with their flag pole for the Fourth's festivities' [726].

The factory and mill with their mechanic sinews are waking the echoes, painting their silhouettes of smoke on the sky, and spreading their silvery clouds of steam in the golden abyss of the busy day.

From Pacific Beach, on the northwest, from Roseville to Coronado and around the bay to National City, and South San Diego is growing up a cordon of plants, in easy reach of railroad and wharf.

One cannot write of the industrial development of the San Diego Bay region without writing of the Story & Isham Commercial Company, the members of which have done, and are still doing, so much to develop the manufacturing and commercial interest of the bay region. Messers H. L. Story (President) A. H. Isham (General Mgr.) E. A. Wells (Secretary), compose the company which extends its business over the entire Southwest and into Mexico, and far up the sea coast.

After praising Story as 'one of the strongest and most substantial men in San Diego . . . one of the chief manufacturers of San Diego . . . bought, named and developed Coronado . . . developed a water system for San Diego, then the street car system . . . his name and capital gave strength to the successful system of banking', the article continued:

Now Mr. Story has turned his attention to the great field of manufacturing development, and in company with Messrs. Isham, John D. Hoff, of Asbestos and paint fame, F. A. Wells, J. D. Schuyler, and others, has put his means, capacity and enterprise into a number of manufacturing corporations whose plants are dotting the bay region and giving to it an industrial character.

Mr. A. H. Isham is a born man of business, who after years spent in business and industrial development, far and near, in other connections, is now the managing man, in close counsel with Mr. Story, of the great business of the commercial company, and the manufacturing corporations with which Mr. Story himself, and Messrs. Hoff and Wells are connected.

John D. Hoff, who has done much and was the original man, in developing asbestos, coal, etc., at Elsinore, is a practical and constant experimenter and scientific investigator. He has had extended experience in geologic observation and mining in Indiana, Georgia and on this coast.

E. A. Wells, the secretary of the Commercial company, and the several corporations with which it has more or less connection, is a young man of fine business character, or sterling integrity and great moral worth. He is a member of the First Baptist church of San Diego, a son of Mr. E. F. Wells, a leading and successful horticulturist of Sweetwater valley.

The John D. Hoff Asbestos Company

This company, lately incorporated has its steam manufacturing works at Pacific Beach, where they were established by Mr. Hoff in a smaller way, a year or two ago. Mr. Story's purchase into the Hoff mines and plant were made after thorough personal examination, and the development and progress making in the business of utilizing Asbestos has proved the wisdom of the investment. The plant has been newly fitted with 30-horse engine power, improved paint mills, etc., and must soon double its room and capacity, and the business can be developed and extended indefinitely. The company owns and controls all the Asbestos mines yet discovered on the Pacific coast, and does all the manufacturing for the west.

JOHN D. HOFF.

Asbestos is utilized at this factory for combining with pure white lead and pure linseed oil in making liquid or prepared house and cottage paints, in twenty-four beautiful shades. It is utilized for fire-proof roof paint, for fire-proof roofing, for boiler and steam piping, effecting a saving of half the fuel; for paints for iron and tin work, and Prof. Hoff has recently produced the "California Asbestos Lubricant," which prevents "hot boxes" and outwears all other lubricants. Tons of Asbestos and tons of pure white lead are used, and all the great power plants are having boilers, pipes, etc., covered; and the roof and house paints are becoming universal in their use [291].

The December 1890 issue of *The Golden Era* was entirely devoted to an novel by Madge Morris, author, poet and wife of editor Harr Wagner, and included a testimonial which stated that the author 'wrote the narrative at her Villa Home, Pacific Beach – made attractive and beautiful – both interior and exterior – by Hoff's Glossy Asbestos Paints' and that the views 'through her open casement windows reflect on the shores of the Bay – a net-work of buildings – alive with busy men Amalgamating, Packing and Shipping, HOFF'S ASBESTOS PAINTS AND LUBRICANTS'[45]. Not only that, but these 'shipments to distant lands, and incoming ships from the World around – with proud, black hulls – glistening with Hoff's Asbestos Marine Paints, may have given her thoughts of Nations where laws are hard for the peasantry to bear' - and thus inspired the novel, 'A Titled Plebeian' presumably about the legal burdens born by the peasantry of other nations [292].

---

[45] The Wagners' home is still standing at the corner of Diamond and Noyes Streets, still with a view of the bay.

By 1890 the John D. Hoff Asbestos Company and its factory in Pacific Beach was represented as one of the dozen or so manufactures now in operation in the area that were major factors in the growth of the San Diego Bay Region. However, beginning in 1891 the high profile of the Hoff asbestos business in the local media began to fade. Neither the *San Diego Union* nor *The Golden Era* featured Hoff or the asbestos industry in any further articles after 1890. The Story & Isham Commercial Company's full-page advertisements featuring John D. Hoff asbestos goods disappeared in 1891 and the John D. Hoff Asbestos Co. placed its own, much more modest ads.

The land boom in San Diego had peaked in 1888 and more than half of the population, who might have been customers for house paint and roofing, had left by 1890. The featured client for boiler and steam pipe coverings, the Stonewall Mine, was in sharp decline. Severe winter floods aggravated by the plant's exposed position at the mouth of Rose Creek may have adversely affected production. These same floods also caused interruption to both local and mainline rail transportation that could have affected the flow of raw materials from inland mines and the shipping of finished product. Flooding of the Santa Margarita River in the vicinity of Fallbrook in February 1891 permanently washed out the rail link between San Diego and San Bernardino and points east, putting San Diego instead at the end of a branch line from Los Angeles and ending direct rail service between San Diego and Elsinore.

In addition to these possible commercial challenges, a different sort of problem arose from turmoil within the Story & Isham Commercial Company, where A. H. Isham's ethical shortcomings were coming to light. By the end of 1890 Story & Isham was heavily in debt and unable to obtain credit. In February 1891 Isham engineered the ouster of Story as president and in March he formed the Isham-Miller Commercial Company and attempted to transfer Story & Isham's assets and accounts to his new company. The resulting legal battles among individuals who were also principals of the Hoff company and owners of half of its shares, and the disarray and ultimate collapse of the company serving as its general agents, undoubtedly had an adverse effect on the Hoff company's business.

Isham and his former partner J. S. Gordon had also been swindling Frank Kimball by making unauthorized purchases in Kimball's name. These scandals involving H. L. Story and Frank Kimball, two of the area's leading citizens, ruined Isham's reputation in the legitimate business community and led him into a new career in the patent medicine business, where he went on to achieve further infamy as one of the most notorious medical frauds of the era. Isham's Waters of Life, bottled at a spring at the base of Mt. Miguel, was sold all over the world as a cure, originally for baldness, but eventually for just about any ailment or even as the prescription for perpetual youth. He conducted a marketing campaign that made use of bogus testimonials, fraudulent claims and false news stories and which achieved phenomenal success until he was featured in a series of articles on medical fraud and quackery in *Collier's* magazine in 1905 ('mentally unsound . . . the most arrant and blasphemous faker now before the public' [293]). This exposure caused sales to plummet, and the Pure Food and Drug Act of 1906 (passed partly in response to these articles) outlawed many of his sales practices.

While the demise of Story & Isham and the redirection of Isham's promotional talents to his own Waters of Life brand contributed to the lower profile of Hoff's asbestos company after 1890, it is also possible in view of Isham's later credibility issues that some of the success that Story & Isham had reported for the asbestos business might have been overstated in the first place.

Whatever the reasons, on July 16, 1892, Hoff sold his half-interest in the Pacific Beach real estate to A. B. Cairnes, then serving as San Diego's first Fire Chief, while reserving the 'right to use the one half acre of ground now occupied by the Asbestos Works' [294]. George Hazzard deeded his half-interest in the property to Cairnes unconditionally on August 28, 1892 [295].

Although Hoff had reserved the right to use the asbestos works, he apparently didn't exercise that right for long, if at all. The San Diego City Directory of 1892-93 showed a 'Hoff, John D., Asbestos Co. factory on Pacific Beach Motor Line' [18] and the 1893-94 Directory showed a 'Hoff John D., Asbestos Co factory, Pacific Beach' [296], but by 1894-95 the San Diego directory no longer had an entry for John Hoff or his asbestos factory. The timetable of the San Diego, Old Town & Pacific Beach Railway had included a stop at the Asbestos Works as late as July 1, 1892, but the Asbestos Works was missing from its July 24, 1892, timetable.

The county Lot Books from this era, which list property assessments for tax purposes, has an entry for Pueblo Lot 1788 that shows that John D. Hoff owned '4.6 a. SW Cor' with improvements worth $2000 in 1892; in 1893 the Pacific Asbestos Co. owned '½ A. in SW Cor' with improvements worth $1500 (and A.B. Cairnes owned 4 a., also in the SW Cor with no improvements). In 1894 Cairnes owned all 19 acres in the southwest corner, with improvements worth $150 ($1500 or $2000 was a very large assessment, consistent with a building and machinery that cost 'not less than $4000'; $150 was less than the assessment for a typical house, perhaps representing the value of an empty corrugated iron building). These facts suggest that the asbestos works in Pacific Beach had not only been shut down and abandoned by 1894 but had been dismantled and removed from the property, possibly leaving the empty building behind.

John Hoff may have abandoned Pacific Beach but he was not finished with the asbestos industry, or mining and minerals in general. Los Angeles city directories showed him as manager of the Hoff Asbestos Manufacturing Co. in Los Angeles until 1899. In 1901 he reappeared in the San Francisco City Directory with an entry for the Hoff Asbestos Mfg. Co. in San Francisco and a residence in Oakland. In the ensuing years he evidently branched out into other pursuits involving minerals, including coal, oil and magnesite, a cement-like mineral used as flooring. There was a John D. Hoff Asbestos Company factory at the foot of 22nd Avenue in Oakland and a John D. Hoff Asbestos Co. mine in what is today the Redwood Regional Park near Moraga in the East Bay area.

There is conflicting information regarding the exact location of the Pacific Beach asbestos works. The 1892 Lot Book shows that John D. Hoff owned 4.6 acres in the southwest corner of Pueblo Lot 1788, which matches the size of the parcel stretching 500 feet north and 400 feet east from the southwest corner of Pueblo Lot 1788 deeded by the Pacific Beach Company in 1888. In 1893, after Hoff had sold the property to Cairnes, reserving 'the right to use the one half acre of ground now occupied by the asbestos works', the Lot Book showed that Cairnes owned 4 acres in the southwest corner but also that the Pacific Asbestos Co. owned ½ acre, also in the southwest corner. The Lot Book therefore places the asbestos works within the original 4.6 acre parcel in the southwest corner of Pueblo Lot 1788 but it does not specify exactly where the ½ acre factory site was located within these 4.6 acres. To further confuse the issue, a July 12, 1892, deed which transferred the site from the Hoff asbestos company to Hoff himself specified 'the land on which the asbestos works are located' as the 'E ½ of Block 174 being a subdivision of Pueblo Lot 1788' [297]. The problem with this is that Block 174 was in the Pacific Beach subdivision, in the southeast corner of Pueblo Lot 1789, not Pueblo Lot 1788; the property in the southwest corner of Pueblo Lot 1788 had consistently been described as 'lying directly east and adjoining Blocks <173> and <174>'.

One possible explanation of this discrepancy is that Block 174 was less than half the normal size of a block in Pacific Beach, and it might have seemed natural to describe the parcel of land immediately east of and adjoining it as the east half of the block, even though it was not even in the same subdivision or Pueblo Lot. Another possibility is that the plant actually was in the east half of Block 174 in the Pacific Beach subdivision, and that the reference to Pueblo Lot 1788 (and the entries in the county's Lot Book for Pueblo Lot 1788) was incorrect. A March 31, 1892, deed to John Hoff from Olive Hoff (his sister; formerly a student at the College of Letters in Pacific Beach) and Minnie Hoff (his wife) granted him a half interest in the west half of Block 174 as well as all interest in Block 173 in Pueblo Lot 1788 [298]. Since Blocks 173 and 174 in the Pacific Beach subdivision are the same size west-to-east, their differential treatment in this deed suggests that Block 174 actually was divided, and that might have been because the east half of Block 174 was indeed 'the land on which the asbestos works are located'. Again, this assumes that the deeds describing these blocks 'being a subdivision of Pueblo Lot 1788' and the entries in the Lot Books listing the asbestos works in Pueblo Lot 1788 were incorrect.

The idea that deeds could be recorded with incorrect descriptions of property is not as unlikely as it might seem; several earlier deeds had mistakenly described the property in Pueblo Lot 1788 by metes and bounds starting at the S.E. corner instead of the S.W. corner, an error of half a mile that had to be corrected in a subsequent deed [299]. The Lot Books were probably based on information recorded in deeds rather than from actual inspection and their purpose was to assist in property tax collection; as long as taxes were collected from the property owner the precise description of the property would have been of secondary importance.

Since the asbestos plant was built to process car loads of asbestos mined around Elsinore and shipped by rail, it must have been located next to a railroad line, and one of the *San Diego Union* articles even indicated that a spur line would be built from the San Diego, Old Town & Pacific Beach Railroad, which ran along the north side of what is now Garnet Avenue and on the southern edge of this property. A nautical chart of the San Diego Bay region published in 1889 and republished in 1899 which includes soundings and other features of False Bay (now Mission Bay) also shows topographical features of Pacific Beach, including Rose Creek, the racetrack, a railroad labeled Pacific Beach and San Diego Steam Motor Rail Road, and the few buildings standing in Pacific Beach at the time, one of which is located just north of the railroad (and the near turn of the racetrack) and west of Rose Creek. This may represent the asbestos works, which was in operation at that time.

Considering all the evidence, the plant must have been located north of the railroad line, now the northern side of Garnet Avenue, and near the boundary between Pueblo Lot 1789 (and the Pacific Beach subdivision) and Pueblo Lot 1788, which today is the western side of

Soledad Mountain Road. The site may have actually been in the east half of Block 174 in Pacific Beach (the southeast corner of Pueblo Lot 1789) or a location just to the east in the southwest corner of Pueblo Lot 1788 but near enough that contemporaries described it as the east half of Block 174. Block 174 today is the location of the Bayview Child Development Center just west of Soledad Mountain Road and north of Garnet, and the area to the east, in Pueblo Lot 1788, would include Soledad Mountain Road itself (about 75 feet wide) and the residential units on its east side.

Why was an asbestos factory built at this location in Pacific Beach? The asbestos mines near Elsinore were served by a rail spur and there

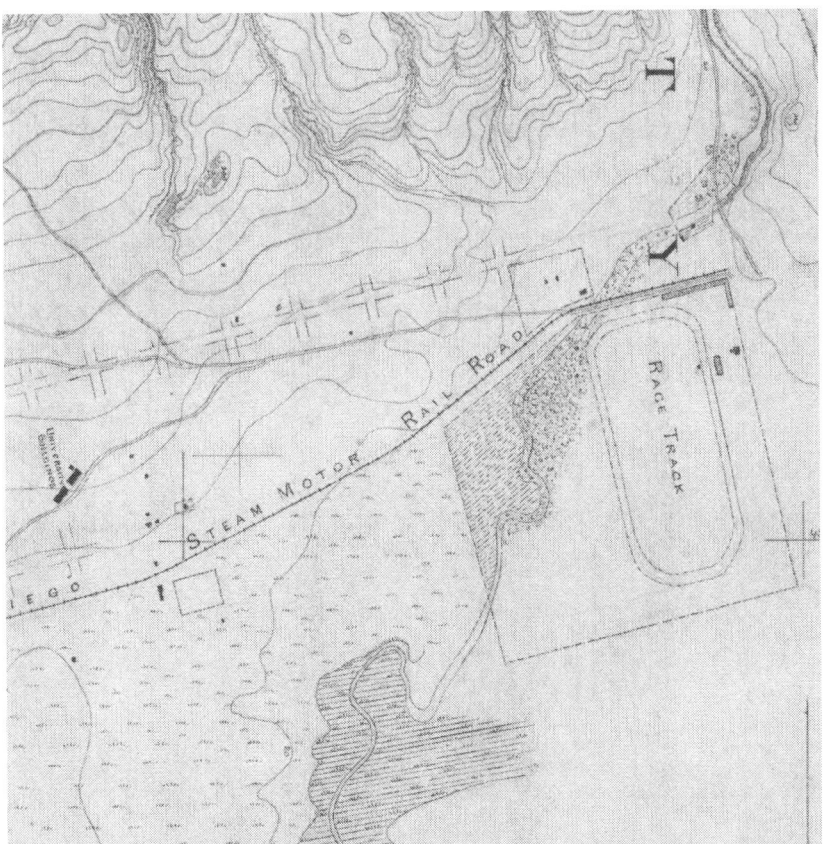

Detail from U. S. Coast and Geodetic Survey chart of the Pacific Coast from False Bay to La Jolla dated 1889, showing features of Pacific Beach including the 'Pacific Beach and San Diego Steam Motor Rail Road', 'University' Buildings, the Race Track (with club house, grandstand and judges stand) and the course of Rose Creek. The building across the tracks and the creek from the Race Track may represent the Hoff Asbestos Works, which was in operation at that time.

was direct rail service between Elsinore and San Diego and local rail service between San Diego and Pacific Beach. San Diego was also a seaport through which equipment and raw materials could be brought in and finished product shipped out. The Stonewall Mine in the mountains east of San Diego would be a major local customer. In addition to being free and on the local rail line, the land at the mouth of Rose Creek was well supplied with fresh water, a necessity for the steam-powered machinery of the day (in a deed from 1889 the Pacific Beach Company asserted that despite granting the land to Hoff and Hazzard it retained the right to sink wells and run pipes on the property [300]).

Today nothing remains of the asbestos works or the railway, but a block north, on the northwest corner of Soledad Mountain Road and Felspar Street, you can still (2013) see retaining walls, fallen gateposts and other ruins on the side of the hill. This is what survives from the A. B. Cairnes estate, built between 1906 and 1908 on the northern half of Block 173, property Cairnes acquired from John Hoff and George Hazzard in 1892. When the surrounding area was expropriated in 1941 to build the Bayview Terrace housing project for defense workers, the Cairnes home was spared and served as the Bayview Terrace Community Building. The Bayview Model Railroad club created a layout in the basement [301] and held public exhibitions on Tuesday evenings [302] until the building was demolished in the late 1950s to make way for the current Navy housing project and Soledad Mountain Road. Unlike the asbestos works, the ruins of the Cairnes home have remained undisturbed for over half a century.

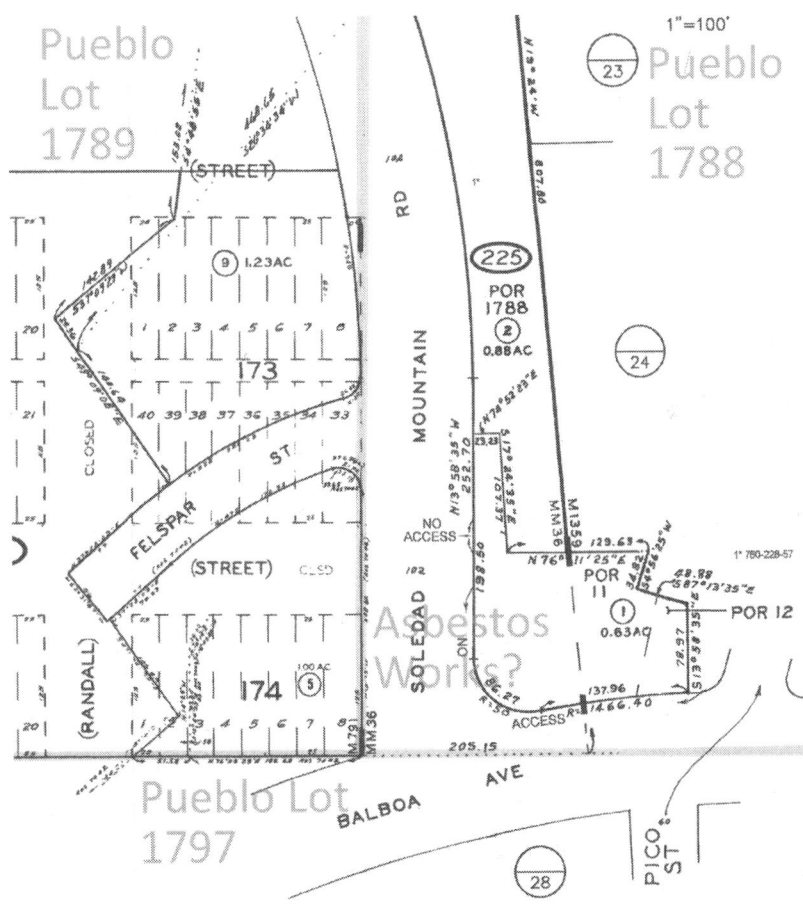

The asbestos works was located in the southwest corner of Pueblo Lot 1788, or possibly in the east half of Block 174 of Pacific Beach (in Pueblo Lot 1789). The site would be in or near today's Soledad Mountain Road and just north of Balboa (then Grand, now Garnet) Avenue. At that time the San Diego, Old Town and Pacific Beach Railway ran along the north side of Balboa/Grand/Garnet Avenue.

6 Lemons

In 1887 the Pacific Beach Company had acquired most of the property between the Pacific Ocean and Rose Creek and from Crown Point to the Mount Soledad foothills and subdivided it into uniform residential blocks of 40 25- by 125-foot lots. The lots went on sale in December 1887 in the midst of San Diego's Great Boom, when trainloads of would-be settlers arrived in San Diego hoping to buy property for homes or to resell to other settlers at inflated prices. However, the Great Boom collapsed in early 1888, just a few months after the Pacific Beach Company's opening sale, and the market for residential lots in Pacific Beach dwindled to practically nothing, the local economy collapsed and the community's propects dimmed.

On March 2, 1892, however, the *San Diego Union* Local Intelligence column reported on new developments in Pacific Beach; George N. Havice had purchased 200 lemon and 200 deciduous trees which he intended setting out on his property at the Beach[46], Miss Ida W. Snyder of Omaha had purchased 5 acres at Pacific Beach and had made arrangements to have her property put out to lemons[47] and Dr. Thomas Cogswell at Pacific Beach had sent a cluster of 16 Bonnie Brae lemons as well as several boxes of oranges and lemons from his property to the citrus fair in Los Angeles [303][48].

A few weeks later the Local Intelligence was that a Mr. Bowers,

---

[46] George Havice was the brother-in-law of San Diego College of Letters co-founder Harr Wagner; his wife Jennie was Harr Wagner's sister. Their property, presumably where the trees were to be set out, was Block 213, between what is now Garnet Avenue and Noyes, Hornblend and Morrell Streets [649].

[47] Miss Snyder purchased the west half of Acre Lot 20, approximately five acres, on March 1, 1892 [640], and the remaining 4.7 acres of Acre Lot 20 on March 15 [641]. Acre Lot 20 is now the two-block area east of (and including) Lamont Street between Beryl Street and Kate Sessions Park; the 1900 blocks of Wilbur, Loring and the north side of Beryl.

[48] Dr. Thomas Cogswell was a dentist with a practice in the Bon Ton Block ('furnished rooms and offices, corner of Sixth and D downtown'). The Cogswell home was on the northwest corner of what became Diamond and Jewell Streets. In May 1892 Hannah Cogswell acquired the west half of Acre Lot 48, five acres on the east side of Jewell between Diamond and Chalcedony Streets (and the eastern portion of Acre Lot 47 that is now Jewell Street itself) [638].

---

who had come west the previous fall from Tennessee and had purchased a thirty acre tract at Pacific Beach[49], was having 4,000 feet of water pipe laid over his property. The property was to be put in lemons during the next few weeks [304]. On April 21, C. H. Raiter, a banker from Alexandria, Minnesota, joined the new land rush, sending instructions to have a ten-acre tract at Pacific Beach put equally in oranges and lemons and to reserve a good building site. The property was also to be piped, fenced, broken and planted as soon as possible [305][50].

By mid-1892 fruit cultivation in Pacific Beach had become prominent enough that it was reported to have influenced Boston industrialist J. Malcolm Forbes' purchase of the San Diego, Old Town and Pacific Beach Railway. According to the July 17, 1892, *Union*, it was understood that the purchaser (a 'wealthy eastern resident' whose identity had not yet been disclosed) had made a casual trip over the railroad and noticed the great improvement taking place near Pacific Beach by the planting of lemons and oranges and, learning that the railroad was for sale, had purchased it 'at the figure at which it was offered' [166]. Later that month George Hensley of the Pacific Beach Company reported that 170 acres of citrus planted near Pacific Beach were 'making a fine growth' and that they had lately located 17 families on tracts near Pacific Beach and nearly all were planting orchards [306].

The January 1, 1894, *San Diego Union* contained a status report

---

[49] R. C. Wilson and G. M. D. Bowers had purchased Acre Lots 34 and 50 for $1850, $100 an acre, on February 12 [642], and Acre Lot 33 for $990, also $100 an acre, on March 4, 1892 [643]. These three 8 – 10 acre lots met at the corner of what became Lamont and Chalcedony, lot 33 on the northeast corner, 34 on the northwest and 50 on the southeast. Wilson and Bowers later extended their holdings between Chalcedony and Diamond to Noyes Street, acquiring the western half of adjoining Acre Lot 51 on June 28, 1892 [644], and the entire lot in June 1893 [681].

[50] The ten-acre Raiter tract was Acre Lot 61, between Reed Avenue and today's Pacific Beach Drive, from Lamont to the west side of Kendall Street [645]. Two years later the Raiters bought the adjoining Acre Lot 62, extending their holdings between Reed and PB Drive to the west side of Jewell [646]. Although they owned these tracts totaling about 20 acres in Pacific Beach, they remained residents of Alexandria, Minnesota, being counted there in the United States census of 1900 and 1910 and the Minnesota census of 1905. Apparently the properties were piped, fenced, broken and planted, and on their second visit, in 1897, the sight of his orange and lemon grove with its surrounding hedge of cypress trees 'surpassed his most sanguine expectations' [653]. Although they occasionally spent winters in Pacific Beach and announced their intention of making it their retirement home they instead sold their property to D. C. Campbell in April 1902 [659].

from the various communities around San Diego and the report from Pacific Beach was provided by E. C. Thorpe. After acknowledging that fruit culture for profit was in its infancy and to some extent experimental, Mr. Thorpe reported that lemons did nicely there and that Pacific Beach expected much from its future lemon culture. He noted that the sandy soil near the bay was not considered as valuable as the heavier soil on higher lands where the trees made the best growth and required less water. He had noticed that his young orchards, set out a year or two before, made as fine and vigorous a growth as those of the same age where an unlimited supply of water was available [307][51].

The 1895 New Year's report from Pacific Beach was provided by George H. Corey and included his explanation for the extraordinary fertility of Pacific Beach:

> The soil is rich in all the chemical qualities which furnish life to vegetation. The plant food has never been leached out by the heavy rains and snows of ages, as they are in the countries with normal rain fall, and the minerals from the high hills on the north have been dissolved by time, and have found their way down with the crumbling deposits which have filled the foothills with the richest of soil; rich in every element for producing the most perfect fruit, both citrus and deciduous. During all the idle centuries of the past these lands have been enriching themselves, preparing for their intelligent tillage by man, and anything can be grown by the application of water and a little industry.

He also commented on the expansion of lemon cultivation in Pacific Beach:

> Two years ago last May there were not fifty fruit trees on the beach, now fully 30,000 thrifty trees, (mostly lemons) are coming into bearing, and the profit soon to be realized will be something handsome.

Mr. Corey went on to explain that water for irrigation was furnished through the city system and that the cost was 'very trifling'; his total expense for water for ten acres, used in abundance, was less than $20 for 1894 and would probably be cheaper in the future as the city acquired a larger supply [308][52]. By the end of 1895 the *Union* was

---

[51] The Thorpes owned Block 167, between today's Lamont, Diamond, Morrell and Emerald Streets [682].

[52] George H. Corey's lemon orchard was in Acre Lot 19, 9.7 acres between what today are Lamont and Kendall Streets from Beryl Street north to the boundary of Pueblo Lot 1785, the city-owned land that is now Kate Sessions Park. The property had been purchased in February 1892 by Lucien F. Burpee of Waterbury, Connecticut, trustee for Martha Dunn Corey and her children [660]. In February 1895 the Common Council also granted Corey a lease in the adjoining city land; Joint Resolution 550 allowed Corey to use 20 acres of the south portion of Pueblo Lot 1785 for a term of three years 'and that said Geo H Corey shall clear said land from all brush for use of same' [695].

able to report that Pacific Beach was the center of a flourishing farming colony, citrus fruit orchards forming the chief industry [309].

For some of the early investors in Pacific Beach acreage lots, the handsome profits were to be realized from selling the land and the thrifty trees that were coming into bearing, not the lemons that the trees were expected to produce. In the fall of 1895, R. C. Wilson and G. M. D. Bowers disposed of their original 30-acre investment, selling Acre Lot 33 (9.3 acres) on September 20 to Ozora P. Stearns for $5,500 [310], Acre Lot 50 (9.9 acres) on October 19 to Lewis and Elizabeth Coffeen for $3,000 [311], and Acre Lot 34 (8.6 acres, together with improvements) on November 20 to William B. Davis for $5,500 [312]. In these transactions Wilson and Bowers realized $14,000 for property they had bought three years earlier for $2,840 (although they had also paid for installing an irrigation system and for setting out and cultivating 30 acres of trees for three years).

The *Union's* 1896 New Year's Day report on Pacific Beach was again provided by E. C. Thorpe, who introduced himself as 'one who has watched the rapid transition of Pacific Beach from sage brush to lemon orchards, from the monotonous desolation of California's coast region to cultured homes'. Reviewing the 'early history' of Pacific Beach, Thorpe wrote:

> The depression that followed in the wake of the boom necessitated the closing of the college and disbanding of its company. At the close of the college as an institution of learning in 1890 many of those to whom this had been the attraction moved away, and the following year but three or four families remained in the college settlement. In the fall of 1891 the tract was placed upon the market as acreage property and in a few weeks a force of workmen were clearing the first hundred acres preparatory to planting lemon orchards[53]. Rabbits and rattlesnakes were driven back to mesa and canyon, and the sunny southern slopes were soon clothed in fragrant lemon foliage. In place of the few discouraged, depressed settlers in 1891 are more than a hundred contented, ambitious inhabitants now [313].

Thorpe added that several of the ranchers had begun to market lemons and the prices they had received for them had been 'encouraging in the extreme'.

During the remainder of 1896 the lemon industry was the subject of regular comment in the Pacific Beach Notes column in the *Union*. The May 21 column reported that Mr. Hinkle, who had bought the

---

[53] Actually, the acreage property was first described in Pacific Beach Subdivision Map 697, which was approved and ordered filed by the Pacific Beach Company on January 2, 1892. The first deed, for the east half of Acre Lot 48, was filed January 3 by Milton Trumbauer [698]. Twelve acre lots, totaling 112 acres, were sold over the next five months.

'Tutton ten acres set to lemons'[54], was building a fine residence, and that the lemon festival was a great success [314]. The May 26 column noted that 'our ranchmen' were busy irrigating their lemon trees and that W. B. Davis had shipped forty boxes of choice lemons for which he received a high price [315]. On June 20 the report was that Col. Corey had shipped 20 boxes of lemons from his young lemon grove and that Miss Davis had shipped $4 boxes of choice lemons from Ondewa ranch. F. W. Barnes & Sons were buying lemons on the tree for 1¼ cents; 'Many of our lemon growers find it to their advantage to sell at that figure, as it saves expense of picking, curing and shipping' [316]. The July 11 column noted that carloads of baled hay and boxes of lemons were being daily shipped to San Diego [317][55].

Lemons continued to be news in 1897. The Local Intelligence column in the January 12 *Union* reported that E. Y. Barnes of Pacific Beach had picked seventy-two boxes of lemons in December from 280 4-year-old trees. His record for the year was 1,200 boxes, netting $1 per box. Barnes had also erected a curing house[56] and expected even better results in the future [318]. While some growers were netting $1 a box by working their lemon groves and curing and packing lemons, others continued to profit by selling their groves to those hoping to get a start in the lemon business. The January 19, 1897, *San Diego Union* carried an advertisement offering 10 acres in bearing lemons, 4 years old, with water under pressure and a 6 room house at Pacific Beach, just back of the college; an exceptional bargain at $3,800. Presumably this was the same advertisement referred to in the April 7 *Union's* Pacific Beach Notes column:

> Maj. Hall, a new arrival, who spent three years in Phoenix, Ariz.,

---

[54] Victor A. Hinkle purchased Acre Lot 36, 10.2 acres, from A. W. and Betsy Haight in February 1896 [733]. The Haights had bought the property from George Tutton in September 1892 [732].

[55] A box or packing case held approximately 40 pounds of lemons. A carload was approximately 600 boxes, or about twelve tons of lemons.

[56] Tree-ripened lemons tended to be too large and were graded down by buyers. Better grades, and prices, could be achieved by picking the lemons when they reached an ideal size, when they would not slip through a metal ring of the desired diameter. These lemons were generally still dark green when picked and were then 'cured' in a curing house for 30 – 60 days until they had attained the desirable waxy 'lemon-yellow' color. Inside the curing house batches of lemons were placed in tents where temperature and humidity could be moderated by raising or lowering the sides to adjust air circulation. Cured lemons not only had a more acceptable and uniform appearance but also thinner rinds and better keeping qualities [720].

---

seeking restoration to health, was induced to visit Pacific Beach to examine a ten-acre improved tract, by an advertisement in the Union. Three days after first sight, Maj. Hall was the proud possessor a four-year-old lemon grove beautiful for situation, commanding a view of Mission bay, the breakers at Ocean Beach, Point Loma, San Diego city and Coronado. He has already erected a curing house and has a hundred boxes of lemons packed therein [319][57].

The April 7 Notes column also referred to the relocation of the hotel and pavilion from the beach to a block of land near College station, claiming that the move had 'greatly improved the appearance of this place'[58]. The Pacific Beach Company had originally built a hotel and dance pavilion in 1888 at the beach near the terminus of the San Diego, Old Town and Pacific Beach Railway to attract riders and would-be settlers to the new community. However, in November 1896 the Pacific Beach Company sold the hotel and pavilion to Sterling Honeycutt, along with the northern half of Block 239, the south side of today's Hornblend Street between Lamont and Morrell. The agreement stipulated 'that said hotel building and said pavilion shall be moved to and placed upon the said north half of said Block 239 within six months' [21].

When the move was made in early 1897 the hotel was put down on the western end of the block, the corner of Hornblend and Lamont, and the pavilion on the eastern end, the corner of Hornblend and Morrell. Lamont is where Grand turned from its generally west-to-east route from the beach to a more northeasterly direction, the section which today has been renamed Balboa Avenue, cutting diagonally through the south half of Block 239. In 1897 the right-of-way of the San Diego, Pacific Beach and La Jolla Railway ran along the northern side of Grand (Balboa) and thus passed immediately south of the pavilion's new location. The railway had built a siding to service the West Coast Lumber Company on the south side of the block near Lamont and this siding now also provided service to the pavilion.

A large empty building in the center of a growing expanse of lemon orchards and serviced by a railroad siding was apparently ideal for lemon curing, packing and shipping, and the July 19, 1897, *Union*

---

[57] Henrietta Carlisle Hall, wife of William B. Hall, had purchased Acre Lot 50 for $3,000 'as her separate property' from the Coffeens in March 1897 [639]. Acre Lot 50 is east of Lamont between Diamond and Chalcedony Streets.

[58] In 1897 the San Diego, Pacific Beach and La Jolla Railway stopped near the corner of Grand and Lamont, about two blocks from the former college and a block from the relocated buildings. This 'college station depot' had recently been 'very much enlarged and improved' [182].

reported in its Notes for Fruit Men column that Pacific Beach had enough faith in lemons to propose to turn its pavilion into a packing house. Notes for Fruit Men also included practical advice from local lemon ranchers. C. H. Turner 'the original pioneer of Pacific Beach' who had 'twenty as fine acres as the sun shines on'[59], rid his orchard of cottony cushion with vedalias[60] and disposed of the rest of the scale with water. Miss W. B. Davis's ranch, in charge of her brother, showed thoughtful, diligent cultivation, as did the prim ranches of J. B. Esden for Mrs. Judge Stearns[61], who had an admirable packing house, and S. Honeycutt[62]. Barnes & Son had a home and ranch to be proud of and experience had shown them that severe pruning could be injurious; two rows of their trees were cut back and had never borne again. Maj.

---

[59] Calvin H. Turner was the bidder who won 113 lots for $136.50 when the college company's property was auctioned at the courthouse door in 1894 [99]. This property totaled about 9 acres but was scattered across the community in twelve separate parcels. His wife Eliza owned about 9 acres in two adjoining blocks, Blocks 249 and 272, between Grand Avenue and today's Lamont, Reed and Kendall Streets, purchased in June 1896 [647]. They later purchased Acre Lot 63, also about 9 acres between Reed, Jewell, Pacific Beach Drive and Ingraham, in January 1899 [661]. Originally a furniture merchant, he was described in 1891 as a director of the Pacific Beach Company [662] and in the 1893 and 1895 city directories he was listed as being with the 'Pacific Beach Land Company'. It had been Turner's 'casual remarks' about lemons and oranges on the train to Pacific Beach that caught the attention of J. Malcolm Forbes and led him to purchase the railroad in 1892 [166]. Whether or not C. H. Turner qualified as an 'original pioneer', his son Marcus C. Turner did become a major player in Pacific Beach real estate, first in partnership with Frank Barr and later with Barr's ex-wife Madie Arnott. Marcus and Madie Arnott Turner subdivided Turners Sea Shell Park in 1909 [684] and Hollywood Park in 1910 [683].

[60] Cottony cushion is a scale insect that feeds on citrus; vedalia beetles are a species of ladybug that feed exclusively on cottony cushion. Vedalia beetles were introduced to California from Australia in 1888-89 to combat a severe infestation of cottony cushion (which had also invaded from Australia) and were a spectacular success, credited with literally saving the California citrus industry and establishing the practicality of biological pest control [736].

[61] Mrs. Judge Stearns, Sarah P. Stearns, owned Acre Lot 33, east of today's Lamont Street between Beryl and Chalcedony Streets, now the 1900 blocks of Law and the north side of Chalcedony and the south side of Beryl. Ozora Stearns, a former judge from Minnesota, had purchased the ranch in 1895 from Wilson and Bowers and after his death his widow Sarah had gained 'exclusive use' of the property when the estate was settled in October 1896 [734]. She was assisted by daughters Stella and Susan and Susan's husband John Esden.

[62] In 1897 Sterling Honeycutt raised lemons on the four blocks between Lamont and Jewell Streets and Grand and Garnet Avenues, immediately south of the college campus [675].

W. D. Hall was delighted with soil, location, climate and environment and most of all with the low cost of water; he paid less to irrigate his entire ten acres as he paid in Phoenix to irrigate an acre and a half [320].

The Horticultural Notes column in the August 4, 1897, *Union* included a number of items of interest to Pacific Beach. Mrs. Mary E. Rowe had a ranch that from the raw condition had been developed to one valued at $9,000[63]; 'The ladies at Pacific Beach are justly proud of their ranches'. Dr. Berkebile depended on water and red lady birds to destroy his black scale and what the birds left he hand-picked[64]. Maj. Hall treated a tree with purple scale by cutting it back and coating it with tar and oil, giving it a greasy black appearance; 'A lady friend, evidently not versed in horticulture, congratulated the major on the beautiful appearance of his rubber tree'. V. A. Hinkle had trouble with some roots being balled in adobe but cleaned it out with force from the hose, leaving the grown roots washed clean. Mrs. Martha Dunn Corey had some finely grown trees and would use ricini[65] for a wind break for her younger trees exposed to the ocean wind; 'Her ranch and trees are an evidence of how a woman can manage. There are some men who could get pointers there on keeping a ranch clean' [321][66]. On September 8 the *Union* noted that a 'good report' had come from a carload of lemons that John Esden had shipped to Duluth [322] and on October 18 the news was that John Esden was making further improvements to the Stearns Ranch, including an up-to-date curing house [323].

The conversion of the dance pavilion to a lemon packing house was apparently completed by the fall of 1897. Honeycutt had sold the east half of Block 239, including the pavilion building, to F. W. Barnes and F. J. Marshall[67] in November, 1897 [324], and the November 12

---

[63] Mrs. Rowe's ranch was Acre Lot 49, on the west side of today's Lamont Street, between Diamond and Chalcedony and where Kendall would be if it ran between these two streets [685].

[64] John Berkebile had purchased Block 213 from the Havices in 1893 [650].

[65] Presumably the castor bean plant, Ricinus communis, sometimes planted as a wind break.

[66] Martha Dunn Corey was a physician and wife of George Corey, a mining consultant who was often away on business. She apparently managed their ranch in his absence.

[67] Marshall owned a lemon ranch on Acre Lots 30 and 53 [324].

Union's Pacific Beach Notes column reported that E. Y. Barnes had fully equipped the pavilion for a curing house and was buying lemons for the fall and winter trade. The report added that 'The outlook is very promising. Pacific Beach lemons having already a good reputation' [325]. The December 8 Notes added that E. Y. Barnes shipped from seventy-five to one hundred boxes of lemons and oranges weekly [326].

News of the new packing house continued in the December 15, 1897, *Union,* which reported that 'E. W. Barnes and Son' had the most commodious packing and curing house in the county, 'a house built in the great pavilion, giving even temperature and ventilation', and that their five-year-old Lisbons, five acres each, had from January '97 to December '97 yielded fourteen tons of merchantable lemons[68]. Also, Maj. Hall had received $200 from five acres of bearing trees in an abandoned orchard he took in charge a year earlier, W. D. Davis used the McBain-Hewitt wash 'with very gratifying results' and J. T. Martin used a home-made insecticide consisting of a twenty gallon solution of boiled tobacco stems, 1½ pounds of baking soda and one pound of cayenne pepper; 'After this dose the scale's remarks are unprintable' [327][69].

F. W. Barnes himself was the author of an article in the February 13, 1898, *San Diego Union* in which he described the natural advantages of Pacific Beach for growing lemons and recounted the short history of lemon cultivation in Pacific Beach:

PACIFIC BEACH
The Lemon's Natural Home – Trees Are Now Loaded with Golden Fruit

Eight miles northwest of San Diego court house, on the San Diego, Pacific Beach and La Jolla railway, is one of San Diego's most beautiful suburbs. Pacific Beach, a village consisting of stores, a fine hotel, schools, church, and all that goes to make up the desirable California settlement.

Surrounded by beautiful and thrifty looking orange and lemon orchards, artistic residences overlooking the ocean on the west; the bay region on the south, and the grand old mountains of Cuyamaca on the east; with a society of cultured people who unite in promoting the best interest, intellectually and materially, of their adopted home, Pacific Beach may truly be called an ideal part of "our Italy."

Pacific Beach is one of the few localities in the whole United States

---

[68] Actually, the father was F. W. Barnes and the son E. Y. Barnes. Their lemons were grown on Acre Lot 64, south of what is now Diamond Street and north of what was once Emerald Street, between Jewell and Lamont. In 1897 F. W. Barnes owned the eastern half and E. Y. Barnes the western half of this approximately 10-acre lot.

[69] Mrs. E. V. Martin had purchased Block 179 (between Morrell, Emerald, Noyes and Felspar Streets) in May 1893 [648].

---

where the conditions are almost perfect for the successful culture of the lemon. Frost and extreme hot weather are practically unknown here. Few places during the weeks just passed have escaped the blighting effects of the unusually cold weather, but the tenderest bud on the lemon trees was uninjured in any orchard lying in Pacific Beach. A climate tempered by the balmy salt breezes both summer and winter; a soil free from stones, or hard-pan, easy to work, sloping gently south to the shores of Mission bay, make this the natural home of the lemon.

The first lemon orchards were planted here about five years ago, and there are at the present time about 25,000 lemon trees in bearing, and our own experience has been that lemon raising has not been a failure. During the year '97 we picked 1,400 boxes from 600 four-year-old trees, and are now picking from the same trees 200 boxes per month. Lemons grown here cure and keep well. The Lisbon, Villa Franca and Eureka are the leading varieties raised. The output from this locality last year was estimated at about 7,000 boxes. Considering the fact that there were no trees over five years old, we claim it a good showing.

We have a large packing house in the midst of the settlement with railway facilities for handling and shipping, the San Diego prices being paid at our door. Although this part of the San Diego bay region is known as the home of the lemon, oranges thrive quite as well here, and the branches of the orange trees bend earthward loaded with clusters of golden fruit, as perfect and of as fine quality as can be found anywhere in the state.

This locality comprises 5,000 acres of land finely situated for lemon culture, and when the Morena water system is completed, this land will be planted to oranges and lemons, and Pacific Beach will then become the crown and glory of the San Diego bay region in the culture and production of the lemon and orange [328]. F. W. BARNES.

Although Barnes and others had praised the quality of the soil as a factor in the success of lemon culture in Pacific Beach, some ranchers apparently did not share this view (or their ranches were in less favorable locations). The previous summer the *Union* had noted that V. A. Hinkle's trees had been 'balled in adobe' [329]. The *Union* reported on February 24, 1898, that Mr. Thorpe was resetting his trees in red clay soil by removing the surface soil and refilling with sandy loam. He had also taken the precaution of boring through the clay to the under stratum of sand, 'thus insuring perfect drainage'. Insects also continued to be a problem; J. W. Davis sprayed every two weeks with lye to exterminate scale and J. D. Esden and 'Messrs Barnes, Ash[70], Honeycutt and others' also found a one to twenty lye solution entirely satisfactory' [330].

Despite the many challenges of lemon ranching, some recognized that Pacific Beach held other attractions, even for a rancher. O. L. Gridley of Pacific Beach was quoted in the July 18, 1898, *Union* as being

---

[70] W. A. Ash's ranch was in Block 205, directly east of the college and surrounded today by Garnet Avenue and Lamont, Felspar and Morrell Streets.

'in no wise discouraged by reason of the seemingly unfavorable season'. He had found health for his family, a most delightful community, people who mix the joys of life with its duties, where the entire community got together to enjoy an exhilarating bath in the bay of in the surf of the ocean; 'Ranching at Pacific Beach is not all of life' [331][71].

While the lemon ranchers of Pacific Beach were learning how to deal with bugs and clay in 1898, events in the wider world were also bringing attention to lemons. On February 13, 1898, the USS Maine, a battleship of the United States Navy, blew up and sank in the harbor of Havana, Cuba. The United States government blamed Spain, then the colonial power in Cuba, and after some diplomatic maneuvering war was declared on April 25. American troops invaded Cuba on June 22, landing on the southern coast and advancing on the strategic port city of Santiago de Cuba where the Spanish garrison surrendered on July 17.

Although fewer than 400 Americans had been killed in the fighting, thousands contracted tropical diseases such as yellow fever and malaria, and thousands more became sick from the unsanitary conditions of their camps. Prevailing medical opinion at the time considered lemons and lemon juice to be a remedy to many of these disorders. According to San Diego physician Dr. P. C. Remondino, quoted in the August 6, 1898, *Union,*

> Lemons and limes are as indispensable to the health of the European in the tropics as they are in the arctic regions. In the latter, lime juice is the great preventative against scurvy, while in the former it is the remedy furnished by nature against the jaundiced conditions and many forms of liver diseases so prevalent in that climate, as well as against most forms of malarial ailments.
>
> In Italy, Spain and in the south of France, lemon juice is the great corrective against the prevailing diseases of the hot season, and the juice is employed in many different ways to relive the effect of sunburns. Intestinal summer complaints in the semi-tropics often yield readily to its use while most superficial non-malignant skin diseases of the tropics and semi-tropics find in lemon juice a universal remedy.
>
> Take it all in all, I cannot advise the Red Cross society a more useful method of assisting our soldiers in the tropics than by supplying them with lemons. They must, however, be used with discretion[72].

---

[71] Orrin L. Gridley's property was the east half of Acre Lot 48; the west half belonged to the Cogswells. Acre Lot 48 was between Diamond, Jewell and Chalcedony, and where Kendall Street would be if it ran between Chalcedony and Diamond Streets.

[72] Dr. Remondino also endorsed A. H. Isham's Waters of Life, plain spring water from Spring Valley which was marketed internationally as a cure-all and anti-aging agent until Isham was exposed as a fraud in 1905 [737].

With this sort of endorsement from the medical profession, the Red Cross Society of San Diego determined to send a carload of lemons to the 'fever-stricken boys in blue at Santiago' and patriotic citizens rushed to do their part. F. W. Barnes, owner of the Pacific Beach packing house, not only gave a number of boxes of choice lemons but offered to pack free of charge all lemons left at his packing house. Manager Herbert Dabney of the Pacific Beach railway 'tendered the free use of the road'. Dr. Cogswell of Pacific Beach was 'drumming up the residents to show their gratitude in a substantial way' [332].

By August 8 the news was that the Red Cross Society was on the road to success in securing a carload of lemons to be sent to Santiago de Cuba. Grapefruit, oranges and other fruit were also being donated, and it was even suggested that dried apricots be sent since they made a very refreshing drink when soaked in water. 'The car will bear a banner with the words San Diego to Santiago and will be an advertisement not only for the generosity of this county but its fruit also' [333].

On August 14 the car was loaded and ready to go and the *San Diego Union* story reported it would leave the following day:

RED CROSS CAR FULL.
WILL LEAVE TOMORROW WITH FRUIT FOR SICK SOLDIERS.
Bedecked with Flags and Bunting, and Eloquent Banners, the Car Was an Object of Interest Yesterday - Report of Chairman Bennett Submitted.

The carload of fruit raised through the efforts of the Red Cross to be forwarded to the sick soldier boys of Gen. Shafter's army attracted great attention yesterday at the foot of Fifth street. The committee in charge of the work has decorated the car with red, white and blue bunting, flags and large signs bearing the red cross and the following inscriptions: "San Diego to Santiago - Lemons for the Boys in Blue."

On placards is the following: "This car contains lemons, oranges, grape fruit, dried peaches, pears, prunes, and raisins, all raised in San Diego county, California, and contributed by its citizens through the Red Cross to the boys in blue. Trainmen: This is a good thing – push it along. Santa Fe to Kansas City, Missouri Pacific to St. Louis, Wabash to Buffalo, West Shore to New York. Deliver to Col. J. Morris Brown, U. S. A., Staten Island Military Hospital. (Signed) Red Cross Society."

The article went on to describe the route the car would take (as far north as possible, even passing through Canadian territory between Detroit and Buffalo) and to report that since many of the sick men had already been transported to the hospital on Staten Island and many others would have by the time the car arrived in New York, the fruit would be used in the hospital there and not be carried to Cuba. A list of contributors including Honeycutt, Dr. M. Corey, Dr. Cogswell, J. B. Esden & Co., and F. W. Barnes & Son from Pacific Beach as well as growers from San Diego, La Mesa, Chula Vista, Fallbrook, Otay, El

Cajon, South San Diego, Sunnyside, Sweetwater and Chollas was included [334].

Pacific Beach's importance in the regional lemon industry was recognized when the County Horticultural Society held its quarterly meeting at Stough Hall in October 1898. Rev. W. L. Johnston of the Pacific Beach Presbyterian Church invoked a divine blessing on the meeting, E. C. Thorpe gave a humorous recitation[73], 'The Huckleberry Picnic', Master Willie Ash, the 7-year-old son of Pacific Beach lemon rancher William Ash, acquitted himself most creditably in another recitation, 'King Lemon', composed by Mrs. Rose Hartwick Thorpe, Mesdames Woodworth and Johnston entertained the convention with a piano duet and J. B. Esden entertained with a song. On the business side of the convention, F. W. Barnes presented a session on 'How We Handle Our Lemons' in which he recounted his experience; he had paid $300 for a piece of land, planted 300 lemon trees, put in $230 in pipes, and expended $200 a year for cultivation, water, etc. The orchard paid $40 the third year, $300 the fourth, and so far had paid $1,100 in the fifth year, practically balancing his ledger. His son Edward's results were similar [335].

Another testimonial to the superiority of Pacific Beach as a center of lemon cultivation appeared in the December 19, 1898, *San Diego Union*:

> The winter of '97-'98 was the coldest experienced for many years in southern California, and many lemon orchards were more or less severely injured. In some orchards, a part of the trees were frozen back, while others escaped. In other orchards the trees all suffered from the unusual cold. One tract, however, containing several hundred acres, escaped entirely. This tract, lying north of the city of San Diego, and about one mile back from the ocean, is one of the most favored in natural location of any in Southern California. Some of the finest lemons in the state have been shipped from Pacific Beach. The entire tract slopes gently from the mesas to False bay on the south, and westward to the ocean. It is a true home of the lemon, and a pretty one. To the west is the white-capped, restless ocean, to the south the tranquil blue waters of the bay, framed in a circle of green, dotted with white cottages and small settlements. Beyond the bay lie San Diego, Coronado and Old Town, with grim Point Loma standing like a sentinel on duty keeping watch and guard over the harbor that lies in the bend of its mighty arm. Away beyond the white-walled city and the glint of San Diego bay rise the mountains of Mexico, hazy and dim in the distance with nature's landmark, Table mountain, conspicuous through fifty miles of space. Overtopping the nearer mesas, at the east, is the rugged outline of old Cuyamaca, snow-capped a part of the year, thus affording the people who live among the

---

[73] Thorpe was well known for his talent of writing and speaking in the 'broken English of a Dutchman'. One example was his poem Dot Bacific Peach Flea, 'vot schumps und viggles und bites. . . und keepen me awake effry nights' [719].

roses a glimpse of winter as they once knew it. Lemon trees at this place, when properly cared for, make a phenomenal growth. One five-acre orchard of five-year-old trees at a recent picking yielded 266 boxes.

The lemon has many natural enemies, but man's inexperience may well be called its greatest enemy. A retired banker, recovering from la grippe comes to this farfamed health resort, and drinking deep of its exhilarating atmosphere becomes intoxicated, and straightway buys a lemon ranch for a plaything, and finds it anything but an amusing toy. A Boston dentist, with more knowledge of teeth than trees grows a lemon orchard between molar extractions. A "sto' keeper" from Tennessee decides to make the proverbial California fortune by cultivating lemons while recovering his lost avoirdupois. A Michigan carriage maker concludes to apply his knowledge of seasoned timber to the needs of the growing tree[74].

Miners, doctors, widows, photographers, ministers, in fact representatives of every vocation, except that of lemon culture, are those who, in a large majority, are growing the California lemon today. Is it any wonder that there are discouragements and failures? It is not more of a wonder that here are really profitable shipments? Men plant orchards who do not know the least requirements of the tree, and have not even the rudiments of an education in this respect. A man must be a mechanic to build a house; an engineer to run an engine; a doctor deal out physic; but the moment he sets foot upon this California soil, and inhales it mesmeric atmosphere he imagines himself equal to any undertaking, even to the successful growing of lemon orchards.

The question is frequently asked: "Does lemon culture pay?" One is informed that "figures will not lie," and unless they prevaricate in this instance the question may be answered in the affirmative. When lemon trees have attained the age of five or six years it becomes necessary to pick the fruit every four weeks during the entire year. A thrifty five-acre lemon orchard six years old should yield between two and three hundred field boxes to a picking, and the trees increase in bearing as they grow older. An ordinary field box contains forty pounds of fruit. The grower receives from one-half a cent to four cents per pound for the green fruit. This summer's prices ranged from two and one-half to four and one-fourth. If the grower averages but one cent per pound for his fruit his orchard will prove a most satisfactory investment, for instead of one crop a year, there are twelve.

---

[74] Franklin W. Barnes had been a banker in Nebraska before moving to Pacific Beach for his health in 1880s. He planted lemons and became a leader in the local lemon industry (and eventually a state assemblyman). Dr. Thomas Cogswell had lived in Needham, Massachusetts, outside Boston, before relocating to San Diego where he combined a downtown dental practice with lemon ranching on Acre Lot 48. Sterling Honeycutt had moved to Pacific Beach from Tennessee. Edmond C. Thorpe had been a carriage maker in Litchfield, Michigan, which is also the town where his wife Rose Hartwick Thorpe had written her then-famous poem 'Curfew Must Not Ring Tonight' as a schoolgirl (a bell with the slogan 'Curfew Shall Not Ring Tonight' is now the city's symbol, appearing on its web site and on city vehicles and badges). The Thorpes were among the first Pacific Beach residents to attempt lemon cultivation. William B. Davis and George Corey were involved with mining, Martha Dunn Corey was a doctor, and Sarah Stearns and Mary Rowe were widows. There was also a former judge and apparently a former photographer and minister among those who imagined themselves equal to the successful growing of lemons in Pacific Beach.

In other days men put forth herculean efforts in order to reach "the land of gold," and endured untold hardships and privations that they might find the hidden treasure and appropriate it to themselves. Today they travel in a Pullman coach into the "land of sunshine" and grow a lemon orchard on the shores of the peaceful sea [336].

The favorable growing climate of Pacific Beach was mentioned again in February 1899 when no damage was observed to the fruit and tender shoots were only 'slightly nipped' after one of the coldest nights in the history of San Diego county [337]. The news in May was that 'Mrs. Dr. Corey' had given charge of her orchard to Mr. Isben[75], and the Snyder ranch was in charge of Maj. Gleason [338]. In June the *Union's* Hints for Fruit Growers column noted that Pacific Beach residents were realizing a better output of lemons than they anticipated: 'Maj. Hall just got a picking from about four acres that netted him $100. Barnes & Son are busy packing and buying. Isben & Co. have just sent out a car, and the prices paid are encouraging' [339]. The October 8, 1899, *Union* reported that Messrs. Barnes and Esden had shipped a carload of lemons to eastern points during the past week [340].

Lemon rancher William Hall took his turn describing Pacific Beach in the traditional New Year's report on suburban areas in the January 1, 1900, *San Diego Union*:

Pacific Beach Described
Wm. D. Hall

When Moses viewed the promised land from Mount Pisgah he beheld a country beautiful almost beyond description, but that view cannot be compared with the picturesque scenery of Southern California as seen from Point Loma, looking to the north, northwest, east and southeast; and of all the beautiful spots seen from this point there is none so lovely and attractive as Pacific Beach and its surroundings. From the Pacific ocean to the foot hills on the north there is a gradual rise of 80 feet in two miles, the same slope extending eight miles east and west containing over ten thousand acres of the best soil for lemons in Southern California.

---

[75] Also in May 1899 the *Union* reported that Martha M. Corey [sic] had brought suit in the superior court for divorce from George H. Corey [658]. The San Diego History Center has no record of a divorce case but the 1900 United States Census listed her as divorced and the head of her household (although the 1910 and 1920 census listed her as widowed). What is clear is that the Coreys went their separate ways before 1900 and that George Corey died before 1910. Dr. Corey and her three sons spent the years between 1900 and 1906 in Marion, Ohio, then returned to resume her medical practice in La Jolla. After retiring from medicine about 1926 she moved back to Pacific Beach, living in the home at 872 Grand Avenue that is now the Needlecraft Cottage. She also owned the cottage at the northeast corner of Diamond and Noyes Streets that was originally the home of college founder Harr Wagner and Madge Morris Wagner. Martha Dunn Corey's sister Elizabeth Dunn had purchased the property from the Wagners in 1894 [663] and Dr. Corey acquired it about 1905.

It is not only the most beautiful spot to look at from Point Loma, but the view from Pacific Beach looking to the east, southeast and west, is finer than from any other place about San Diego. From here we see the whole of San Diego bay with all its shipping, Coronado island and hotel, the most of the city of San Diego, and the grand mountainous country east and southeast extending into Mexico, and the blue waters of the Pacific to the west as far as the eye can reach. This beautiful view – new every morning and fresh every evening – is inspiring and dispels depressing feelings and helps one to live a cheerful, hence a happy life.

LEMONS AND OTHER FRUITS

Nearly in the center of this beautiful spot are clustered about three hundred acres of lemon groves from three to seven years old, including a few orange trees, also apple, peach, apricot, nectarine, quince, plum, prune, almond, cherry, pear and loquat trees, interspersed with guava, blackberry and raspberry bushes. The orchards are from 2 ½ to 10 acres each.

Dotted here and there are fine residences with well kept yards, beautiful with every variety of flowers, in bloom all the year round.

During the past year there have been raised and shipped from this place thirty carloads of lemons and two of oranges.

Some of the older five-acre ranches have netted the past year 10 per cent on a valuation of $6,000. The coming year the product of these orchards will nearly double if properly cared for.

By looking at the map one will see that Pacific Beach is more favorably situated for lemon raising than most other suburbs of San Diego. The lay of the land, extending out into the Pacific, with Mission bay on the southeast, gives it water on three sides. This with the foothills only two miles back from the ocean, makes it absolutely frost proof, and so diverts the wind that Pacific Beach escapes almost entirely the fogs that occasionally come in on this southern California coast.

In addition to the lemon, orange and other varieties of fruits raised at Pacific Beach, there are grown from three to four thousand acres of grain each year.

AN UP-TO-DATE SUBURB

Pacific Beach is up-to-date as a well-bred suburban town. We have three trains to and from San Diego, eight miles distant, each day, with an extra train at night when necessary. Soon the smoking engine will be replaced by the electric motor, and then the number of trains each way will be increased. This place boasts of two curing and packing plants, one of which is the largest and finest in the state; one up-to-date grocery store, run on the accommodation plan, which makes the proprietor very popular; a flourishing Union church, fine school house, with an excellent teacher; two college buildings at present used only for dwellings, but soon to be occupied as institutes of learning.

The woman's club and the Shakesperian club are a source of pleasure and profit to the cultivated ladies of the Beach, and are well sustained. One whist club never fails a quorum. The young people of the Beach have a prosperous tennis club and there are quite a good many expert players among them.

The ranchers sustain a farmers' club and once a month meet to discuss everything pertaining to their welfare.

Mission bay is an ideal bathing place and from the floating dock and dressing rooms one can take a plunge every day in the year. The young people here own several sailing and row boats, and almost any day in the year one can witness an exciting yacht race on the bay.

As to healthfulness, Pacific Beach cannot be excelled by any place on earth. Thus endeth the lesson for 1899 [341].

Lemons and lemon ranchers were again a frequent topic in the Pacific Beach Notes column throughout 1900. On January 18, Mr. Roxburgh was said to be having his orchard thoroughly fumigated, Mrs. Mary E. Rowe was moving back to her ranch and Frank Woodworth's family was moving into the house Mrs. Rowe had recently occupied, known as the dormitory building[76], Charles Belser had arrived to assume the management of the ranch recently purchased by his sister, Mrs. Linck[77], and Mr. Huntington, nephew of Sterling Honeycutt, had bought the ranch formerly owned by Ben Colvin[78] [342]. The March 8 column reported that the large number of so-called cull lemons that went to waste every year would now be used to extract juice for bottling and shipping east and north. There was nothing wrong with the great bulk of these lemons except that they were not just the right shape or size to suit the particular eye of the buyer, and it was hoped that this new process would be made to 'pay big'. With the dry season approaching, Mr. Conover would not set out any more trees or finish his place [343][79].

In the April 11 column the ranches were again reported to be busy picking lemons and the outlook was very encouraging, F. W. Barnes and Son had shipped two carloads of lemons, making ten carloads for the season, and C. F. Belser had at last opened up his packing house.

---

[76] Presumably the home she owned on the northeast corner of Lamont and Hornblend. This property had previously been owned by the San Diego College of Letters and may have been the 'College House' where young men lived while attending the college (women lived in the main college building, also known as the 'Women's Hall').

[77] Carrie Linck (nee Belser), a 35-year-old widow, had purchased the Stearns ranch on Acre Lot 33 in November 1899 [722] and, according to the 1900 census, lived there with her mother, Caroline, three unmarried sisters, Louise, Minnie and Nettie, and brother Charles F. Belser. Another brother, William Belser, lived elsewhere in Pacific Beach with his wife and reported his occupation on the census as 'Works in Packing H.'.

[78] This ranch was the west half of Acre Lot 51. Colvin had bought it from Wilson and Bowers in October 1895 [667] and sold it to Thomas McConnell in November 1897 [666]. McConnell granted the property to Lizzie Huntington in February 1900 [668].

[79] Wilbur Conover's 'place' was in Block 212, between Garnet Avenue and Hornblend, Noyes and Olney Streets, although he was not the registered owner in 1900. His brother Harvey as trustee for Wilbur recorded the purchase of the west half of the block in July 1901 [664] and the east half in November 1901 [665].

He had three carloads of lemons curing and had sent a consignment north the previous week [344]. The June 13 Pacific Beach Notes included the news that Belser & Co. were rushing out a carload of lemons every few days, a good rain Sunday night had been much appreciated by the farmers, and Mr. Hinkle was plastering and finishing up his house, which when finished would be one of the most commodious and elegant on the Beach [345][80]. The July 31 column reported that the packing houses were doing a 'land office business' and that the price of lemons had reached a point where the growers would soon be wearing diamonds and saying 'Ither and nither' (also, the church needed a bell and the columnist appealed to 'some rich man with doubts about his future' to donate one) [346].

1900 was also the year that the decennial census was conducted in the United States. In Pacific Beach the enumeration was undertaken between June 21 and 26 and consisted of visits to 54 dwellings, presumably every residence in existence at the time (counting 'near race track' but not Rose Canyon or Morena). A total of 185 individuals were recorded and of these 80 included a response in the 'occupation, trade or profession' column (including 12 students or 'at school'). Fourteen were listed as lemon rancher (or 'L Rancher' or 'L Packer and Rancher'), three more men worked in packing houses ('Works in Packing H.', 'Laborer in P. H.') and another ten described themselves simply as ranchers or their profession as ranching. There was also a 'contractor and rancher' (E. C. Thorpe) and 'carpenter and rancher' (Francis Manning). An additional nine were farmers, or their trade was farming, and four more were described as 'farm laborers' or 'farm help'. Some of the ranchers (e.g., Orrin Gridley) and farmers (e.g., Nathan Manning) and residents who reported other occupations (e.g., Thomas Cogswell, 'Physician') or no occupation (William Conover) were actually either full- or part-time lemon growers. Altogether, 23 of the 54 households responding to the United States census in Pacific Beach in June of 1900 had some involvement in the lemon business.

The locations of the lemon ranches in Pacific Beach in 1900 cannot be determined directly from the census forms since addresses were not filled in (the 'Street' column on the census form simply says 'Pacific Beach') but most of those identified as lemon ranchers also indicated they owned their homes and the ownership and location of property (and assessed value of improvements) is listed in the San Diego County

---

[80] The Hinkle's house is still one of the most elegant in Pacific Beach, although it was moved a short distance from its original location in Acre Lot 36 to the northwest corner of Ingraham and Law Streets about 1926.

assessor's Lot Books. When the locations are plotted on a map it is apparent that the property owned by these lemon ranchers in 1900 was clustered around the college campus, north of Pacific Beach Drive and east of Ingraham Street (then Pacific Avenue and Izard Street[81]), the areas that slope gradually up to the Mount Soledad foothills.

In January 1901 the *Evening Tribune* posed the question 'can lemon culture be engaged in at a profit in San Diego county?' and after the visit of a *Tribune* representative to Pacific Beach the answer was 'decidedly in the affirmative'. Although the total area planted there did not exceed 325 acres, the statements of owners showed that the lemon industry could be made to yield a good profit over expenses. The *Tribune* article advised that lemon culture should not be undertaken without some capital, since little return can be expected until the trees are six years of age and in the meantime they required almost constant attention. The ground must be plowed at least twice a year to keep the soil porous and mellow and money spent on irrigation and fertilizers. The ten-acre orchard owned by F. W. and E. Barnes was cited as a good example of the rewards for properly caring for lemon trees; the trees were among the finest in the county and the total income from 650 eight-year-old trees was $2000. Mr. E. Barnes told of his experience in lemon culture at Pacific Beach, 'We find the orchard needs constant care, and have a man steadily employed, with an occasional assistant. We find it necessary also to replenish the soil with fertilizers, and the essential feature of all is plenty of water'.

Mr. Martin was another fortunate owner of a well-kept five-acre lemon orchard and he reported that his net income from five acres of 6-year-old trees was a little over $580, 'I care for the orchard myself, and my only expenses were for fertilizers and water'. Mrs. Linck's orchard showed every evidence of being well cared for, and according to the owner's statement yielded a substantial income over all expenses. Similar reports were collected from Major Hall, whose five-acre lemon tract was evidence of untiring labor and constant attention and who reported income of about $750 and Tom McConnell, another happy lemon grower who had purchased a five-acre tract from Mr. Honeycutt for $2000 a year before and whose profit on fruit sold from that time was $700 [347][82].

---

[81] Pacific Beach streets were renamed by city ordinance 755 in May 1900. However, the new Izard Street reverted to Broadway in 1907, then Ingraham Street in 1913 when D Street downtown was changed to Broadway. Pacific Avenue became Pacific Beach Drive in 1935 when Atlantic Street downtown was changed to Pacific Highway [705].

[82] Thomas McConnell had purchased Block 216 from Sterling Honeycutt [686]. Block 216 is south of Garnet Avenue, between Kendall, Hornblend and Jewell Streets.

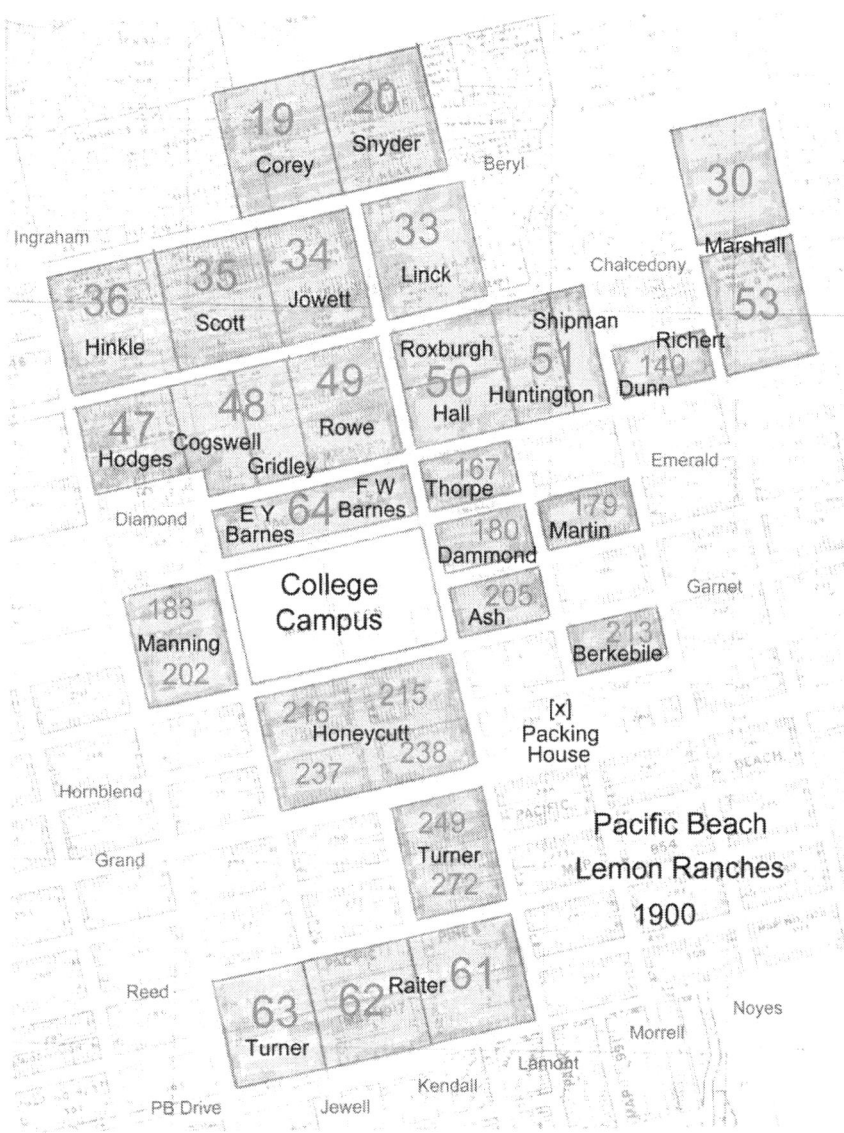

Locations and ownership of Pacific Beach lemon ranches in 1900. Numbers indicate Acre Lots (2-digit) or Blocks (3-digit). The College Campus and Acre Lot 64 are today the location of Pacific Plaza and the Plaza Condominiums.

The Pacific Beach Notes columns in the *Union* and *Tribune* maintained their interest in lemons throughout 1901. The April 3 *Union* reported that Major W. D. Hall was having his orchard sprayed and the Baker packing house was getting out two carloads of lemons in addition to some dozen carloads packed waiting for cars [348][83]. Hall and Baker were also featured in the April 12 *Tribune,* which noted that Major Hall had sold his lemon orchard to Mr. Baker[84] and would move to San Diego to live. The Raiters, who owned a lemon grove in Pacific Beach and who had been spending the winter, had left for the east [349]. On April 23 the *Tribune* reported that the price of lemons still stayed in the depths; cold weather in the east and a large importation of foreign lemons were said to be the cause, and the columnist added the humorous observation that those foreign lemons were 'known to be loaded with the germs of bubonic plague and delirium tremens and yet some people will use them' [350].

The price of lemons still had not advanced as early as was expected by June 17 but the *Tribune* columnist had an explanation, 'when we read of snow in Dakota and Iowa, and it [is] June, and that the rest of the east has had cold rains, the continued low price is explained. But the time is close at hand when the unfortunate people of the east will be obliged to take to lemonade to keep alive, and we will read the cheerful news that there is unheard of hot weather in the east' [351]. Lemons were 2 cents a pound on July 18 [352] and on August 21 Messrs. Wilson and Cole were buying and shipping lemons from the Baker packing house [353]. On October 14 the Horticultural Notes column in the *Union* reported that the Martin orchard in Pacific Beach was evidence to prove that low trimming and cleanly attention would produce a profitable class of trees; also that D. W. Rannels proposed to put the Rowe premises in good shape, T. Londry had the Dammond ranch in charge[85], and Mr. Smith the Corey place [354].

Wilbur Conover, a Pacific Beach lemon rancher, contributed an article titled 'Pacific Beach and the Home Seeker' to the December 1, 1901, *Union.* In addition to having the best and most healthful climate, a delightful location between game-filled hills, an ocean full of fish and a warm bay for swimming and boating, Pacific Beach was one of the few places where the lemon comes to perfection. According to Conover, Maj. Gleason and E. C. Thorpe planted the first lemon trees at

---

[83] F. W. Barnes had sold his half-interest in the packing house property to R. M. Baker in February 1901 [637], giving Baker an undivided interest in the property and the packing house.

[84] The Halls sold the southern half of Acre Lot 50 to R. M. Baker in April 1901 [723].

[85] R. P. and L. M. Dammond owned Block 180 [687], but apparently were not full-time residents and left the ranch in charge of others.

Pacific Beach, but the Hon. F. W. Barnes[86] had set out the first orchard about ten years before and now, over the previous 12 months, over 50 cars of lemons had been shipped, bringing growers at least twenty thousand dollars. Mr. E. Y. Barnes, for example, picked over twelve hundred boxes of lemons at one picking from his 5 acres of 8-year-old trees, which at 40 pounds a box represents 48,000 pounds of lemons. Even at 2 cents a pound, not a large price, this would be $960, from one picking of a 5-acre lemon orchard. The Gridley, Jowett[87] and Honeycutt orchards and many others had all produced large quantities of very fine fruit that summer. Another example cited by Conover was Thomas McConnell, who had purchased a 7-year-old bearing lemon orchard for $1,800 and cleared over $800 over expenses in his first year [355].

The importance of the lemon industry in Pacific Beach at this time is documented again in the 1901 San Diego City Directory, where 33 of the 54 residences with Pacific Beach home addresses listed the occupation of the resident as 'fruit grower'. The fruit growers included many of the residents who had reported their occupations on the 1900 census as farming (e.g., John Hodges[88] and Nathan Manning[89]) or ranching (e.g., Orrin Gridley and Sam'l Berkebile[90]).

Pacific Beach Notes continued to feature lemons and lemon ranchers in 1902. On April 19 the *Tribune* reported that Mr. Baker packed something over a thousand boxes of lemons from his ranch this picking [356]. The July 11 *Union* reported that the Gridley five acre

---

[86] Franklin W. Barnes had been elected to the State Assembly from the 79th Assembly District in 1900. Members of legislative bodies, even today, are entitled to be addressed as 'the Honorable' or 'the Hon.'.

[87] Sarah Jowett had acquired Acre Lot 34 from the Davises in May 1898 [636].

[88] John Hodges owned Acre Lot 47, except for the eastern 80 feet which had been 9th Street and would become Jewell Street [676]. That strip of land had been deeded to the Cogswells in 1892 [638].

[89] Nathan Manning owned the lemon ranch on Blocks 183 and 202, between Garnet Avenue and Ingraham, Emerald and Jewell Streets [677]. This property later belonged to the military academy, which used it for athletic fields, and to Safeway, which had a store on Garnet between Ingraham and Jewell. The Pacific Beach Pony League played on a baseball field here in the 1950s. It is now occupied by retail stores and a parking lot.

[90] Samuel Berkebile's owned Block 213, where George Havice reportedly 'set out' the first lemon trees in Pacific Beach in 1892. Berkebile purchased Block 213 from the Havices in September 1893 [688].

lemon ranch had been sold to eastern people for $5,500 [357][91]. The Advice to Lemon Packers column in the July 15 *Tribune* noted that R. M. Baker & Son had taken charge of the packing house and were shipping for themselves and others, finding a good market for lemons [358]. The Pacific Beach Notes in the *Union* for November 4 reported that the packing house was running full-handed and that there were plenty of lemons on the Beach [359].

News reports had frequently pointed out that prices for lemons, and consequently the fortunes of local lemon ranchers and packing houses, depended on factors such as the weather in the east and overseas competition. Toward the end of 1902 the San Diego Chamber of Commerce announced an agreement with the Santa Fe Railroad and the Western Cold Storage Company designed to stabilize prices through better supply chain management. According to the November 8, 1902, *Evening Tribune* it was only too well known how a Californian would send east a carload of lemons and by the time the fruit reached Chicago a shipload of Sicilian lemons would arrive at New York and 'completely demoralize the market', leaving the California shipper with his lemons, plus freight charges. The Santa Fe proposed an experiment under which the California growers would ship two carloads of lemons a month to the cold storage company at a 'fair and reasonable price', the railroad company would transport the fruit to Chicago at a rate of $1 per hundred pounds, the cold storage company would place them in storage, making careful experiments as to temperature, etc., and charging 10 cents per box per month. The lemons would be carried in storage until they could be disposed of to the best advantage, or as may be necessary because of their condition. The total charges of the three parties, the growers, the railroad and the cold storage company, would then be pooled and each would share in the loss or profit on the lemons in the ratio that their charges bear to the total charges. F. W. Barnes of Pacific Beach was appointed to the committee to cooperate with the railroad and the cold storage company [360].

Lemons continued to dominate the news from Pacific Beach in 1903, but another topic of local interest began to attract increasing attention in the press. Notes and Personals from Pacific Beach in the January 10 *Union* included the fact that Ed Barnes was getting out a car of lemons and that the Baker packing house was running full handed.

---

[91] The 'eastern people' were Francis Kinney, of New York City, who bought the east half of Acre Lot 48 from the Gridleys in August 1902 [678]. Less than a year later, in July 1903, Kinney sold the property to J. W. Stump [679].

Mr. and Mrs. Williams of the Race Track had sold their lemon ranch and were moving to San Diego; the ranch had been bought by Mr. Stephens who intended occupying it shortly[92]. Mr. Quackenbush of Chicago, who had lately purchased the upper Baker ranch[93], was on the beach and the Turner orchard was being put in better shape [361].

However, this Notes and Personals column also observed that 'every morning train brings quite a number of buyers and lookers for the new addition, Fortuna'. Fortuna Park Addition was a new subdivision laid out in the eastern half of Pueblo Lot 1800, south of Pacific Beach Drive (then called Pacific Avenue), from Lamont to just west of Jewell Street and south to what is now Moorland Drive. Second Fortuna Park Addition, a subdivision of the western half of Pueblo Lot 1800 extended the newly subdivided area westward to Riviera Drive[94]. Buyers and lookers were not only taking the morning train to Fortuna, but they were looking, and buying. The County Lot Book for 1904 showed that dozens of lots in the Fortuna Park and Second Fortuna Park Additions had been sold to individual purchasers (although only one lot had actually been assessed for improvements).

The News and Notes from Pacific Beach on March 14, 1903, was that the February and March crops of lemons were simply immense [116]. The orchards were laden with bloom, not only with orange and lemon blossoms but also with peach, pear and plum, according to the April 30 *Union*. Also, Mr. Baker was shipping three cars of lemons east and the recent rains had made fishing in False Bay very good, an

---

[92] The Williams' ranch was lots 1, 2 and 3 of the Eureka Lemon Tract, east of the racetrack in Pueblo Lot 1208, at the extreme eastern edge of Pacific Beach [724]. Lots 1, 2 and 3 were south of Bunker Hill Street between the Pacific Beach railway line and the Santa Fe. Mission Bay Drive has replaced the former right-of-way of the Pacific Beach railway and Interstate 5 now covers the eastern portion of this property.

[93] The upper Baker ranch was Acre Lot 30, now in the Admiral Hartman Community between Chalcedony and Beryl Streets and what would be the northern extensions of Olney and Pendleton Streets. Chauncey W. Quackenbush had purchased it in December 1902 from R. M. Baker [725]. Baker continued to own Acre Lot 53, which extended south of Chalcedony to Diamond Street between Olney and Pendleton and was lower both in elevation and in its orientation on a map.

[94] Pueblo Lot 1800, as well as 1801, 1802 and 1803, had been included in the original Pacific Beach subdivision map of October 1887, but these pueblo lots had all been removed in subsequent amended maps of Pacific Beach. A subdivision map for Fortuna Park Addition in the eastern half of Pueblo Lot 1800 was filed in January 1903 [691] (although buyers and lookers had apparently already been taking the morning train to look and buy). A subdivision map for Second Fortuna Park Addition, the western half of Pueblo Lot 1800, was filed in April 1903 [692].

attraction which kept anglers busy when not employed in the orchards [362]. The *Tribune* reported that Mr. Vessels from Nebraska, who some months before had bought the Major Hall place from Mr. Baker, had come out to take charge[95].

On the other front, now that water was assured the Fortuna Park people were setting out five hundred palm trees and would start to build cottages in the near future [363]. The May 20 *Tribune's* At Pacific Beach column reported that a large number of residences were to be built in the next few months at Pacific Beach and Fortuna Park, 'the choicest bit of home land in all Southern California is to be occupied now that abundant water is assured'. Although the water may have been abundant, the quality apparently left something to be desired. The *Tribune* reported that the water that came through the new pipes from the river was very much in the nature of ink on account of the tar in the pipes but it was 'not unwholesome to drink on that account although unsatisfactory just now to wash with'. The *Tribune* also noted that many automobiles were in evidence out this way and that the horse didn't seem to fancy them and, in other news, the heavy shipment of lemons was about over and prices were not all that could be wished [364].

The July 7, 1903, *Evening Tribune* contained a column headlined A Newsy Letter from Pacific Beach. Among the newsy items was the fact that Mr. E. Y. Barnes had ordered an automobile from the east and that Mr. Manny, formerly of St. Louis, who had bought the Boycott ranch, had moved onto it with his family [365][96]. The August 15 *Union* added that Mr. Manny had changed the name of his ranch from Oradawa (rushing waters) to Los Flores[97]. It was also noted that Mrs. Rowe's ranch had been sold and the new people had taken possession [366][98]. The turnover in the ownership of lemon property continued in the

---

[95] Mary Vessels had purchased the south half of Acre Lot 50 from the Bakers in July 1902 [654]; the Halls had sold the property to the Bakers in 1901.

[96] Abraham and Adelaide Manny had purchased Acre Lot 34 from the Boycotts in June 1903 [651].

[97] The *Union* had previously referred to this ranch as 'Ondewa' when it was owned by Miss Davis in 1896.

[98] Mary E. Rowe's ranch on Acre Lot 49 was sold to John and Julia Hauser in July 1903 [674]. In another sign that the pendulum was swinging away from agriculture and back toward residential development, the Hausers filed a subdivision map for Hausers Addition in September 1904, restoring Acre Lot 49 to its original configuration of two blocks of residential lots separated by Missouri Street on the west side of Lamont [680].

---

following year when 'Vancesecola Ranch' [367] on Acre Lot 33, formerly owned by the Stearns and Lincks but since 1901 by three other families in as many years, was sold to the Laymans of Des Moines, Iowa in May 1904 [368][99].

Although lemons were still newsworthy in 1904, agricultural news was balanced with news about the growing residential real estate market. The Notes and Personals column from Pacific Beach in the April 13, 1904, *Tribune* ('The following budget of news is at hand from the *Tribune's* correspondent') reported that two cars of lemons were shipped in the preceding week which netted $385, 'so some of our growers will again have an opportunity to see what a dollar looks like'. On the residential front, the population of the beach had more than doubled in the last six months [369].

In November 1903 the Folsom Bros. Co. had acquired O. J. Stough's majority share of the property in Pacific Beach. With their huge portfolio of Pacific Beach real estate, the Folsom Bros. Co. embarked on a campaign to market Pacific Beach, including the Fortuna Park additions, as a residential community. The January 9, 1904, *Union's* Past Week in Pacific Beach column reported that the first week of 1904 had seen not only an influx of a large number of new residents and visitors but a great advance in building and development by Folsom Bros. 'A large force of men is kept constantly employed and, in addition to a continuance of the work of street improvements and building operations, heretofore commenced, the foundations of two new houses were laid during the past few days. Nearly every train lands a number of prospective lot buyers, but few of these, it is said, leave without purchasing' [118].

Needless to say, many of the lots purchased by the trainloads of prospective lot buyers had previously grown lemon trees. The same article noted that one of the considerable transfers of real estate during the week was that of thirty lots located at Tenth and Vermont avenue. 'The property is very desirably situated and was formerly owned by E. Y. Barnes, who has just sold it to Frank M. McCrary of Independence, Mo., for $5,000'. Tenth Street and Vermont Avenue (actually, since 1900, Kendall and Emerald Streets), was the southwest corner of Acre Lot 64, site of the E. Y. Barnes lemon orchard, once considered the

---

[99] The Laymans continued the tradition of giving their ranch a name, deciding on 'Seniomsed' (Des Moines, their former home, spelled backward) [696]. The Layman family remained on the property for the next 30 years.

model for lemon cultivation in Pacific Beach[100].

In an April 12, 1906, article titled Pacific Beach Attracts Many, the *San Diego Union* noted that Dr. Corey, who had been away from her Pacific Beach home for five years, was delighted with the changes and found the growth and improvement remarkable, 'every old resident of Pacific Beach and San Diego as well should be willing or glad to thank Folsom Bros. company, and all interested, for what they have done' [370]. And, in another shift of the balance towards the housing market, the same article reported that J. W. Stump transferred all of the east half of Acre Lot 48, except the southeast corner on which his home was situated, to 'Sterling & Nancy Honeycutt & McCrary'[101].

Not everyone in Pacific Beach was willing or glad to thank the Folsom Bros. and other 'boomers' for what they had done for their community. The January 8, 1907, *San Diego Union* published the text of a letter from Wilbur Conover to the city Board of Works complaining that the 'real estate town lot boomers' were destroying numbers of fine trees while 'grading useless and silly 80-foot streets that there is no need for, and no one wants'. The Folsom Bros. Co., which was doing the grading, explained to the Board that the trees were in the street and had to come down and Conover's complaint generated nothing but ridicule [371]. Momentum was definitely on the side of residential growth; an article in the January 20, 1907, *Union* titled Many Sales at Pacific Beach began by listing dozens of real estate transactions and improvements in Pacific Beach and Fortuna Park, ending with the statement that other larger deals would be given to the press later [372].

With fewer lemon groves producing fewer lemons, the lemon

---

[100] E. Y. Barnes' property in the west half of Acre Lot 64 was indeed broken up into lots, although far fewer than 30. Most remained undeveloped and were reunited and appended to the Army and Navy Academy campus in the 1920s, and the property is now incorporated into the Plaza Condominiums. Barnes went on to become a retail grocer (and postmaster) in Pacific Beach, then partner in a wholesale produce business downtown, but he also resumed fruit cultivation and marketing, raising apples on his property in Pine Hills near Julian and selling them at his popular Manzanita Ranch fruit stand in Wynola. Manzanita Ranch remained in the Barnes family until it closed in 2000.

[101] Actually, Stump sold all of the east half of Acre Lot 48 except the southeast corner, the east 125 feet of the south 270 feet, to Sterling Honeycutt in April 1906 [670]. Honeycutt then sold the west 150 feet of the south 270 feet to Charles McCrary in April 1907 [669]. The Honeycutts and McCrary soon broke up their properties and sold them off as residential lots. The existence of the home at the southeast corner of Acre Lot 48, encroaching on what would have been Kendall Street, probably explains why Kendall was never re-opened between Diamond and Chalcedony.

---

packing business in Pacific Beach had also gone into decline. The former dance pavilion turned lemon curing and packing house on the railroad siding at the corner of Hornblend and Morrell had passed from Sterling Honeycutt to Barnes & Marshall and, when the Marshalls sold their lemon grove to R. M. Baker in December 1900, to Barnes & Baker. When the Barnes quit lemon ranching they also conveyed their interest in the packing house to Baker and in 1903 Baker sold the former dance pavilion back to Sterling Honeycutt [373]. In 1906 the Honeycutts donated the property and the building to the First Pacific Beach Methodist Episcopal Church (of which Sterling Honeycutt was a trustee) and after $2,500 had been spent on repairs the new church was dedicated on February 10, 1907 [374][102].

In the early 1900s there were no aerial photographs which might have illustrated the extent of lemon cultivation in its peak years in Pacific Beach, but the San Diego History Center does have a number of photos taken from high points in and around the community in the early 1900s which do show lemon groves and their changes over the years. One photo taken in 1906 from the high ground to the east of the Santa Fe railway tracks and looking west toward Pacific Beach shows the adjoining lemon ranches in Acre Lots 30 and 53, between Diamond, Olney, Beryl and Pendleton Streets. The trees are set out in neat rows and surrounded on the windward side by a wind break of what look

1906 view of Pacific Beach from Bunker Hill, east of the Santa Fe railway line, showing the adjoining lemon groves in Acre Lots 53 and 30, from Diamond Street at left to Beryl Street at right. (SDHC #283)

---

[102] The Methodists continued to own their previous church building on Emerald Street until that property was sold in 1913 to Bessie Davis, wife of the San Diego Army and Navy Academy founder Thomas Davis, and they built their home next door. The church eventually sold the pavilion property to Herbert D. Mason in December 1922 [671] and the pavilion disappeared from the tax rolls in 1924.

1904 view from College Campus toward corner of Garnet and Lamont with packing house in center, former hotel at right and lemon orchards on Blocks 205 (left) and 215 (right). (SDHC #23535)

like cypress trees. The homes of the lemon ranchers stand in the corner of each lot.

Other photos were taken in 1904 from a site in the very center of Pacific Beach, the college campus, presumably from the tower of Stough Hall. One shot looks in a southeasterly direction toward the intersection of Lamont and Garnet, with the lemon packing house in the former dance pavilion in the center background and the former hotel building on the right. The blocks on both the northeast and southwest corners of the intersection are covered with orderly rows of lemon trees. A second photo, also dated 1904 and presumably taken from the same vantage point at the same time, looks in a southwesterly direction toward the corner of Garnet and Jewell, where the Presbyterian Church and the schoolhouse just beyond are also flanked by lemon groves on the southeast and northwest corners.

The decline of the lemon industry can be appreciated by comparing these photos with another pair of photos, both also taken from the college campus, one in 1908 and the other after 1912. The 1908

1904 view from College Campus toward corner of Garnet and Jewell with church and schoolhouse in center and lemon orchards on Blocks 216 (left) and 202 (right). (SDHC #266)

1908 view from College Campus toward the corner of Garnet and Lamont (left). The lemon orchard in Block 215 looks untended and there are more buildings and street improvements. (SDHC #395-A)

photo again looks to the southeast, toward the corner of Lamont and Garnet, and also includes the former dance pavilion and hotel in the background, but the lemon grove in the center of the photo appears to be yielding to the forces of urbanization; the streets have been widened and graded and some have curbs and sidewalks, there are fewer lemon trees, and those that remain do not look like they are being actively cultivated. There is also a new building on one corner of the grove and power or telephone lines in the alley that cuts through the block. In the foreground, the college campus (which by then had become the Hotel Balboa) has been landscaped with decorative palm trees.

The 1904 photo from the college campus toward the southwest can be compared with a similar shot that is undated, but must have been taken after the large house in the center of the photo appeared on the site in 1912. Both photos show the identical house at the southwest corner of the block (on the left of the older and right of the newer photo), but in the more recent photo only bare ground, stumps and a

View from College Campus toward southwest after 1912. The lemon orchard formerly in Block 216 is dead or dying, replaced by new construction and power or telephone lines. (SDHC #14589)

few trees that appear dead or dying can be seen where a lemon grove had been in 1904. Even more houses and other signs of urbanization (and progress), including graded streets and more and taller power and telephone lines are seen in the more recent shot.

The two blocks across Garnet Street from the college campus which appear in these photos are representative of the transition from lemon ranching to residential development that took place in the central part of Pacific Beach in the early 1900s. These blocks, Block 215 and 216, and the two blocks immediately south of them, 237 and 238, had been the Honeycutts' initial acquisitions when they first came to Pacific Beach in 1893 [375], and although they were subdivided as city blocks Honeycutt initially treated them as acreage for his lemon ranch. There were no improvements before 1900 and early photos show lemon groves on each of the four blocks. After 1900 Honeycutt began selling lots and then entire blocks, and the purchasers began building on their property. In 1904 the county Lot Book indicated that Honeycutt still owned Blocks 215 and 237, but Blocks 216 and 238 had been sold to separate buyers and three improvements had been assessed. By 1908 these four blocks had been divided into a total of 25 separate holdings by 15 different owners with 9 improvements, two of which can be seen in the 1908 photo above. In 1908 Honeycutt no longer held any property in what had been his lemon ranch.

The San Diego History Center Oral History Program has a transcript of an interview with George Waddell Brooks, conducted in September 1961, in which he recounts moving to Pacific Beach in 1906 when he was 32 years old. He recalled that at that time there were lemon orchards and a lemon packing plant, and that lemon packing continued for many years until there was trouble with the duty on lemons. In his account, the Federal Government had placed a duty on first class lemons but Italian lemons arriving in New York were condemned as culls to avoid the duty and then put back on the market as first class lemons. 'That killed the lemon business in Pacific Beach' he said, 'There was subterfuge by the Italians and collusion with the Americans'[103]. 'Then they started in with more subdivision and the lemon orchards were destroyed' he added [376].

In April 1910 an enumerator for the decennial United States

---

[103] Southern Italy, and Sicily in particular, was a major producer of lemons and the lower costs of production and shipping by sea to the major markets on the east coast largely offset the cost of the duty on foreign lemons. Although California may have been losing a trade war with Italy over lemons it is doubtful whether the conspiracy suggested by Brooks was the reason.

Census once again made the rounds of Pacific Beach, visiting 95 locations (again not counting Morena and Rose Canyon) and collected 379 names, nearly twice the number of homes and over twice the number of residents counted in the 1900 census. Ninety-one of the entries included the 'trade or profession of, or particular type of work done' by the respondent (not counting 'Own Income' or 'None') and the 'general nature of industry, business, or establishment' in which the respondent worked. Of these, only twelve listed agricultural occupations, including 7 farmers, 4 ranchers, one ranch manager (George W. Brooks) and one farm laborer. Four of the farmers and ranchers indicated that they were 'working out', presumably for hire, two were truck farmers, one was a poultry farmer and one (Joseph Richert) a stock farmer[104]. None mentioned lemons or even fruit as the general nature of their business. Victor Hinkle, who had been listed as 'L. Rancher' in 1900 was listed in 1910 as 'Farmer'.

On the other hand, 27 residents in 1910 listed occupations associated with residential development. There were seven real estate agents (including former lemon rancher Sterling Honeycutt and his son and the two Folsom brothers), three others worked for real estate companies (a salesman, secretary and teamster) and 17 were employed in construction trades; six carpenters, two contractors, a builder and a stonemason described the general nature of their business as 'houses' or 'buildings', four concrete or cement workers worked on 'streets' and three worked at the lumber company[105]. Although Pacific Beach had been fertile ground for lemons it was also an ideal location for home sites, and in the end the trees gave way to houses. Even George Waddell Brooks, the ranch manager in 1910, spent 12 years doing 'outside work' for the San Diego Beach Company (successor to Folsom Bros. Co.) grading streets and maintaining their properties, then another 25 years as a real estate agent.

Property in the central corridor of Pacific Beach was already subdivided into residential lots but many of the lemon ranches were at the edges of the community where the original residential blocks had been remapped in the early 1890s as 'acre lots' of about 10 acres for agricultural purposes. With the pendulum swinging back from

---

[104] Although the Richerts owned property and a home in Pacific Beach, they also had a livestock operation in Rose Canyon.

[105] There were also other signs of progress in the 1910 census; seventeen-year-old Susie Ravenscroft was a telephone operator and the staff of the Scripps mansion at Braemar included a chauffeur (in addition to two gardeners, a nurse and a cook).

agriculture to residential development some owners of acre lots followed the example of the Hausers by re-subdivided their property into blocks of residential lots and placing the lots on sale. In October 1904 Henry Scott, owner of Acre Lot 35, and O. J. Stough, who had acquired Acre Lots 17 and 18 adjoining Acre Lot 35 on the north, filed a subdivision map which returned their properties to the configuration of the original Wheeler map of 1887, recreating the streets and avenues which had been removed when the acre lots were formed[106].

Acre Lot 20, east of Lamont Street below today's Kate Sessions Park, was re-subdivided in December 1906 into its original Wheeler configuration, reopening Lamont Street and restoring Blocks 53 (between Loring and Wilbur) and 66 (between Wilbur and Beryl) [377]. The southwest corner of Block 66 (lots 37-40) was sold in September 1907 to Ella MacFarland [378] and the MacFarlands built the Classical Revival home with the red steps which now stands on this property at the northeast corner of Lamont and Beryl. Construction of the $4000 home had begun by October [379] and they had moved in by February 1908 [380][107]. Between Lamont and Kendall Streets, Acre Lot 34 was

---

[106] On Scott's property in Acre Lot 35, Map 931 recreated Kendall and Law Streets where Tenth Street and Florida Avenue had been on the Wheeler map. Between Jewell and Kendall Streets, Block 89 was restored between Beryl and Law and Block 105 between Law and Chalcedony [673]. The straight streets and rectangular blocks of the Wheeler map proved unsuitable for the topography of Acre Lots 17 and 18, in the relatively steep foothills region, and they were re-subdivided (again) in 1914 as Congress Heights, with the new Collingwood and Monmouth Drives and Malden Street [693].

[107] Andrew F. MacFarland had been in the life insurance business in Spokane before moving to Pacific Beach. He was also apparently a serial bigamist; the newspapers called him a 'Bluebeard mate' and 'hymeneal champ' [656]. In 1911 he persuaded Ella, his third wife, to seek an annulment so he could have his second marriage annulled. Ella apparently understood that they would then be remarried, but when the second marriage was annulled he instead married a fourth woman, Ethyl Groom. On returning from an extended honeymoon in the east the newlyweds found that the annulment of his marriage to Ella had been vacated, making him once again a bigamist, which was once again resolved by having the latest wife seek an annulment on the understanding that they would remarry after he divorced the previous wife. Once again he changed the plan, instead taking up with his first wife in Ohio. Miss Groom then claimed that he had looted their safe deposit box and had him arrested and charged with grand larceny. The jury in his first trial deadlocked and a second trial in September 1912 ended in acquittal (which he celebrated by telephoning his first wife) [655]. The granting and vacating of annulments left him married to Ella and they seem to have resumed their previous domestic life; the San Diego city directory for 1914 has an entry for 'MacFarland Andw F (Ella C), ins, h 3154 B' (another corner lot with concrete steps to the sidewalk). They were finally divorced in 1919. His complaint for divorce alleged that she acted in a cold and unaffectionate manner and visited upon him a continuous tirade of abuse, accusing him among other things of squandering money in riotous living, which made it impossible to co-habitate with her and still preserve his peace of mind. Her cross-complaint alleged

re-subdivided into original Wheeler Blocks 90 (between Beryl and Law) and 105 (between Law and Chalcedony) in October 1907 [381].

Other owners of acre lots waited until later to re-subdivide their properties. Acre Lot 47 was eventually subdivided as Kendrick's addition in 1925 [382], Acre Lots 61 and 62 became Pacific Pines in 1926 [383], and Acre Lot 19, owned by C. M. Doty since 1904 became C. M. Doty's Addition in 1926 [384]. Another round of subdivision occurred in the 1940s with most of Acre Lot 33 becoming Lamont Terrace in 1947 [385][108], the portion of Acre Lot 36 on Law Street becoming Chalcedony Terrace in 1947 [386] and the portion on Beryl becoming Chalcedony Terrace Addition in 1948 [387]. Other acre lots have never been re-subdivided; Acre Lots 48 and 50, for example, are divided into odd-sized parcels that are still described in terms like 'The Westerly 50 feet of the Westerly 165 feet of the Easterly 290 feet of the South 165 feet of the North 310 feet of Acre Lot 48 of Pacific Beach, according to Map 854. Excepting therefrom the South 40 feet thereof'.

Most of the lemon growers in Pacific Beach lived on their properties and a few of their homes have survived to this day. The Hinkle's 'commodious and elegant' home stands on the northwest corner of Ingraham and Law, having been moved a few hundred feet from its original location on Chalcedony east of Ingraham about 1926[109]. The house at 1860 Law Street was built for Wilson and Bowers about 1892 and was also the home of the Davis, Jowett, Boycott, Manny and Ravenscroft families when they grew lemons on Acre Lot 34[110]. On

---

that he deserted and abandoned and lived separate and apart from her, and also prayed that the bonds of matrimony between them be dissolved (and that he be required to pay a reasonable sum to defray the cost of this action). Judge Marsh found that all the allegations in the cross-complaint were true and granted Ella a divorce (and costs) [694].

[108] One parcel on the north side of Acre Lot 33 had been sold to Henry Gross in August 1908 [672] and was not included in the re-subdivision. The Gross home, built in 1909, is still standing at 1921 Beryl.

[109] Carrie Hinkle, Victor Hinkle's widow, sold Acre Lot 36 to Lawrence L. Adams in September 1922 [657]. In January 1924 Adams bought the property at Ingraham and Law, lots 21-24 in Block 87 [689]. County Lot Books show that the value of improvements in Acre Lot 36 decreased from $210 in 1926 to $40 in 1927 while improvements on lots 21-23 in Block 87 increased from $30 to $600 in the same years. The San Diego City Directory showed that Adams lived at 1620 Chalcedony (in Acre Lot 36) in 1926 and 1596 Law (lots 21-24 in Block 87) in 1927. The Adams sold both properties in 1928 [690].

[110] This house was also apparently moved about 1912 from a location south of Law and west of Lamont Streets (lots 16-20 in Block 105) to its current location on the north side of Law (lots 25-27 in Block 90), at least according to the Lot Books.

Acre Lot 50, east of Lamont Street between Diamond and Chalcedony, the ranch houses on the south half, built by the Coffeens in 1895, and on the north half, built by the Roxburghs in 1904[111], are both still standing, although both are now obscured from the street behind newer buildings. The landmark home which stands today at the northwest corner of Diamond and Olney belonged to the Richert family, ranchers and fruit growers who had owned the property since 1896, but this house was actually built about 1914, after the lemon era had passed.

Other houses on the former lemon ranches have not survived. The Corey's home on Acre Lot 19, near the northwest corner of Lamont and Beryl, disappeared about 1932. On Acre Lot 33, the ranch house where the Stearns, Linck and Layman families had lived was torn down in the late 1940s when the property was re-subdivided and redeveloped as Lamont Terrace. The developers scraped the new subdivision down to bare earth in preparation for building new streets and homes but spared a Moreton Bay Fig tree which had shaded the ranch house in the center of the tract and which still stands in front of 1922 Law Street. The house on Mary Rowe's lemon ranch on Acre Lot 49, which also served as the parsonage for the Presbyterian Church from 1918 to 1939, was demolished in the late 1950s and replaced by the apartments at 1828–1840½ Missouri. A large palm tree that once stood in front of the ranch house remains to mark that spot. Nothing remains to mark the spot of the Cogswell home at the northwest corner of Diamond and Jewell, next to their lemon ranch in the west half of Acre Lot 48. It disappeared about 1958 and was replaced by the Jewell Manor apartments. The ranch house built in 1896 for Mrs. Gridley on the southeast corner of Acre Lot 48 was demolished in the late 1960s to make room for the Tiffany apartments on Diamond Street.

The Barnes homes in Acre Lot 64 were acquired by the San Diego Army and Navy Academy in the 1920s. The F. W. Barnes home on the southeast corner of the lot (the northwest corner of Lamont and Emerald) and the E. Y. Barnes home on the southwest corner (the northeast corner of Jewell and Emerald) were put to various uses including residences for academy staff. Both were torn down after the academy was sold in the 1950s and the site converted to a shopping center and apartment complex. Acre Lots 30 and 53, site of the Marshalls and Bakers lemon ranch, became the site of a public housing

---

[111] The Roxburghs' home was 'both substantial and artistic looking being built largely of stone' [652]. The artistic looking stone exterior which characterized this house for decades has now been plastered over.

project in 1941. The original ranch houses were demolished and the entire area was reconfigured to allow the construction of hundreds of temporary homes for defense workers.

The lemon industry had revived Pacific Beach and dominated its economy for more than a decade, from the first sales of acreage property in 1892 to the resurgence of the residential real estate market in the mid-1900s. Lemon cultivation represented an opportunity for 'the few discouraged, depressed settlers in 1891', as E. C. Thorpe called those (like himself) who had been involved with the College of Letters and remained when the college closed in 1891[112]. Their existing properties and the unexploited acreage nearby were ideal in terms of climate, soil and the availability of water and transportation facilities. These early settlers were joined by others who, like them, were generally not experienced citrus growers but 'miners, doctors, widows, photographers, ministers, in fact representatives of every vocation, except that of lemon culture' as the *San Diego Union* phrased it in 1898 [336]. The lemon industry included investors who purchased and developed lemon ranches for resale, absentee owners who hired managers to operate their ranches and many who labored on their own ranches, sometimes with hired help. Once lemons were picked they were gathered into packing houses where they were cured, packed and shipped, providing additional employment opportunity for residents, including many women. However, as the land allocated to lemon orchards became more valuable as homesites for a growing population, the lemon industry gradually died out and, like the other institutions and industries which were vital to the early development of Pacific Beach, few traces remain today. The lemon era is remembered by a few century-old farmhouses which once stood alone among acres of lemon trees and are now squeezed between apartment buildings and condominiums along residential streets.

---

[112] The Thorpe, Barnes, Cogswell and Rowe families had lived in Pacific Beach while their children attended the former college and became lemon ranchers after the college closed. Lemon rancher E. Y. Barnes and his wife, the former Lulo Thorpe, had themselves been students at the college.

7 The Scripps and Braemar

Frederick Tudor (F. T. or Fred) Scripps was born in 1850 in Rushville, Illinois. His widowed father had emigrated from England with six children from his previous marriages (among whom was Ellen Browning Scripps), married again, and raised five more children in the Rushville area. Fred was the third of these children; the youngest, Edward Willis (E. W.) Scripps, born in 1854, went on to establish a newspaper empire which eventually became the E. W. Scripps Company, a media conglomerate which exists to this day.

While E. W. and Ellen had joined her brother (his half-brother) James and prospered in the newspaper business in several Midwestern cities, Fred remained a farmer in the Rushville area. He was described as the 'problem' sibling in the Scripps family; never settling on a career, moving from one venture to another, and losing money along the way [388]. Nevertheless, the Scripps family remained close and in 1890 Fred and Ellen travelled to California to visit his sister (her half-sister) Annie who had moved to Alameda for her health. After a month in northern California Fred and Ellen travelled to San Diego to visit cousins and spent some time travelling around the region, including Pacific Beach, La Jolla and what was then called Linda Vista but is now better known as Miramar or Scripps Ranch.

Both Ellen and Fred were impressed with the San Diego area, particularly Fred who, like his sister Annie, suffered from arthritis and felt that he would benefit from the milder climate. They convinced E. W. to visit later in the year and he also liked what he saw and agreed to join Ellen in purchasing property in Linda Vista. They began by purchasing three tracts of land totaling 400 acres north of Carroll Canyon, extending east from approximately where Interstate 15 runs today [389] [390] [391] [392]. They later added other property surrounding their original tract.

Fred sold his farm in Rushville and moved to San Diego to oversee development of the new Scripps ranch. The January 7, 1891, *San Diego Union* noted his return to San Diego:

The Game Went On.
By last night's train arrived Fred T. Scripps of Rushville, Ills, who spent a portion of last season at the Horton. What he considers a coincidence is that he found the old circle of whist players just at a point in the game that characterized the breaking off of his last contest with them, and he accordingly resumed to finish the game. Mr. Scripps is here to remain [393].

Construction of a palatial home on the ranch, which E. W. Scripps named Miramar, began in 1891 and proceeded throughout the decade; when completed in 1898 it had grown to 49 rooms.

Sarah Emma Jessop was born in England in 1871. Her father, Joseph Jessop, a jeweler, had been told by his English doctor that his 'chances for health' depended on moving to Southern California. His doctor also prescribed a change of careers, giving up his jewelry business in favor of the outdoor life of a rancher [394]. Accordingly, the Jessops moved to San Diego County in 1890 and bought a 50-acre ranch in Linda Vista, a location which is between today's Black Mountain Road and Interstate 15, north of Miramar Road and south of Carroll Canyon Road [395]. The Jessops and the Scripps thus became neighbors; the northeast corner of the Jessop property met the southwest corner of the Scripps.

In October 1891 Fred Scripps entered into an agreement with Gordon, Howard and Vincent Surr, who owned property north of the Scripps ranch, in which he was granted a forty-acre tract of land in exchange for his agreement to build a dam and reservoir on the property and supply the Surrs with a fifth of the water impounded by the dam [396]. Scripps then began work on what became known as the Surr Dam, the precursor of today's Miramar Lake, reportedly with Joseph Jessop's assistance[113]. Fred Scripps and Emma Jessop became acquainted and in December 1993, when he was 43 and she was 20, they were married [397].

E. W. and Ellen Scripps had intended for their ranch to become a home not only for themselves but for other members of their extended family, but even with the addition of separate wings it apparently was never large enough to hold all of them. Ellen Browning Scripps made her departure from the family estate and began her long association with La Jolla when she bought property on Prospect Street in 1896 [398] and built the home she named South Moulton Villa[114]. Fred and Emma

---

[113] Although the Jessops retained the Linda Vista ranch, Joseph Jessop soon gave up the outdoor life and opened a shop at 1317 F Street downtown first, in 1893, as a watchmaker [296] and by 1895 as a jeweler [19]. In 1896 he 'renounced all allegiance to Queen Victoria' and became a United States citizen [701] and despite his English doctor's concerns lived to the age of 83. Jessop Jewelers is still in business in San Diego today, owned by a great-grandson of Joseph Jessop.

[114] South Moulton Villa was named for South Moulton Street in London, where Ellen had grown up. This original home burned down in 1915 and Miss Scripps commissioned architect Irving Gill to build a replacement on the same site, which she also named South Moulton Villa. Today it is the Museum of Contemporary Art in La Jolla.

Scripps followed soon after, accumulating property on the shore of Mission Bay in the southwest corner of Pacific Beach in 1900 and building their bay front home Braemar (or Brae Mar) Manor.

The land in this corner of Pacific Beach, along the northwest shore of Mission Bay, had once been the property of James Poiser, who had apparently raised sheep there and watered them at freshwater springs in the area[115]. Poiser had purchased 40 acres in the north end of Pueblo Lot 1803 from Alonzo Horton in 1885 [399] and was among those whose land was acquired by the Pacific Beach Company in 1887 [400]. Poiser's deed granted the Pacific Beach Company 40 acres in the north end of Pueblo Lot 1803 'excepting therefrom 1 acre previously sold, and one acre around the house now occupied by me to be taken off the end of any block that may be laid out to cover said ground'[116].

The Pacific Beach Company's first subdivision map, the Wheeler map of October 1887, left a portion of Pueblo Lot 1803 between Hensley Avenue and the shoreline of the bay unsubdivided, presumably the property that had been reserved to Poiser. In 1892 the first revision of the subdivision map, Map 697, no longer included Pueblo Lot 1803 south of Hensley Avenue in the Pacific Beach subdivision at all, although the portion of Pueblo Lot 1803 north of Hensley was re-subdivided as Acre Lots 70 and 71. Map 791, in 1894, reconfigured the area again, removing the southern portion of the new Acre Lot 70 to restore the south half of the former Pacific Beach Block 387 to its original location. Map 791 also specifically identified the parcel along the shore of Mission Bay south of Acre Lot 71 as 'Poisers 1 Acre'.

The bayside Poisers 1 Acre tract passed through the hands of several other owners before being sold in December 1899 to F. T.

---

[115] Pacific Beach resident Wilbur Conover wrote in the December 1, 1901, *San Diego Union* that 'A Mr. Poiser owned and pastured this land to thousands of sheep. His ranch house was down on the bay near where Mr. Fred Scripps has just built his beautiful residence. There were then, and would be now, if dug out, some very fine springs at this point' [355]. The high water table implied in this account is consistent with a history of flooding in this area. In 1916 the *San Diego Union* reported that the home of F. T. Scripps was practically surrounded by water left by a storm (the 'Hatfield flood' of 1916) and that city employees were sent out to help drain the pool [712]. A city official reported in 1964 that in storms of any magnitude 'ponding' begins at the Mission Boulevard-Pacific Beach Drive intersection [711].

[116] James Poiser's son Richard had also acquired 20 acres in nearby Pueblo Lot 1793 in November 1885 [703] which he also sold to the Pacific Beach Company in November 1887 [704]. The Pacific Beach Company honored the Poisers by naming one of the avenues in their first subdivision map after them. In the Wheeler map of 1887 Poiser Avenue was approximately where La Playa Avenue is today.

Scripps for $325 [401]. Scripps also paid $360 for Acre Lot 71, at the southwest corner of the streets that became Bayard and Pacific Beach Drive and separated from the Poiser tract by what had originally been Hensley Avenue [402][117].

Scripps wasted little time developing his property. The *San Diegan – Sun*[118] noted on October 5, 1900 that 'F. Scripps is making a fine home on the old Poiser place near the bay. The inside finish of his house is of white cedar. He has also a fine, commodious barn, wharf and all conveniences of a seaside home' [403]. Landscaping of the 7-acre site was also underway; the November 21, 1900 *Evening Tribune* reported that Mr. Scripps was improving his place at the ocean front by putting in roses and bulbs [404].

By the end of 1901 the home had become 'Mr. Fred Scripps beautiful residence on the bay' [355]. County Lot Books show that the assessed value of improvements on Acre Lot 71 went from nothing in 1900 to $250 in 1901 and 1902, roughly comparable to other large residences in Pacific Beach at the time. In 1903 and 1904 the assessment for improvements on Acre Lot 71 increased to $750, the highest assessed value of any private home in Pacific Beach (by comparison, in 1904 the improvements on the College Campus, the original college building or Girls' Hall, designed by Reid Brothers, and Stough Hall, were assessed at $1000).

The Scripps mansion was built facing Mission Bay, perhaps 100 feet from the shoreline. Early photos showed a large two-story home with a central gabled section which featured a balcony overlooking the bay, dormer windows to each side and a covered porch extending the full width of the building on the bay side. The home was surrounded by ornamental stonework, trees and gardens.

In April 1905 the *Union* commented on the Scripps home on the occasion of what was apparently an annual Scripps family sojourn at the Tent City in Coronado:

> "Why should they come to Coronado?" Their own lovely, commodious and modern home at Pacific Beach, 'Braemar Manor', is most charmingly located within a stone's throw of the ocean; they have their own

---

[117] The 75-foot strip of what had been Hensley Avenue in the original Wheeler map of the Pacific Beach subdivision had been left out of subsequent subdivision maps. Scripps petitioned the city to close Hensley Avenue and the petition was granted September 3, 1901 [707]. Apparently the land formerly dedicated to the street reverted to the surrounding landowner, namely F. T. Scripps.

[118] The *Sun* was the Scripps newspaper in San Diego; Edward W. Scripps was president of the San Diegan – Sun Publishing Company.

Braemar Manor, the Scripps Mansion, before its 1926 renovation. (SDHC #93: 18888)

> private pier and pleasure craft – a yacht, a launch, row boats, canoes, big
> boats and little boats. Each member of the family has his or her own pet boat
> and there is good fishing at their own front gate.
>
> Mr. and Mrs. Scripps entertain many house parties each year, for the
> host and hostess of Braemar Manor are hospitable people, so they need not
> come to camp for the sake of company.

(The *Union* concluded that they came for the novelty of the charmed outdoor life, 'camp life under ideal conditions', and that there were many who considered Tent City on the same high favor as did Mr. and Mrs. Scripps) [405].

While the Scripps' home was notable for its size and architecture (and its assessed value) the landscaping was equally impressive. Emma Scripps was an avid gardener and, with Kate Sessions, one of the founding members of the San Diego Floral Association in 1907. In an article she wrote for the association journal *The California Garden* in 1909, she figuratively led visitors through her garden:

> Come, walk with me in my garden on the shore of False Bay. The sun
> is just sinking into the ocean, and shedding its golden and rosy rays over
> water and land, soothing all nature as a sweet mother sooths and puts her
> little ones to sleep. It is this peaceful influence that rests and quiets me after
> a full and busy day. How I wish that all who are tired and weary might join
> me where silence heals the wound of sound. How quiet nature is in all its
> workings!
>
> Sauntering through the geranium walk, the first bed reached is the
> asters, planted late, but I enjoy flowers planted in season – that is the English
> season I remember as a child. The aster always made me sad, because with
> the dying of the aster the summer departed. Of course, here there is no
> death of summer, as the next bed of penstemon will show. It is full of
> delicate, spikey blooms, and has been so for two years. There is nothing
> more satisfactory, for it is always in bloom, and after our first year, if cut
> back, it will send out new growth and bloom again.

Our next bed is dahlias. What a glorious mass of color, with their thick stem, dark green leaves and spidery petals. It gives one strength to look at them.

One of our prime favorites is the cactus variety. Planted at the end of May, they bloom from the last of June to December. The more blooms you pick the more you have.

Now comes to us the most beautiful bed of all – wonderful because we think we have coaxed nature into doing double duty. At present there is nothing but dead leaves to show for what was a few weeks ago a glorious bed of gladiolus flowers, containing over 600 bulbs, and each one of them bore a stem of cherry-red blossoms, 18 inches in length, and all were in bloom at the same time. Put in the ground the last week of May, by the first of July they were in their prime. The bulbs are ready now to take up and dry for two weeks, when we shall plant them again, and they will repeat the performance. The ancestors of these bulbs were given to me four years ago. I think there were six or eight of them; now we have over 100 good ones and have given as many away.

Here is the Japanese garden, and leading us through the pergola of cypress logs, are flat stepping stones I picked up on the beach. I never go to the beach that I do not find some treasure – flat stones for the walks, or perhaps a piece of worm-eaten rock for the fish pond. If I cannot bring my find with me, I put it aside until a wagon can go for it. . .

The chrysanthemum bed is bordered with a rustic edging of fig tree twigs, saved from the last pruning, and, by the way we do not throw a stick away, for the more twisted it is the more likely it will fit just the right place in making a garden seat or flower basket.

Peeping through the pines, I see the cane summer-house made from our own canes. Less than five years ago I brought the parent root from Coronado in my pocketbook, and now we have enough to plant acres. We cut it down in early spring, saving the cuttings for garden work, cover large barrels with it, weaving the cane together with string, and in these we grow the sprengeri. We also use it for staking the carnations and chrysanthemums. There is no end to the uses for it; it is such a cheerful grower, and the young growth is very beautiful [406].

Fred Scripps had also been accumulating other property in Pacific Beach. In 1903 he acquired Acre Lots 43 and 44, between Diamond, Allison (now Mission Boulevard), Chalcedony and Cass Streets [407] and subdivided it as Ocean Front Addition [408]. Closer to home, he extended his bayside property another block east by purchasing Acre Lot 70 and Block 387 (except for lots 33 and 34) [409]. In 1904 he added another 1 1/3 acres of land west of and adjoining his original Poisers 1 Acre property, between the bay shore and Acre Lot 71 [410]. He also purchased the 'unnumbered lots east of the Depot Grounds'[119] [411]

---

[119] The original Wheeler map and first revision (Map 697) of the Pacific Beach subdivision had left the entire 4-block area between First and Third Streets (now Mission Boulevard and Cass) and Reed and Hubbell Avenues (Pacific Beach Drive) unsubdivided and designated as the 'Depot'. Subsequent subdivision maps (791 and 858) had reduced the 'Depot Grounds' to a smaller area around First Street but had not re-subdivided the area to the east, which became known as 'the unnumbered lots east of the Depot Grounds'.

and Acre Lot 69 [412], extending his holdings north to Reed Avenue and east to Dawes Street. In 1907 Scripps filed a map for Braemar Subdivision, consolidating his holdings in this corner of Pacific Beach east of Bayard Street. The 6.2-acre parcel south of Pacific Avenue (Pacific Beach Drive) and west of Bayard Street where the Scripps home and gardens were located was also included and designated Lot A [413][120]. Development of the Braemar Subdivision began with improvement of the surrounding streets. Bayard Street between Grand Avenue, where the stop on the railway line had become known as Braemar Station, and Braemar Lane was graded, sidewalked and curbed at the expense of the property owners, primarily Scripps [414].

Scripps also turned his attention to La Jolla, filing a subdivision map for F. T. Scripps Addition to La Jolla Park in June 1903. F. T. Scripps Addition covered the westerly portion of Pueblo Lot 1261, extending east from La Jolla Boulevard to Mabel Bell Lane and from north of Marine Street south to Westbourne Street. One street in the center of the Scripps addition was named Rushville Avenue (now Rushville Street) in honor of Scripps' birthplace[121]. He also took the initiative for what became La Jolla Boulevard; the *Evening Tribune* reported on June 22, 1903, that 'work was commenced this morning by F. T. Scripps on the new boulevard from Pacific Beach to La Jolla' [415]. The *Evening Tribune's* Week's Newsletter from Pacific Beach in April 1904 declared that thanks to the generosity of Fred Scripps 'the road between this place and La Jolla' was 'no doubt the best drive of its length in the county' [416][122].

On February 6, 1904, a 'splendid specimen of a whale' washed up

---

[120] Richard Poiser had purchased Lots 33 and 34 of Block 387 from the Pacific Beach company in 1889 [708] and although these lots were directly across Bayard Street from the Scripps mansion and were surrounded by the Braemar subdivision they were not included in it. Scripps finally bought lots 33 and 34 in 1925 [709] and they were included in the 1926 Braemar Extension. The property in the 'unnumbered lots' north of Pacific and west of Bayard was also subdivided, as First Addition to Braemar, in 1917 [710].

[121] There is also a Scripps Street and Scripps Park in Rushville, the county seat of Schuyler County, Illinois. Another Schuyler County native who migrated to Pacific Beach was Mary Bryant Webster, Mom, a 1933 graduate of Rushville High School, who moved into the De Luxe Trailer Park, now the site of the Pacific Beach branch library across Reed Avenue from the Braemar subdivision, in 1947 and then to Diamond Street, next door to the former Gridley ranch house and across from Brown Military Academy, in 1950.

[122] F. T. Scripps' real estate interests were not limited to Pacific Beach and La Jolla. The 7-story Scripps Building at the corner of 6th Avenue and C Streets downtown was opened in 1908 and is still standing today.

Originally Pacific Beach

Map of Braemar Subdivision, filed in 1907. The Scripps bay front mansion and gardens were located in Lot A. The tract north of Pacific Avenue (Pacific Beach Drive) and west of Bayard Street was subdivided as First Addition to Braemar in 1917.

on the beach directly in front of the Scripps Mansion and 'little Tommy Scripps and his cousin George Jessop' who were playing nearby were the first to discover it. Apparently they tied a rope to the whale and secured it to a staple driven into the sand and then charged admission to view it; in the words of the *Evening Tribune* writer, they 'sold the captured whale at a goodly sum for exhibition purposes' making it evident that they were 'chips from the old block' and that 'the precious scions had already developed the family instinct of an eye for the main chance'. Others also benefited by the appearance of the whale; according to the *Tribune*, many of those who came to enjoy the spectacle had been so 'fascinated by the charms and advantages of this beautiful suburb that they have availed themselves of the opportunity to examine the lots placed on the market by Folsom Brothers. It is said that as a result of the whale's unexpected visit, the sales of building sites during the week have been largely augmented' [417].

Given the social status of Fred and Emma Scripps, and of their relatives, Braemar Manor was a frequent topic in the social columns of the local newspapers, particularly when the event featured one of their large extended families. The June 6, 1906, *Tribune* reported the engagement of a Miss Elsie Simpson to Armand Jessop, 'one of Southern California's popular young bachelors and successful business men, who is associated with his father as a member of the firm of Joseph Jessop & Sons' (and was Emma's brother). The article noted that 'several delightful social functions are being planned in compliment to the fair bride-to-be, at one of the most elaborate of which Mrs. Frederick Tudor Scripps, who formerly was Miss Jessop of Braemar Manor, will be the hostess' [418]. Later in the year, two carriage loads of La Jolla ladies drove to Mrs. F. T. Scripps' beautiful ocean front residence, Braemar, to attend the Ladies' Aid musicale (a guessing contest in which each lady represented some well known song). Iced watermelon was daintily served on the lawn. The La Jollans present included Dr. (Martha Dunn) Corey and Miss (Ellen Browning) Scripps [419].

The Scripps also made their home available for local community events. The October 19, 1906, San Diego Union noted that eight prominent ladies of Pacific Beach had formed a Glee Club[123] and made their initial bow to the public in a benefit program at Mrs. F. T. Scripps' cozy clubhouse [420]. Many ladies from San Diego and La Jolla, as well as Pacific Beach, attended the Pacific Beach Reading Club's regular meeting at Mrs. Scripps in January 1907 [421].

TALENT WORKER'S FAIR
for Hospital Fund
F. T. SCRIPPS' GARDEN, PACIFIC BEACH, Wed. Thurs., Aug. 17-18
Admission Free—Open Wednesday Night.
Take La Jolla cars, stop at Brae Mar. Your fortune told. Fun and jokes. Candy and fancy work sold by San Diego's most charming society girls.

The Scripps property was also host to public events to benefit causes which Mrs. Scripps supported. In 1910, *The California Garden*, journal of the San Diego Floral Association, cordially invited the public to the beautiful garden of Mr. and Mrs. F. T. Scripps, at Brae Mar, which would be converted into Fairyland for the benefit of the Talent

---

[123] Members were Mesdames Hinkle, Baker, Woodward, Woodman, McLaury, Scripps, Johnstone and Miss Lillibell Johnstone.

Workers' Hospital fund[124]. The garden would be decorated in the most lavish manner and there would be Japanese and oriental refreshment booths, a flower booth, fortune teller's booth, candy booth and apron, fancy work and tooled leather booths. The date had been chosen to take advantage of the full moon [422]. The *San Diego Union* added that the booths would be filled with bright articles, not the least of these being the 'pretty and popular girls' who would be in charge of them. 'Misses Violet, Fanny and Linda Jessop, sisters of Mrs. Scripps, are to meet the guests and look after their welfare generally' [423].

In 1914, Mrs. Scripps invited the Floral Association to Braemar Manor for an outdoor meeting. *The California Garden* reported that whereas the only living things on the place when the Scripps took possession twelve years before were a few cypress trees and Bermuda grass, today the grounds were surrounded with double rows of Phoenix Canariensis palms, 'large and sturdy in appearance'. Here and there were various out-buildings, including a substantial wigwam 'built by real red men', filled with 'numberless Indian relics and curios, each having its own story'. There was a lath house, rich in ferns and tuberous begonias and a luxuriant grapevine formed an arbor which the sun could not penetrate. On the bay front were other summer houses, including a Japanese teagarden and a little log hut. Florally, despite sitting just off the ocean front and with sandy soil, Braemar had produced creditable blooms of almost every flower family. Mrs. Scripps' roses had long been famous through having won many ribbons and cups at the flower shows [424].

The Scripps were early supporters of the San Diego Army and Navy Academy when it opened in Pacific Beach in 1910. As early as July 1911 F. T. Scripps was listed as a reference in an Academy advertisement in the *Union* [425] and the Scripps' oldest son Thomas became a cadet in 1911. He was named a sergeant in the band in December 1911 [426] and promoted to captain and quartermaster in December 1912 [427]. Tom Scripps was listed in the saxophone section when the cadet band gave their first concert in front of a 'fair-sized audience' in the U. S. Grant Hotel on May 29, 1913 [428].

The Army and Navy Academy was also a factor in the 1921 marriage of Miss Annie Scripps, the Scripps' youngest daughter, and

---

[124] The Talent Workers was a charitable organization founded in 1910 by prominent San Diego women and dedicated to providing medical aid to the needy. The women would meet weekly to make articles, each member using her talents, 'whether it be art, needlework or any other line'. The articles would then be sold and the proceeds directed to the proposed hospital [713]. Mrs. Scripps was a director of the Talent Workers and held regular meetings at her home in addition to the summer fair.

Austen Brown, an Army and Navy Academy graduate. The October 17, 1921, *Evening Tribune* noted that the romance had been one of long standing and many rumors of the engagement were started before the announcement was made. When Miss Scripps attended The Bishop's School in La Jolla[125] she was a 'frequent attendant at the A. and N. dances' and the previous summer they 'were seen much together swimming at La Jolla and were frequently dancing together at the Grant and Coronado'. The wedding took place at 'Brae Mar Manor, the Scripps home in Pacific Beach' and was solemnized in the conservatory of the home; 'The bride looked very pretty in her white velvet gown and veil, and her sister Miss Mary Scripps, set her well off in a charming dark frock' [429].

The roles were reversed two years later when Mary Scripps married William Gardner Corey, son of Pacific Beach pioneer Dr. Martha Dunn Corey, in July 1923. The wedding took place at Saint James-by-the-Sea in La Jolla with Mrs. A. G. Brown (nee Annie Scripps) as matron of honor, followed by a wedding reception at the home of the bride's parents in Pacific Beach [430].

Braemar Manor had always been an impressive residence but in the mid-1920s it underwent an extensive renovation. The April 1925 *Evening Tribune* listed a building permit for F. T. Scripps at 4036

Braemar Manor after renovation in 1926. The room at left, later the Wedding Chapel and now the Rose Creek Cottage, was added and the entire building upgraded to the English cottage style with half-timbered walls, leaded windows and tall brick chimneys. (SDHC #87:16174)

---

[125] The Bishop's School was a legacy of her aunts Ellen Browning Scripps and Virginia Scripps, who provided much of the funding, especially for the architecture of the campus.

       Originally Pacific Beach

Bayard, Lot A, Braemar, for a 'foundation only' valued at $1000 [431]. In March 1926 another building permit for a $500 pump house was listed for F. T. Scripps, 'foot of Bayard' [432]. By the end of 1926, improvements to the Scripps' property in Lot A of Braemar subdivision were assessed at $3700, over three times the 1925 assessment of $1050 and far more than other homes in Pacific Beach, which ranged from about $200 to $500[126].

The renovations involved both new construction and a change in style. The new construction included the addition of a dining room with an arched ceiling that was attached to the west end of the estate (and which is the only surviving portion of the home, although now in a different location). The new dining room was finished in the then-popular half-timbered look with leaded windows called English cottage style, and the original portions of the house were also upgraded with leaded windows, towering brick chimneys and exposed exterior woodwork to match.

Scripps also took steps during 1926 to make the surrounding neighborhood more to his liking. In May the Common Council adopted Resolution No. 37638, closing the half-block of Bayard Street that had continued south of what is now Braemar Lane to the former Hensley Avenue, then called Braemar Lane, which was also closed to public access [433]. In June, the Scripps filed a subdivision map for Braemar Extension, incorporating the closed portion of Bayard Street, the rest of the Braemar subdivision east of Bayard and south of Pacific Beach Drive and new property acquired by Scripps extending another block east to Dawes Street [434]. The current Braemar Lane and Briarfield Drive were dedicated as city streets.

Lot B of the new subdivision, east of the closed portion of Bayard Street and south of the new Braemar Lane, was divided into three parcels fronting on Mission Bay which were distributed to three of the four Scripps children (F. Tudor, Jr., the youngest, was only 18 at the time). Thomas Scripps, the oldest, received the western-most lot [435], separated from his parents' property by the closed portion of Bayard Street, and his own bayside home was completed by the end of the year[127]. The closed portion of Bayard Street was designated Lot C of

---

[126] By comparison, improvements on the 16-acre college campus then occupied by the San Diego Army and Navy Academy, which included some new construction in addition to the original college buildings, were assessed at $3900.

[127] Annie Scripps Brown was allotted the eastern 115 feet [714] and Mary Scripps Corey the middle 100 feet [715].

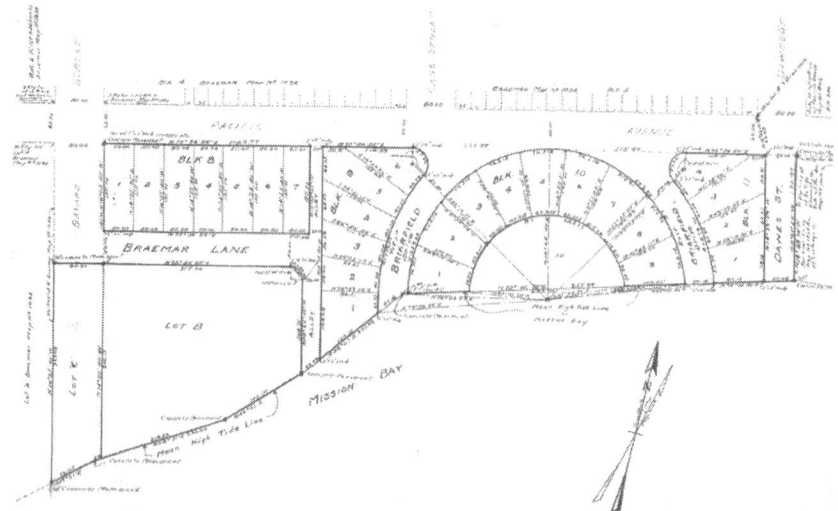

Braemar Extension and effectively became a private drive into the grounds of the Scripps compound.

The Braemar Extension subdivision map had specifically excepted from the described property 'any portions thereof heretofore or now lying below the line of mean high tide of Mission or False Bay'. However, to further enhance the value of their bayside property, the Scripps also obtained a 50-year lease from the Board of State Harbor Commissioners for use of the tidelands extending from their property lines at the mean high tide mark offshore to a proposed seawall (which was never built).

Scripps then spent 'considerably more than $100,000' in improvements for the remaining portions of the surrounding Braemar, First Addition to Braemar and Braemar Extension subdivisions, including concrete streets, alleys, sidewalks and curbs, and even a cove for boating (Braemar Cove, surrounded by Briarfield Drive). The Braemar tract would be 'one of the most highly developed residential beach properties yet presented' according to the *San Diego Union* on July 18, 1926, the day of its opening; 'All public utilities, including gas, electricity, water and a complete sewer system are in and ready for connection' [436]. Braemar wasn't for everyone, however; the advertisement by Barney & Rife, Sales Agents, stressed that the development was 'carefully restricted'. No homes could be built which cost less than a minimum value, which ranged from $3500 to $7500 depending on the value of the lot. Braemar being strictly a high-class residential section, there were uniform set-back restrictions and restrictions against flats or apartment houses [437]. Prospective buyers would also presumably have recognized this heavy emphasis on

Originally Pacific Beach

'restrictions' as a coded reference to another condition which was spelled out in purchasers' deeds:

> No part of said property, or any building thereon, shall ever be used or occupied by any person not of the Caucasian race, either as owner, lessee, licensee, or in any capacity other than of a servant or employee of the occupant nor shall said property ever by mortgaged, sold or transferred to any person not of the Caucasian race [438].

By October 1926 Barney & Rife had warned of a 'price advance' and then a few days later advertised that they were extending the deadline by a few days because the warning had brought them so many eager customers [439]. In November they warned that with the steady demand for the property there was a probability of the tract being entirely sold out with the next few weeks [440][128].

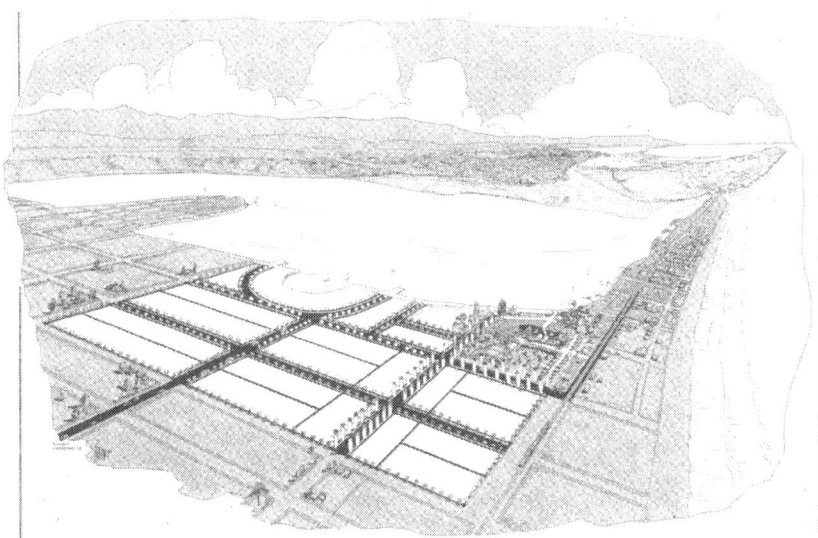

'Braemar, a setting of enduring charm for your permanent home', from a Barney & Rife sales poster in1926. This illustration also emphasizes the proximity to the San Diego Electric Railway line between downtown and La Jolla (an electric train is shown at the foot of Oliver Street) and shows that the highway from downtown through Mission Beach and Pacific Beach to La Jolla passes through Braemar, from Mission Boulevard to Pacific Beach Drive to Cass Street (Mission Boulevard was not a major route at the time and the causeway across the bay to Crown Point had not yet been built). The trees actually did exist and many are still growing. (SDHC #AD1049-078 F5D6)

---

[128] Actually, county Lot Books indicate that of the 26 lots in the numbered blocks of the new Braemar Extension (not counting lots B and C, which were not for sale) only 5 lots had been transferred to 4 new owners by 1928 (one of whom was Joseph Jessop). None of these lots had been improved by 1928; the only improvement in the Braemar Extension belonged to Thomas Scripps on his allotment of the western 100 feet of Lot B.

Development of the northwestern shore of Mission Bay had attracted the attention of water sports enthusiasts and in October 1926 Braemar Cove was the scene of the San Diego Rowing Club regatta which included not only rowing races but swimming events. Duke Kahanamoku, the famous Hawaiian swimmer, was one of the featured performers in the swimming events and he easily won the 50-yard open swimming race [441]. In December the ZLAC Rowing Club, a women's rowing club founded in 1892, decided to relocate from busy San Diego Bay to the quieter waters of Mission Bay and purchased two bayside lots on the east side of Dawes Street, across from the Braemar Extension subdivision, as a location for a new clubhouse[129] [442].

Throughout the renovations to their properties and development activity in the neighboring tract, the Scripps continued to host social events. In June 1926 Emma Scripps and two of her sisters gave an elaborate garden tea in honor of their other sister, Fannie, Mrs. Frederick C. Sherman. Mrs. Sherman was moving to Long Beach soon to join her husband, who was an officer aboard the battleship USS West Virginia[130]. The *Union* reported that the affair, to be given at the Scripps' home, Braemar, at Pacific Beach, would present a lovely setting with colorful awnings and umbrellas throughout the gardens, and on the beautiful strip of beach which adjoined the garden. An orchestra would provide special music during the afternoon on the spacious lawn [443].

The Scripps also continued to make Braemar Manor available for the benefit of other causes they considered worthy. Their neighbors, the ZLAC Rowing Club, needed funds to build a clubhouse and according to Lena Polhamus Crouse, one of the ZLAC founders[131], 'money was raised by selling tickets to the popular May fetes in the beautiful and spacious gardens of Mrs. F. T. Scripps who is now an honorary member of the club' [444]. The garden fete given by the ZLAC Rowing Club in the beautiful gardens at the Fred Scripps home in Braemar on June 2, 1928, was one of the most important social

---

[129] The ZLAC clubhouse, built in 1931, and an adjoining boathouse remain at this location today.

[130] Frederick Sherman, a 1910 Naval Academy graduate, remained in the navy through World War II. He was the commanding officer of the USS Lexington when she was sunk in the battle of the Coral Sea in 1942. He later served as commander of carrier divisions, task groups and task forces and retired after the war as a four-star admiral.

[131] The other founders were Zulette Lamb and Lena's sisters Agnes and Caroline Polhamus; ZLAC is an acronym of the first letters of their first names.

Part of the 'spacious lawn' in the Braemar gardens, with awnings and umbrellas on the adjoining strip of beach and Mission Bay (and Mission Beach) in the background. The bow of the replica Mayflower, the 'pirate ship' of the Scripps' garden parties, is visible between the trees at right. (SDHC #2380-5)

functions of the season, according to the *Evening Tribune*. 'The Scripps gardens are among the show places of San Diego, and include many interesting features, among them being the log cabin, where a dark mammy will tell fortunes; an adobe house built by the Indians of Mesa Grande, and an unusually attractive lath house' [445].

A year later, in April 1929, the *Union* announced that Brae Mar, the charming home of F. T. Scripps at the head of False Bay, with its colorful gardens and walks, had again been chosen by the ZLAC Rowing Club as the setting for its annual garden fete. In addition to an open air dancing pavilion, a crystal gazer to read fortunes, a Japanese tea room and a novel Indian house, special entertainment for children had been planned. 'On the Scripps private beach is a replica of the Mayflower and around this boat will be treasure hunts, ponies to ride, and story tellers to interest the little ones' [446].

By 1931 the ZLAC fete had become a 'brilliant function' on the 'social horizon' of the 'elite sets' in San Diego. The May 2 *Tribune* heralded the 'Fourth Annual Garden Fete of the ZLAC Rowing Club, one of San Diego's most prominent social organizations' as 'the most important of forthcoming affairs'. 'Ever since the first Garden Fete was given four years ago, this function has climaxed the social activities of each Spring season'. The outstanding feature of the afternoon's entertainment was expected to be the Tom Thumb Wedding in which the little four- and five-year-old sons and daughters of older ZLAC members were to come down through the Grape Arbor to the open garden where the ceremony was to be solemnized [447]. After the

(SDHC #2380-2)

event, on May 22, the *Tribune* reported that the colorful garden fete in the beautiful gardens of Mrs. Fred T. Scripps at Braemar had been one of the most successful ever, with over 1500 guests and over $1000 collected for the new club house fund. An unusually large number of children were present to enjoy the pirate ship, puppet show and Tom Thumb wedding [448].

While Emma Scripps was an honorary member of the ZLAC Rowing Club, most of the participants and entertainers at the ZLAC garden fetes were actual members. A photo of Miss Ann Packard and her twin sister Mrs. Norman Karns, the former Frances Packard, in their 'colorful pirate costumes' appeared in the May 9, 1931, *Evening Tribune*. The Packard twins, members of ZLAC crew 11, were in charge of the exciting pirate ship at the ZLAC garden fete [449]. The *San Diego Union's* society column 'Tete-a-Tete with Eileen Jackson' (the topic for Halloween 1934 was 'Do you believe in witches?') revealed that Myra Rife Smith, a popular San Diego socialite and ZLAC member[132], had been the 'veiled occult' at the ZLAC fete for years [450].

ZLAC garden fetes were held again in 1932 and 1933, 'heralded annually by society as the opening event of the early summer season' and definitely marking 'the beginning of those highly enjoyable out-of-doors events, which, with their spirit of informality, make summer a season of gayety':

> Perennially the setting for this outstanding social affair, the beautiful Scripps gardens provide an ideal locale with rustic garden cottages, a rose garden, Japanese garden and sandy beach, sloping down to the waters of the bay, offering interest to all [451].

No fete was held in 1934 however, and in 1935 the *Union* noted that while Garden Mayfairs are in San Diego's social tradition, the ZLAC

---

[132] Myra Rife Smith was also the sister of Thomas Rife, prominent realtor and partner in Barney & Rife, sales agents for the Braemar development.

162   **Originally Pacific Beach**

Rowing Club had given up its annual garden party in May at Braemar. Fortunately, the Neighborhood House was carrying on the tradition by opening the George Marston gardens each springtime for a similar fete [452].

The end of the ZLAC fetes did not mean an end to other social events on the Scripps estate, including gatherings of the Scripps' and Jessop's large extended families. The September 28, 1935, *San Diego Union* carried a photo spread ('Young Society Splashes in Good Old Summertime'), showing cousins Billy Corey, Mitch Corey and Carroll Scripps ready for a slide at Braemar, home of their grandparents, Carrington Corey, Jack Sherman, George Jessop and Tommy Scripps being taught to swim, and Virginia Corey ready for a plunge, at Pacific Beach [453].

Frederick T. Scripps died at the age of 85 in January 1936. He was described as a 'real estate operator' and brother of the late E. W. Scripps and the late Ellen Browning Scripps, and was said to have lived quietly, devoting himself to his family and real estate activities [454]. His widow, Emma, remained on the family estate for many years and continued the tradition of gracious entertainment for the community. In July 1936 the *Union* reported that many of the same attractions seen at the ZLAC affairs were again put to use for a charming English garden fete arranged by the Pacific Beach Presbyterian Church in the lovely bayside home of Mrs. F. T. Scripps; 'booths and tables common to this sort of outdoor "fair", fortune tellers of mystic powers, pirate ship and treasure chest attractions for the youngsters, wandering troubadours and Spanish and Mexican dances on the green'. Refreshments would be served in the music room with the assistance of a group of 'charming sub-debs' [455].

In 1937 the lovely gardens of Mrs. F. T. Scripps at the foot of Bayard Street in Pacific Beach were scheduled to be the scene of one of the prettiest garden parties of the opening of summer, this time under the auspices of the Pacific Beach Women's Club. Again, fortune tellers would peer into the future and would reveal what is in store for inquirers and there would be a fish pond and puppet show and treasure chests for the youngsters aboard the old 'pirate ship' which stood on the water's edge of the big estate which borders Mission Bay. The *Union* even carried a photo of Little Miss Annie Linda Brown and Miss Diana Scripps, cunning granddaughters of Mrs. Scripps, contemplating the beauty of the garden as they planned which of the many exciting things to interest small folk they would patronize at the garden party the following afternoon [456].

Mrs. Sarah Emma Scripps continued to live at Braemar until her death in September 1954[133]. The 7-acre estate was then acquired by Vernon Taylor and Clinton McKinnon, who began the process of rezoning so that a 3 million dollar hotel could be constructed on the property. Local residents, led by *Evening Tribune* city editor (and later chief editorial writer) Ralph Bennett, opposed the initial rezoning proposal but eventually accepted an ordinance for multiple residential zoning except for a 60-foot strip of commercial zoning on the west side in 1955.

Braemar Manor was razed in 1959. On May 31, 1959, the *San Diego Union* reported that construction was underway for the 'Catamarran Resort Hotel', an oriental-styled modern hostelry on Mission Bay, with completion anticipated for early summer. The *Union* noted that the 'chapel' of the old Scripps Estate was being preserved as a historical landmark alongside the new hotel [457].

Eileen Jackson, still writing the *Union's* society column 'Straws in the Wind' in January 1960[134], reported on a party at the hotel's Kontiki Room which attracted groups from all parts of the city and gave 'social scribes' a 'news-gathering field day'. Many 'oldtimers' in the crowd had attended similar parties on the same grounds when they were the site of the 'Stratford manor house of the late Mr. and Mrs. F. Tudor Scripps', 'looked for some Braemar landmarks at the Japanese-Hawaiian inspired Catamaran' and 'found a few of them':

> The wedding chapel now being developed on the property was once the dining room (with cathedral arches) of Braemar, setting for the Scripps-Jessop family reunions for many years. Braemar's fine old palms which outline the property look with superiority over the transplanted Torrey pines and other pine imports from Mt. Baldy. The Old English garden, setting for the Zlac "fairs" of two decades ago, are now severely simple Japanese walks paved with grey beach pebbles from Mexican beaches.
>
> Most intriguing features of the new landscaping are giant boulders brought from Poway and a sapphire blue waterfall tumbling into the swimming pool. The huge stag horns at the entrance were out of historic

---

[133] A week before her death the *Union* published a letter from Mrs. F. T. Scripps, 4004 Bayard St., commenting on their editorial 'A Tragedy Could Result' pointing out the dangerous conditions of Mission Bay. She wrote that she had lived there for 55 years, her children enjoyed their boats with other children and not one accident happened, but now children are not safe in their small sail and row boats. 'These wild men and young boys driving their power boats at top speed seem to have no thought but to outdo each other'. She concluded that the northwest corner of Mission Bay should be reserved for the children and the speed boats should have a portion of the bay to themselves [702].

[134] Eileen Jackson retired from the *San Diego Union* in 1976, but returned to work for the *Evening Tribune* in 1981. She finally retired in 1990 at the age of 84.

Braemar [458].

Weddings at the Catamaran Wedding Chapel began in 1962 and were popular events until the chapel was again moved to make way for a parking garage in 1986. The building was donated to the Pacific Beach Town Council and moved to a site on the other side of Pacific Beach, a 'useless and vacant lot' owned by the Navy on the south side of Garnet Avenue, across from Soledad Mountain Road and bordering Rose Creek [459]. The site had been acquired by the government as part of the wartime Bayview Terrace public housing project and later transferred to the Navy for its Capehart housing project. Nothing was ever built on that particular parcel and the Navy offered to lease the property as a community service. Now known as the Rose Creek Cottage, it is still available for weddings and other special events[135].

In 1926 F. T. Scripps and other landowners with bay front properties had been granted a 50-year lease to the Mission Bay tidelands beyond the high water mark where their properties actually ended. Many of the leaseholders had built piers, docks, fences and other improvements on this leased land, which had become known as Crescent Beach. The leases had stipulated that on termination of the lease the lessee would remove all improvements 'of whatsoever kind, nature or character placed thereon'. When the leases did expire on May 31, 1976, many of the Crescent Beach leaseholders, which the *Union* characterized as 'some of the wealthiest and most influential people in San Diego'[136], refused to comply with the terms of the lease [460]. After a year spent attempting to reach a compromise with the former leaseholders the city had the offending docks and piers demolished and billed the owners for the demolition. Sand dredged from the bottom of the bay was deposited on shore to extend the beach beyond the former high water mark and a concrete boardwalk was built on the reclaimed land outside of the private property lines. Today the actual beachfront is open and accessible to the public and

---

[135] From the historical perspective, the Rose Creek Cottage is on the former right-of-way of the San Diego, Old Town and Pacific Beach Railway, across the street from the site of the asbestos works and Kate Sessions' nursery site and monument, and just across Rose Creek from the former racetrack.

[136] According to the *Union*, these people included 'A U. S. congressman, a county sheriff, a county supervisor, a San Diego port commissioner, an ex-congressman, an ex-city councilman, and owners of banks, airlines, broadcasting companies, newspapers, manufacturing companies, amusement parks and hotels. They are friends of presidents and governors.' The airline owner, C. Floyd Andrews, of Pacific Southwest Airlines, even had a helicopter landing pad on his pier [706].

the private land inside the boardwalk, including Braemar Cove, is high and dry, cut off from the bay. Only the Catamaran Hotel has a pier extending into Mission Bay.

Braemar Manor and the extensive landscaping that once existed on Lot A of the Braemar subdivision, formerly Acre Lot 71 and Poisers 1 Acre, have long since been replaced by a modern resort hotel, but some reminders of the past can still be found in the surrounding neighborhood. The curbs and sidewalks along Bayard Street between Grand Avenue and the Scripps property on the bay that Fred Scripps and his fellow property owners had built in 1907 still exist, and many of the palm trees surrounding the former Scripps property and lining Bayard Street are still growing today. Several other homes inspired by the English cottage style of architecture were built in the Braemar subdivision and some are still standing. The Cass Street entrance to the Braemar subdivision at Reed Avenue was originally distinguished by 'artistic entrance gates' designed by Frank W. Stevenson in 1926, said to be faithful reproductions of the stately entrances to be seen on the picturesque old estates in England [461]. Tall stone gateposts marked with the letter 'B' stood on either side of Cass, and shorter sections extended beyond the sidewalks. These shorter sections still exist, on either side of Cass south of Reed.

Sketch of one of the 'artistic entrance gates' that once marked the approach to the Braemar residential tract. A matching gatepost stood on the opposite side of the street. The sidewalks passed between the two sections of the gateposts.

Only the shorter segments of the Braemar Gates survive today. The gatepost on the east side of Cass (left) is covered with red geraniums and on the west side (right) it has been incorporated into the resident's brick wall.

While little remains of the F. T. Scripps family's presence in Pacific Beach, the enduring legacy of the extended Scripps family is familiar to most San Diegans. E. W. and Ellen Browning Scripps provided support for the Marine Biological Association laboratory in La Jolla in 1903; the lab later merged with the University of California, becoming the Scripps Institution for Biological Research, then, as the Scripps Institution of Oceanography, was the foundation of the University of California, San Diego campus in La Jolla. Scripps Hospital and Scripps Metabolic Clinic, established by Ellen Scripps in 1924 and originally located near her home in La Jolla, have evolved into Scripps Health, now considered San Diego's premier health care provider. Ellen Scripps and her sister Virginia also supported The Bishop's School, founded in 1909, again near her home in La Jolla, and which is still one of San Diego's, and the country's, top independent college-prep schools. In 1926 Ellen Scripps founded Scripps College, a women's liberal arts college on the Claremont Colleges campus in Claremont, California. Miramar, the Scripps' ranch and their first home in the San Diego area, was sold by the Scripps heirs in the 1960s and the area is now the San Diego community of Scripps Ranch.

8 The Military Academy

The Pacific Beach Company and the San Diego College Company had joined forces in 1887 to create an educational institution on a 4-block, 16-acre campus in the heart of Pacific Beach. The cornerstone for the original college building had been laid in January 1888 and by September construction had been completed and 37 students began classes. A year later a second building, Stough Hall, had been added. However, the college company found itself unable to repay the construction costs and when the contractors sued, and won, the college closed in 1891. The plan for an educational institution on the College Campus site appeared doomed, and in fact today it has become a shopping center and condominium community. But in the intervening years an educational institution did arise on the site and over nearly 50 years grew to become the educational landmark that the original planners of Pacific Beach had hoped it would be.

After the San Diego College of Letters closed and the college company underwent voluntary insolvency proceedings in 1891, the College Campus and its empty buildings were involved in a series of trustee sales at the courthouse door which ended in 1898 with Thomas J. B. Rhoads in possession. Pacific Beach residents banded together and formed the Pacific Beach College Company, led by the Presbyterian minister William Johnston, which bought the campus property from Rhoads with the intention of reviving the college. This effort went nowhere and instead the college buildings were used for lodging and a community center until they were leased (1904) then sold (1905) to the Folsom Bros. Co., who had already acquired most of the other property in Pacific Beach. Folsom Bros. refurbished the college buildings and they opened as the Hotel Balboa in 1905. In subsequent years further improvements were made to the buildings and grounds, and to the surrounding streets and sidewalks, but the hotel apparently did not attract sufficient occupancy and the owners sought other uses for the property. In 1909, for example, the Pacific Beach Country Club sub-leased a portion of the Hotel Balboa to be used as a clubhouse [462].

Captain Thomas Alderson Davis was a former officer in the 6th Volunteer Infantry who saw service in Puerto Rico during the Spanish-American War in 1898 and had founded the El Paso Military Academy in 1907. In an oral history interview by the San Diego Historical Society in 1957 Davis recalled that he was attracted to San Diego through advertising by the D. C. Collier Company and was so pleased with what he saw that he decided to stay and start a school in Pacific Beach [463]. On November 22, 1910, the *Evening Tribune* announced that the first army and navy academy in the history of San Diego would open the following morning in the Balboa Hotel at Pacific Beach and that Capt. Davis had invited the public to 'attend the opening exercises, inspect the academy and take a stroll over the spacious grounds' [464]. The *San Diego Union* followed up with a report on November 24 that the San Diego Army and Navy Academy had been formally opened the day before in Hotel Balboa in Pacific Beach with appropriate exercises attended by a large number of representative citizens [465]. The date of this formal opening, November 23, would be celebrated for years at the academy as Founder's Day.

The newspaper articles covering the opening of the San Diego Army and Navy Academy emphasized that the current class was expected to be only the nucleus of an institution Capt. Davis hoped to develop to such a standard that it would become 'one of the recognized academies of the United States'. The academy would occupy the entire Balboa hotel property, including twenty acres of surrounding grounds and would fit young men to enter larger and higher eastern institutions or even the service academies at West Point or Annapolis. Capt. Davis added that he had expected to open the academy the following year but was persuaded to open at this time by several San Diego residents with children they were anxious to send to an institute of that kind. Classes were to begin the following Monday with about a dozen pupils[137] from among some of the best known families in San Diego, and with the promise of additional cadets after the Christmas holidays.

Apparently a few more cadets did enroll after the holidays and a photo in the January 22, 1911, *Union* showed a total of 16 neatly uniformed cadets on the campus of the Pacific Beach academy. The attractive suits for the student soldiers and sailors were patterned after those used at West Point and Annapolis and added 'a becoming military finish' to the young men. 'Resplendent in attractive new uniforms the students of the San Diego Army and Navy Academy are drilling with renewed vim nowadays and present the appearance of trained soldiers as they wheel about the campus of the Pacific Beach institution' [466]. A notice from Capt. Thos. A. Davis, Supt. ('Parents,

---

[137] Actually a baker's dozen; in his oral history interview Davis recalled that he began classes 'with thirteen little dazed students and I was all the faculty'. In later years, nearly every reference to the academy's past noted that it was founded in 1910 with 13 students.

Attention!') appeared in the *Union* from January to March advising parents that a few more 'manly boys' may be enrolled at this time in the San Diego Army and Navy Academy. Other ads for the academy continued on a regular basis throughout 1911.

Capt. Davis was encouraged by his inaugural year in the Pacific Beach location and according to the June 18, 1911, *San Diego Union* he had completed arrangements to continue the school in its present location in the building formerly known as Hotel Balboa at Pacific Beach [467]. On August 17 the *Evening Tribune* reported that the military and naval academy would begin its fall and winter operations the following month in the handsome building formerly known as Hotel Balboa [468].

In his oral history interview with the San Diego Historical Society Capt. Davis noted that in the first year there were grade subjects only; only in the second year did he begin to add high school subjects preparatory for universities and the government academies. An advertisement in the July 30, 1911, *San Diego Union* pictured Capt. Davis surrounded by 16 cadets (all resplendent in attractive uniforms), apparently the entire faculty and student body, but indicated that two additional teachers would be added that year [469]. Another advertisement in the September 2 *Union* pictured the academy buildings along with Capt. Thos. A. Davis, Superintendent, and Mrs. Thomas A. Davis, Home Dept., and described the academy as the 'IDEAL SCHOOL FOR BOYS – A school combining the Military Discipline with all the Influences and Training of a Home of Refinement and Culture'. Regarding the accommodations, the living rooms in the buildings formerly known as the Hotel Balboa were 'large, airy, and almost luxuriantly furnished and each room commands a beautiful view of the ocean'. Military drill and discipline would give 'wonderful physical development and inculcate a spirit of manliness and honor'. A distinct, aggressive Christian influence would pervade every phase of school life, and five hundred dollars would cover practically every expense except uniforms and text books. The next session was set to begin Monday, Sept. 18; 'write for a handsomely illustrated catalogue' (Capt. Davis also provided a phone number, Home 27-172) [470].

The academy's second year did show an impressive growth in enrollments; a series of ads in the *San Diego Union* during January 1912 claimed that there were then 73 students in attendance. Growth in the faculty also kept pace; an ad in the August 18, 1912, *San Diego Union* pictured not only Captain and Mrs. Davis but other faculty members including Charles M. Wood (History, Commercial Law), Jesse A. Beadle (Science and Mathematics), Ralph R. Rice (Ancient and Modern Languages), Charles N. Richardson (Superintendent Buildings) and Mrs. C. N. Richardson (Matron), Newell S. Fiscus (Civil Government - English), H. J. Baade (Mathematics) and David C. Wilson (Athletics) [471]. This ad also posed and answered questions that thoughtful parents would want to know; Q: what will be my boy's associations? (A: 'there has never been a body of students that has been more gentlemanly in its deportment or has taken a higher stand for manliness than has the cadet corps of the Academy'), Q: are the courses of study comprehensive? (A: 'the courses of study fill the most rigid requirements for college entrance'), Q: will he be improved physically? (A: 'there is nothing to compare with plenty of exercise in the fresh air and sunshine . . . a winter spent by a boy among the flowers, the palms and pepper trees, with access to the quiet waters of Mission bay, and the Pacific will mean wonders in his physical development'), Q: how much will it cost? (A: 'lower than most schools of its grade . . . five hundred dollars for a boarding student, and one hundred dollars for a day student will cover practically every necessary expense except uniforms and text books').

The ad continued with testimonials taken from letters to the superintendent ('the patrons of the Academy are its best advertisement'), including local luminaries such as Col. Ed Fletcher ('Our son's improvement in his studies and in addition in his general appearance and manly bearing have more than pleased us'). Rev. H. W. Clark was pastor of the Pacific Beach Presbyterian Church, located across the street from the academy[138] and his son Gaylord was one of

[138] The Presbyterian Church and the college campus property had been closely associated from their earliest days. C. S. Sprecher, one of the founders of the San Diego College of Letters, the original occupant of the college campus, had also been the founder and first pastor of the church. Another pastor, William L. Johnston, had been the titular owner of the campus property from 1898 to 1905. As the new Presbyterian minister in 1904, Rev. Clark and his family had lived in the College Inn, as the college building was known at that time [119]. Rev. Clark's daughter Edith later worked at the

the original corps of cadets. Rev. Clark's testimonial stated that the moral tone of the school was high and 'I know of no man under whose personal influence I would prefer to have my boy than your own, and I say this after having had my son in your school from its beginning'. Testimonials for those faculty members who would be joining the academy for the 1912 academic year (Fiscus, Wood, Baade and Wilson) were also provided.

The San Diego Army and Navy Academy reached another milestone in 1914 when it secured official recognition by the war department as a 'Class A' school, a classification that entitled the academy to the detail of a retired army officer to serve on the faculty at the army's expense. According to the June 15, 1914, *Evening Tribune*, securing a detail from the war department was the desire of every military school in the country but generally took years to accomplish and for Capt. Davis' school to secure this recognition in only three and a half years was looked upon as 'almost phenomenal'. The officer detailed to the academy was Lieut. Cyrus W. Street, a retired veteran of the Spanish-American war and the Philippine insurrection and former commandant of cadets at the Mt. Tamalpais Academy and professor of military science and tactics at the Miami Military Institute in Germantown, Ohio. According to the March 12, 1916, *San Diego Union* he had been introduced to the cadets as their new professor of military science and tactics at chapel exercises during the previous week [472].

By 1917 the academy's reputation had apparently established it as the primary attraction in Pacific Beach; a synopsis of San Diego's suburban areas in the *Union* on January 1, 1917, described Pacific Beach as 'a suburb eight miles north of the center of San Diego. It is noted as the home of the San Diego Army and Navy Academy where students from many states are being fitted for college, West Point or Annapolis. The citizens are justly proud of this growing institution' [473].

A fire in a tower on the north wing of the academy threatened destruction of the entire building on December 13, 1917, but the flames were held in check by the Pacific Beach volunteer fire company until the arrival of the fire truck from La Jolla, which soon got the fire under control. The *Union* reported the following morning that the assistant fire chief on the scene had a high opinion of the discipline at the academy; within three minutes of the alarm every student had been evacuated and accounted for and then went to work with the volunteers and aided in saving the buildings [474].

---

academy as a secretary [626]. The Davises continued the association between campus and church, teaching bible classes and singing in the choir [625].

Originally Pacific Beach

Also in 1917 Capt. Davis attempted to expand beyond the local area by starting a junior school on the Annandale Country Club property in Pasadena, but to keep control in the family by appointing his (much) younger brother, John L. Davis, Jr., a 1916 graduate of the University of Tennessee as headmaster[139]. Apparently Capt. Davis had arranged with the property owner, Mrs. Marie C. Henry, for a two-year lease to be extended five additional years if Davis carried out his agreement to provide a standard of scholarship equal to that maintained by the public schools. At the end of the two years Mrs. Henry contended that Davis did not maintain a successful school and demanded the property back. Davis refused and the case went to court. The January 14, 1920, *Evening Tribune* reported that the judge had ruled against Davis, ruling that the evidence did not justify Davis's assertion that Mrs. Henry sought to unduly control the school, that it was 'because Capt. Davis would not permit her to hold the reins and handle the whip that she desires to throw Capt. Davis out' [475].

By 1921 the San Diego Army and Navy Academy was in its tenth year and evidently thriving but was still operating out of rented quarters in the former college campus in Pacific Beach. On February 1, 1921, the *San Diego Union* reported that the Army and Navy academy had purchased the Point Loma Golf and Country club in Loma Portal and that the military school would occupy its new quarters within 30 days and undertake extensive improvements [476].

The Point Loma Golf and Country Club had been built in 1912 by A. G. Spalding, the sporting goods magnate who had also briefly owned the racetrack property in Pacific Beach. In 1919 the Navy and Marine Corps had commissioned training centers on the land reclaimed from San Diego Bay along the shoreline of Point Loma and construction of the Naval Training Center had encroached on parts of the golf course by 1921. The country club planned to move to a new location in Chula Vista and offered the clubhouse, its furnishings and 20 acres of land surrounding it for sale. In an article in the *San Diego Union* on February 15 Capt. Davis described the site as ideal for a military academy, particularly in view of his desire, as evidenced in the name of his school, to provide naval training, an advantage few military schools located inland could offer. He felt there was no doubt

---

[139] John L. Davis, Jr. resigned from the Pasadena Army and Navy Academy and was commissioned a lieutenant in the army in 1918 during World War I. After the war he was made assistant commandant of cadets at the San Diego Army and Navy Academy and became vice president and one of the three directors of the academy (with his brother and their father, John Lynch Davis) when it re-incorporated in 1926.

that the officers stationed at the military training centers 'located just across the street from the Academy' would gladly co-operate in his work by permitting the cadets to come in close contact with the instruction given by their organizations [477].

The move to Loma Portal never happened, however. The *Union* reported on June 10, 1921, that the deal for the Point Loma Golf club property, which had been pending for several months, had been declared off. Instead, the San Diego Army and Navy Academy would make its permanent home in Pacific Beach where it was started in the property then known as the Hotel Balboa. Davis explained that 'We had counted fully on beginning the fall semester at Loma Portal but found it impossible to obtain the terms we wanted. Thereupon we made a proposition to the San Diego Beach company for the purchase of their property at Pacific Beach[140], which we have been leasing, consisting of the two large buildings with their equipment and 20 acres of land. Our proposition was accepted and the final papers were signed day before yesterday' [478]. The transaction was completed in October 1923 when the San Diego Beach Company granted the tract known as the College Campus to Thomas A. Davis, husband of Bessie T. Davis, for a consideration of $40,000 [479].

Davis anticipated further growth in enrollment and his plans for the academy included both the development and expansion of the campus. The *San Diego Union* reported on August 5, 1921, that the San Diego Army and Navy academy was building a large number of cottages and otherwise developing its property to meet the increased demand [480]. The *Union* covered the academy's fourteenth anniversary celebration on November 23, 1924 and noted that the enrollment was more than 200 and that a new mess hall seating more than 300 had just been completed. A new athletic field, four new cottages and two new class rooms had also been built and contractors were just finishing the academy library [481]. On October 24, 1925, the news was that building permits had been issued to the Army and Navy academy for two more frame cottages on the college campus, Pacific Beach, at $500 each [482]. Expansion plans included the purchase of the property north of the campus, in Acre Lot 64, across Emerald Street and bounded by Jewell, Diamond and Lamont Streets, beginning in

---

[140] The Folsom Bros. Co. had changed its name to the San Diego Beach Company in January 1911, control having passed from the Folsom brothers to A. H. Frost, Philip Morse and F. R. Burnham [628].

1923[141], and, in 1925, the property to the west, in Blocks 183 and 202, across Jewell Street from the campus and bounded by Ingraham and Emerald Streets and Garnet Avenue[142].

Enrollment at the academy had increased steadily over the years from the original 13 cadets in 1910 to 73 in 1912, 102 in 1915, 125 in 1923 and 'more than 200' in 1924. This growth of enrollment had so far been accommodated in the original college buildings and by the addition of relatively modest wooden structures built elsewhere on the grounds. In 1926, apparently convinced that this growth would continue indefinitely, the academy began a program of new construction which would eventually cover much of the campus with the large reinforced concrete buildings that became Pacific Beach landmarks, dwarfing the two former college buildings where the academy had originated.

On September 11, 1926, the *San Diego Union* reported that a building permit had been issued to the Army and Navy academy for a $5000 dormitory [483]. A few months later, the November 13 *Union* reported that the Army and Navy academy, which had shown remarkable growth in the last few years, was to have a fine new gym; a building permit had been issued for a gymnasium structure to cost $36,500 [484]. On New Year's Day, 1927, the *Union* indicated that work had progressed steadily on the new buildings, made necessary by the steady and rapid growth of the school, which included a spacious addition to the junior school and a beautiful infirmary building and auditorium 'both of class A construction':

> The lower school annex, accommodating about 20 boys, will include classrooms and dormitory, and adjoins the original junior school building on Emerald street.
> The new infirmary is situated on a knoll just east and south of the main building. It is of Spanish architecture and commands a beautiful prospect of gardens, bay and ocean, and distant mountains. It has broad sun porches, reception and living rooms for the housemother, a large ward, and several

---

[141] The Barnes family had originally owned all of Acre Lot 64 but had sold it off in the early 1900s before moving downtown. Davis began buying up these parcels in 1923 and by 1927 had acquired the entire acre lot with the exception of a 125- by 125-foot parcel at the northwest corner and a 5- by 135-foot strip in the center of the lot. Emerald Street between Jewell and Lamont, which separated the College Campus from Acre Lot 64 and was then entirely surrounded by academy property, was closed by the city in 1931 [622].

[142] Davis bought all the property from Jewell to Ingraham between Garnet and Felspar (Block 202), and between Felspar and Emerald (Block 183) except the seven lots at the northeast corner of Block 183. These lots, at the southwest corner of Emerald and Jewell, were owned by Rev. Clark, former pastor of the Presbyterian Church and father of one of his original 13 cadets [620]. Felspar Street between Jewell and Ingraham and the alleys in these blocks were closed by the city in 1926 [621].

---

private rooms, as well as diet kitchen and supply room.

At the west side of the main building, another large concrete structure is nearing completion. This will be used temporarily as an auditorium, but later, when the plans for the development of the school property are completed, it will be used as a gymnasium. Space has been planned for a large stage, where the plays produced by the cadets from time to time, as well as concerts and other entertainments, may be given. There will also be a projector room, for the placing of a motion picture machine. On the lower floor of this building will be storerooms for the use of the quartermaster and commissary departments, and an indoor gallery range for rifle practice. At the end of the building, adjoining the athletic field, there will be shower rooms, etc., for the benefit of visiting athletic teams [485][143].

Growth continued; in the announcement of the academy's eighteenth anniversary exercises on November 23, 1927, which appeared in the November 9 *San Diego Union,* Davis said that enrollment totaled 316 boys ranging in age from 6 to 19 years [486]. A *Union* article from August 5, 1928, reported that the 1927 attendance had been nearly 350 students and it was expected that the numbers for the fall term would exceed 400. During the previous term the academy had been crowded to capacity and the president and founder, Col. Thomas A. Davis[144], announced a four-year, $400,000 construction program which would give the academy a housing capacity of 1000 students. A $50,000 auditorium and $25,000 infirmary had been built in 1927 and work had already started on a $50,000 dormitory. Five such dormitories and an administration building were planned. The numerous small cottages where the cadets currently resided would be

---

[143] The lower school annex, or addition to the junior school, was presumably the $5000 dormitory project for which a building permit had been issued in September 1926; the junior school building that it adjoined was actually the original Pacific Beach schoolhouse which had been closed and moved from its original location on Garnet Avenue next to the Presbyterian Church to the north side of Emerald Street next to the former F. W. Barnes home. The new infirmary and auditorium/gymnasium surrounded the original college buildings; the infirmary just to the east and the auditorium just to the west of the 'main building'. The infirmary was also the first expression of the Spanish or California Mission style of architecture which characterized future building at the academy.

[144] According to the website of the present Army and Navy Academy in Carlsbad, successor to the San Diego Army and Navy Academy founded by Davis in 1910, he 'garnered' a commission as Colonel in the National Guard of Kentucky in 1922. A biography on file at the San Diego History Center says that he was commissioned Colonel on the staff of Governor Field of Kentucky. Since Davis had been based in San Diego since 1910 and had no known association with Kentucky, his promotion was probably a 'Kentucky Colonel' commission, an honor awarded by the Governor of Kentucky to individuals in recognition of noteworthy accomplishments and outstanding service to a community, state or the nation. He was also awarded a Doctor of Laws degree by Wheaton College in Illinois.

Originally Pacific Beach

torn down to make way for the dormitories. The two blocks adjacent to the academy that had been purchased the preceding year would be transformed into a big parade ground [487].

The August 27, 1928, *Evening Tribune* included a feature on the San Diego Army and Navy Academy – 'The West Point of the West' in a special Schools and Academies section, presumably a promotional piece provided by the academy itself. Under 'Some Interesting Facts', the aggregate enrollment for the previous year was 363, making it the largest private school west of the Mississippi River. It had a campus of nearly thirty-eight acres[145] with ample facilities for all military and athletic activities. There had been four large buildings and over seventy cozy bungalows for housing students and meeting their various needs and there had been added within the last eighteen months a new concrete and tile gymnasium, a well-equipped hospital, a dormitory and band stand and another three-story concrete dormitory was under construction. Eight hundred dollars would cover practically all expenses except uniforms and school supplies. There would be an advance in rates in the coming year, but all students enrolled on the present basis would remain on the same basis as long as they attend the Academy [488].

The new dormitory was completed in time to be dedicated on the academy's nineteenth Founder's Day, November 23, 1928. A photograph in the November 25 *San Diego Union* shows academy cadets in battalion review in front of what the article called a fireproof modern structure in pleasing Spanish architecture, the third unit in the $400,000 building program inaugurated the previous year [489]. It was three stories and was expected to house 60 cadets. This first of what became four dormitory buildings of the same general design was located along Lamont Street near its intersection with Felspar, north and east of the central campus, then consisting of the original College of Letters building, Stough Hall, and the auditorium and infirmary built the previous year on either side of these former college buildings.

The senior class of 1929 also added their own contribution to the architecture of the academy, presenting their alma mater with a triple concrete arch at the main entrance to the campus (the northwest corner of Garnet Avenue and Lamont Street), according to the May 29, 1929,

---

[145] The academy's acreage was consistently exaggerated in news reports. The College Campus property itself is actually 15.37 acres, which in its college days had been expressed as 16 acres, but academy publicity always described the campus as 20 acres. The addition of Emerald Street (1.98 acres), the property in Acre Lot 64 (6.69 acres) and the two blocks west of Jewell (7.12 acres) eventually raised the actual size to 31.16, not 'nearly' 38 acres.

The Senior (Triple) Arch; San Diego Army and Navy Academy (*The Cadet*, 1936).

San Diego Union [490]. Another arch, this one of stone, was added about the same time on the south side of campus, in front of Stough Hall. This arch had originally been built in 1891 as the grand entrance to the Fisher Opera House in downtown San Diego. The Fisher had been acquired in 1903 by Madame Tingley of the Theosophical Institute and renamed the Isis Theatre. When the Isis was razed in 1928, the arch was dismantled, the stones were marked and moved to Pacific Beach, and it was re-erected in its new location on Garnet Avenue across from Kendall Street [491].

Later the same summer the *Evening Tribune* reported that the building program (now priced at $450,000 and with a five year schedule) would continue with the addition of an outdoor swimming pool complex consisting of a 75- by 30-foot pool, a second, smaller pool for junior school students and a chlorination plant 'to guarantee absolute sanitation', which was expected to cost $13,000 [492]. The September 19, 1929, *Union* reported that a building permit had been issued to the San Diego Army and Navy Academy for improvements costing $80,000, including the swimming pool and a new dormitory [493].

A month later, on the other side of the country, the Wall Street stock market crash of October 1929 set the stage for the Great Depression of the 1930s. The depression would have a devastating effect on almost all economic activity, including the education of boys at private military boarding schools in California.

The battalion of cadets, more the 400 strong in 'snappy West Point uniforms' and led by their band, were featured in the 1930 Tournament of Roses parade in Pasadena. A photo in the *Evening Tribune* on January 1, 1930, showed the cadets boarding the special train that was 'to be their home in the northern city' at Pacific Beach on New Year's Eve. The article explained that the cadets would march in the parade and then attend the Rose Bowl as guests of Col. Davis on New Year's Day before returning to Pacific Beach late that night in time for the opening of school the following morning [494]. The January 12 *Union* published additional photographs of the parade, including the 40-piece academy band and Colonel and Major Davis decked out in their own uniforms and accoutrements. The *Union* reported that the battalion of cadets would receive a silver plaque as a special merit prize for its appearance [495].

On January 16, 1930, the *Union* reported that dedication of the new $70,000 dormitory on February 1 and $18,000 swimming pool within the next few days would bring the fall building activities to a close for the remainder of the year. Work had been rushed to completion, necessitated by the overflow enrollment of cadets [496]. The dedication was scheduled for February 6 and would include a parade and appropriate exercises. The pool was located south of the three-story concrete dormitory on the Lamont Street side of the campus. The new dormitory was four stories and of a similar design, located along Lamont Street to the north of the year-old three-story dormitory.

Within months Col. Davis announced another round of construction, this time of two more four-story dormitories estimated to cost in excess of $150,000 and planned to be ready for occupancy at the beginning of the fall school session to take care of the present academy overflow and large increase in the student body expected. The May 13, 1930, *Evening Tribune* reported that the dormitories would accommodate 270 students as well as guest rooms, house mothers' apartments and apartments for three instructors in each building [497].

Commencement exercises for the San Diego Army and Navy Academy were held in June 1930 and the highlight of the event was the presentation to the school by parents of the boys of a portrait of Col. Davis painted by Arnold Mountfort. A June 15, 1930, *San Diego Union* article by Robert Hunter Paterson, Assistant Director, San Diego Fine Arts Gallery, described the portrait as a 'painting of great merit in the traditional English portrait school'.

According to Paterson the artist had received his early training under the impetus of the pre-Raphaelites but was currently painting according to the discoveries of the impressionistic school; his work was exceedingly British and followed the tradition established by

Gainsborough and Reynolds, but was more directly related to the work of Lawrence and Hoppner. Comparison with other work by this painter revealed in this canvas of Colonel Davis a growth of technical power. The agitated quality which characterized his style at the turn of the century had entirely disappeared in the suave, simplified and bold manner in which he has composed this present portrait depicting Colonel Davis in uniform.

> The colonel has been painted standing beside a table against an almost monotone background. One of the finest areas of technical prowess is found in the painting of the right hand, in which Colonel Davis holds a green fountain pen. This fountain pen, incidentally, together with the colors above the left breast pocket of his coat, are the high notes of the painting, the rest being composed of khaki, olive drab and brown, lightened here and there with the addition of steel chain, brass buckles and brass buttons. The kindliness, which is part and parcel of the character of the man who is painted, has been deftly achieved in the face.
>
> As is always the case with paintings of this type, the face is one of the most beautifully painted parts of the picture. In comparison with the earlier work of this artist, there is more a sense of surety exhibited here. His style particularly lends itself to the crisp, smart line of the military, and the trousers, of a lighter color than the coat, have been painted with a dash and warmth of color which, to those persons who enjoy the beauty of texture in paint, will form a source of pleasure.

The *Union* article also noted that Mr. Mountfort was present at the exercises, and spoke briefly to the student body [498].

Once again construction of the two new dormitories was completed in time for their dedication to be the featured event at the twentieth anniversary celebration of the San Diego Army and Navy Academy held on November 23, 1930. The November 22 *Evening Tribune* reported that the celebration would begin with a parade of the 400 cadets in full dress, to which the public was invited, followed by the dedication of the dormitories which had been constructed at a cost of more than $175,000. The new buildings were in modified California-Spanish architecture which is distinguished by graceful arches, long esplanades and a beauty of design that is typically Californian, and which conformed with the other academy buildings recently erected in the current building program [499]. These two newest and largest (and last) dormitories were built along the line of Emerald Street, west of and at right angles to the previous two concrete dormitories, and became the third, northern side of an enclosed quadrangle (with the original College building, Stough Hall and the 1927 auditorium as the southern flank).

A few weeks later, January 1, 1931, the *San Diego Union's* annual New Year's Day review of the community reflected on the growth in attendance and facilities at the academy. While many private schools had reported a marked decrease in enrollments in 1930-1931, the San Diego Army and Navy Academy not only reported the largest student body in its history but also an expansion program that had called for the expenditure of more than $350,000 in the last eight months, necessitated, according to Col. Davis, by the over-taxing of the school's facilities and by his desire to make the school second to none in the United States. With the current building program now complete, the dormitory housing capacity was well over 500 students and Col. Davis indicated that plans were being formulated for the beginning of a new building program with an ultimate capacity of 1000 students or more as the objective [500]. The *Union* article included a photo of the new dormitories and revealed that they had been named the John Lynch Davis hall and Mary Janette Davis hall after the parents of founder Col. Davis and his brother, John L. Davis, Jr., the academy vice-president. The senior John Davis, who had relocated to Pacific Beach in 1920 to join his sons and to participate as a director and business manager of the academy, had passed away in April 1930[146].

However, despite the increased housing capacity of the newly constructed dormitories, the deepening depression of the 1930s meant that fewer families had the resources to send their boys to an expensive boarding school, even one proudly described as the largest private school west of the Mississippi.

The twenty-first anniversary celebration on November 23, 1931, was attended by scores of graduates and students of former years who gathered to pay their respects to the school's genial founder and present head, Col. Thomas A. Davis. The *Union* noted that growth of the school had been remarkable, but this time the *Union* did not supply any actual attendance figures or predictions for the upcoming school year [501]. An article in the June 20, 1932, *Evening Tribune* reported that with enrollment fast approaching 200 the San Diego Army and Navy academy was looking forward to an increased registration of students for the coming year [502]. The *Tribune* did not offer any context for this number, but the fact is that an enrollment approaching 200 would be

---

[146] His widow, Mary Janette Davis, known as 'Mother Davis', continued to live in Pacific Beach, first at their home on the academy campus and, after the sale of the academy in 1937, at 1918 Emerald Street. That home, on the northeast corner of Lamont and Emerald Streets, had been purchased by her son John L. Davis, Jr. in 1924 and was the home originally built for E. C. and Rose Hartwick Thorpe. The January 14, 1951, *San Diego Union* reported that Mother Davis would celebrate her 94th birthday at her Emerald St. home [735]. The Thorpe/Davis home burned to the ground on the night of April 22, 1957, still a vivid memory for a boy who witnessed the blaze from his home at 1804 Diamond Street, a block away [728].

less than half the enrollment of the mid-1920s when the decision had been made to build the rows of dormitories that must have stood largely empty by 1932.

Over the next few years, news from the San Diego Army and Navy Academy shifted from the routine reports of growth in enrollment and new construction to articles stressing the collateral benefits of the school. In the January 6, 1933, *Union*, Col. Davis explained the economic value of the academy to San Diego, that many thousands of dollars of 'new money' would be brought to San Diego by the cadet students and find its way into the pockets of San Diego citizens. He calculated that many millions of dollars had been brought to the community, including over $450,000 during the peak years of 1929-30 [503].

Davis and his staff had always managed to project a positive image of the academy in the local media, and apparently they were able to preserve that image during the depression years by keeping the academy's deteriorating financial position out of the newspapers. A synopsis of what did occur between 1933 and 1936 can be found in the 'ANA Historical Timeline' on the website of the Army and Navy Academy in Carlsbad [504], which traces its origin to the San Diego Army and Navy Academy founded in 1910 in Pacific Beach:

1931 The National economic problems of the pending depression were starting to impact school operations with declining enrollment.

1933 The Security Trust & Savings Bank, and other creditors, which hold to mortgage on the school, seized control of the management of the school.

1935 The Academy starts its twenty-fifth year and should be celebrating their Silver Anniversary. In light of the poor economic situation no celebration is held.

1936 The last graduation for the San Diego Army and Navy Academy is held at the Pacific Beach campus. Bank and creditors foreclose on the school seizing all property and holding of the school.

Further details are provided by public records on file with the San Diego County Recorder. In June of 1930 Thomas and Bessie Davis had transferred the property they had accumulated in their own names, consisting of the College Campus, the various parcels in Acre Lot 64 to the north and Blocks 183 and 202 to the west, to the San Diego Army and Navy Academy corporation [505]. On November 15, 1930, a promissory note was recorded in which the San Diego Army and Navy Academy agreed to repay a debt of $100,000 to Security Trust & Savings Bank of San Diego. The note established a payment schedule in which the principal sum of $100,000 plus 7% interest would be paid in installments of $25,000 or more on the first day of October and

February beginning on October 1, 1931[147]. The note was secured by a deed of trust granting the parcel of land known as the 'college campus' to the bank, in trust, with power of sale[148] [506].

On June 18, 1932, the academy entered into another agreement with the bank under which a debt of $132,000 was divided into promissory notes for $44,500, due September 20, 1931, and $87,500 to be paid in payments of $25,000 or more due on the 20th of September and February, beginning September 20, 1932. This time the notes were secured by a trust deed to not only the college campus property but also to the property in Acre Lot 64 and the property in Blocks 183 and 202 [507].

The financial situation of the academy apparently failed to improve again in 1932 and on August 23, 1932, the San Diego Army and Navy Academy agreed to a 'chattel mortgage' under which 'all the furniture, furnishings and equipment of every kind and character belonging to and used in connection with the operation of the San Diego Army and Navy Academy' was mortgaged to Security Trust & Savings Bank of San Diego. A list of the furnishings and equipment was attached, subdivided into sections labeled beds, tables and desks, dressers, miscellaneous, dramatic club, kitchen and dining room, and band and orchestra. Each subdivision included a detailed list of items; 'tables and desks' included 335 desk tables, 12 large office desks, etc., 'kitchen and dining room' included items ranging from 2 dishwashing machines to '260 knives, 630 forks, 340 soup spoons, 550 teaspoons, 103 serving spoons' and 'band and orchestra' included 4 sousaphones, 140 march books and 1 drum major's baton among dozens of other instruments, music books and furniture [508].

Despite the gathering clouds the academy 'soldiered on' and apparently even resumed growth in enrollment. An open house was held to celebrate its Silver Jubilee on November 23, 1935. The *San Diego Union* report on November 24 noted how the academy had become famous throughout the country and had grown from an enrollment of 13, some of whom attended the celebration, to approximately 300 in 1935. The *Union* article was accompanied by photos of the battalion parade of 271 cadets, and of members of the Davis family; Col. Davis,

---

[147] The installment payment dates were presumably timed to coincide with the receipt of tuition payments for the fall and spring terms.

[148] All the major academy buildings, including the original college and the new additions, were located on the college campus property; the mostly unimproved land also owned by the academy in Acre Lot 64 and in Blocks 183 and 202 was not included in this deed of trust.

his daughter Mrs. J. Sanford Curtis, social secretary of the academy, his wife, his mother, his brother Maj. John L. Davis, Jr., and Maj. Davis' wife [509].

The 1936 yearbook, *The Cadet*, gave no indication that anything was amiss at the academy. Col. Davis was pictured busily at work in his office. Administration, faculty and staff were gathered for a photograph. The exploits of the athletic teams and of the literary and dramatic societies were celebrated. The 237 students who were listed in the yearbook were divided between a 2-year junior college (60 students), a high school (124), a junior high school for seventh and eighth graders (23), and a junior school for students from kindergarten to sixth grade (29). The junior college and high-school students were also organized into two military companies, A and B, and the band. The military companies competed for honors in their military drills, and the best-drilled company was awarded a red, white and blue ribbon to attach to their company guidon[149]. The band marched in parades and held concerts, as well as supporting the team at football games. They were often the only non-players in attendance at away games, 'encouraging them to victory in the face of overwhelming numbers of enemy rooters'. A dance orchestra made up of band members played for balls and dinner dances at which groups such as the Girls Chorus from Phoenix Junior College were entertained [510].

In reality, on March 17, 1936, Security Trust & Savings Bank of San Diego had declared San Diego Army and Navy Academy to be in default on the note secured by the June 18, 1931, deed of trust and also in the payment of taxes, which had been an obligation of the deed of trust itself. City and county taxes from 1934 totaling $15,823.53 together with interest and penalties, plus the first installment of 1935 taxes, had not been paid. Only $15,000 of the installment of principal for the $87,500 promissory note had been paid when due on September 20, 1932, and the installments due on February 20, 1933, and thereafter had not been paid[150]. Security Trust & Savings declared the balance of the note, $72,500 plus interest and other sums, to be immediately due and payable and gave notice of its election to sell the property three months after the recordation of this 'election to declare default' [511].

---

[149] The junior high and junior school students (kindergarten to sixth grade) were not included in the military companies, although they did march in parades, in full uniform, much to the delight of spectators.

[150] However, the $44,500 note due on September 20, 1931, apparently had been paid; it was not declared to be in default in this recording.

Originally Pacific Beach

The August 2, 1936, *San Diego Union* carried a special announcement from Col. Thomas A. Davis, founder and for 25 years president of the San Diego Army and Navy Academy, and Maj. John L. Davis, Jr., Vice President and Commandant, who has been a member of the faculty since 1919, that they had resigned their respective positions and would no longer be associated with the Academy in any way. Personal communications could be addressed to a Pacific Beach post office box or phone number, or care of the Davis Military Academy, Carlsbad, California [512]. An article in the same issue of the *Union* added that the Davis Military Academy had leased the attractive buildings and grounds of the Red Apple Inn in Carlsbad and that the new school would open in September. There was no explanation for the resignations or the creation of the new academy or the future of the academy in Pacific Beach.

On August 8 the *Union* reported that Maj. Edmund M. Barnum, U. S. Cavalry, an active army officer detailed to the academy by virtue of its 'Class M' or 'essentially military' rating by the war department, and who had been professor of military science and tactics, would assume the position of commandant of the San Diego Army and Navy Academy. The remainder of the previous year's faculty had been retained almost intact for the coming year [513].

The August 14, 1936, *San Diego Union* reported that the San Diego Army and Navy Academy would retain its high rating and recognition by the war and navy departments in relation to graduates entering West Point or Annapolis and that 150 students had enrolled for the school term opening September 12. The article added that 20 of the original 30 members of the faculty were remaining with the new management [514].

On March 15, 1937, the John E. Brown College Corp. purchased the San Diego Army and Navy Academy property. According to the March 16 *San Diego Union*, John E. Brown, president of the corporation, and members of his staff, would take charge of the academy and start a program of beautification of the grounds and prepare to add a vocational guidance program to the present curriculum. Present financial policies and curriculum would continue until the close of the current school year. The current enrollment was 181. Col. and Maj. Davis had consented to the sale with the consideration that they would be allowed to retain the name, San Diego Army and Navy Academy, for their military school in Carlsbad beginning July 1, 1937.

The *Union* explained that at the beginning of the depression the academy had executed an extensive building program and the indebtedness had grown until it was unable to meet the demands of its creditors, particularly the Security Trust and Savings Bank which was carrying much of the indebtedness in loans. The attorney for the bank, who had been business manager of the academy since the bank took it over on foreclosure proceedings the previous September, announced that all creditors would receive 'some money'. Total indebtedness was $280,000 when the bank assumed management [515].

An *Evening Tribune* article on April 5, 1937, included an illustration and description of a landscaping project that would transform the present campus into a 'garden of beauty'; a development program designed to make the Brown Military Academy 'outstanding among institutions of this kind in the country'. The centerpiece of the project was the quadrangle enclosed by the Spanish-style barracks, which was to be graded and laid out as a formal garden, flanked by towering palms and with lawns, flower gardens and walks [516]. Work had begun on this project the previous week and in fact the quadrangle was transformed into an attractive formal garden by summer.

After the takeover by the bank and departure of the Davises in 1936 the Pacific Beach academy had continued operations in the 1936-1937 academic year as the San Diego Army and Navy Academy. When the Brown company took over in March 1937 and announced their development program and name change, the Junior College graduates and senior class members of the Class of 1937 voted unanimously to be graduated from Brown Military Academy and to have only its insignia on their rings, which the *Tribune* described as 'indicative of the enthusiasm with which cadets have received word of the change in administration'.

The acquisition of the academy by the John E. Brown College Corp. represented a move by Brown to expand his educational establishment from its base in the rural South. Brown had begun as a fundamentalist evangelist and had established John E. Brown College (later John Brown University) in Siloam Springs, Arkansas, in 1919 as a Christian vocational school where students combined a half-day of classes with a half-day's work in college industries, Bible study, and daily chapel. He believed that schooling should 'meet demands for skilled labor and craftsmen', not 'overcrowding of the white collar field', and intended to develop the academy's military aspects and emphasize vocational training [517]. Presumably Brown saw the strict discipline and regular religious observance at the academy as a natural fit with the educational philosophy of his existing institutions[151]. The

---

[151] Although apparently not strict enough; Dr. Brown banned the balls and dinner dances that had formerly been fixtures of the academy social calendar. 'Social dancing' is not permitted at John Brown University in Arkansas to this day.

Brown Military Academy and vicinity in 1937, shortly after Brown's acquisition of the property and completion of the landscaping project: 1) Administration Building (original College), 2) Stough Hall, 3) Auditorium, 4) Infirmary, 5) 3-Story Dorm, 6) Pool, 7) First 4-Story Dorm, 8) Last 4-Story Dorms, 9) Junior School Annex, 10) Formal Garden, 11) Bandstand, 12) Fisher-Isis Arch, 13) Senior Arch, A) John L. Davis Sr. Home, B) Col. Davis Home, C) Mother Davis (former Thorpe) Home, D) former F. W. Barnes Home, E) former E. Y. Barnes Home. (This photo also shows the locations of former lemon ranches on the Acre Lots north of the Academy: F) Lot 48 (east; Gridley), G) Lot 49 (Rowe), H) Lot 50 (south; Coffeen), J) Lot 50 (north; Roxburgh) K) Lot 34 (Davis-Ravenscroft), L) Lot 33 (Stearns-Layman). (SDHC #83:14603-1; identifying labels added)

August 29, 1937, *Union* reported that Brown Military Academy, successor to the San Diego Army and Navy Academy, would open September 15 and 'a gratifying preliminary enrollment' indicated a student body of upward of 250 [518].

Meanwhile, the Davises proceeded with their new academy in Carlsbad. The *San Diego Union* reported that the first (and last) commencement service of the Davis Military academy would be held June 9, 1937 (on July 1 the Carlsbad academy would reclaim the San Diego Army and Navy Academy brand as one of the conditions of the sale of the Pacific Beach academy to the Brown company) [519]. The (new) San Diego Army and Navy Academy, Col. Thomas E. [sic] Davis, President, Carlsbad, California posted an ad in the January 1, 1938, *Union* ('Best Wishes for the New Year') thanking their many friends and patrons and announcing that registrations were being taken for the second semester classes commencing February 1st, 1938 [520].

Later in the year, in December 1938, Col. Davis resigned the presidency of his new academy. According to the *San Diego Union* on December 18, his letter of resignation cited 'certain situations which have arisen and which affect me personally'. His place was taken by his brother, Maj. John L. Davis, Jr. [521]. A few months after that, on March 31, 1939, the *Union* announced that he had been appointed assistant to the president of the John Brown Schools, which operated the Brown Military Academy on the former San Diego Army and Navy Academy campus, as well as the John Brown university in Arkansas and the Brown School for Girls at Glendora [522]. Within a year, the February 4, 1940, *San Diego Union* reported that Davis had been named president of the Brown Military Academy so that Dr. Brown could devote more of his time to the John Brown University. John E. Brown College retained ownership but Davis had resumed his role, after a short interruption, as head of the academy he had founded 30 years earlier[152].

In his interview with the San Diego Historical Society Oral History Program in 1957 Davis recalled:

> I was with that [Carlsbad] academy until 1939 when I was induced to leave and return to my old school in Pacific Beach, so I resigned as President of Carlsbad Academy and my brother John succeeded me as president there and I took up where I began with in my baby school at Pacific Beach and I was on duty with them as Asst. President, Past President, Tractor [Director?] of Admissions up to the time of my retirement three years ago in 1954. The school is carrying out some of the same ideals with which I established it [463].

On February 9, 1958, less than a year after this interview, the *San Diego Union* reported that Brown Military Academy would relocate to Glendora that summer to make way for commercial development of its 23-acre Pacific Beach campus[153]. The school property was sold to Metropolitan Investment Co. of San Diego in a cash transaction involving more than a million dollars. John Brown Schools issued a statement that the land had been 'released' to meet the community's

---

[152] He also moved to relax some of Dr. Brown's more fundamentalist policies. He wrote to Mrs. Edith Steele, the mother of a former student who now managed an orchestra, 'Steele San Diegans', that Brown had forbidden dancing on campus or even attending dances in the city but that since his return there had been 'something of a change', that the boys 'sometimes arranged social affairs of this kind off campus', and 'I believe they are planning something of the kind the 22d of this month' and offered to bring her orchestra to the attention of the social committee [624].

[153] The property to the west of Jewell Street had gradually been sold off in the 1950s. The remaining property, the College Campus, the former Emerald Street and most of Acre Lot 64 did cover approximately 23 acres.

---

need for its rapidly increasing business expansion; retention of the campus for school purposes would not be wise financially in view of the land's increased commercial value. Most of the 475 cadets and 90 faculty members were expected to move to Glendora[154]. The move had been under study for three years because the school was increasingly being 'hemmed in' by Pacific Beach's growth[155]. The 40-acre Glendora campus in the Sierra Madre foothills was larger and had more adequate buildings than the San Diego site [523].

Academy commencement exercises were held for the last time on June 11, 1958. Col. Davis, who had founded the institution on this spot nearly 50 years earlier (and was actually nearly 85 years old) was on hand to complete the cycle, and as the *Evening Tribune* reported, was the center of attention:

Brown's Founder, 78, Watches 'Last Parade'
400 Salute Col. Davis in Review

The colonel saw his boys pass in review in Pacific Beach today for the last time.

Col. Thomas A. Davis, 78, who founded Brown Military Academy 48 years ago, took the salute of 400 cadets.

Col. Davis was honorary reviewing officer. Maj. Gen. John W. Harmony, commanding general, Headquarters XV, U. S. Army Corps Reserve, was reviewing officer.

They March By

Davis tried valiantly to stand to take the review. Harmony gripped his right elbow to steady him, but he couldn't make it.

He sat at rigid attention, his cane held straight up in his left hand as his gray-clad boys marched by.

His silver mustache bristled but his gray eyes were misty behind their rimless glasses.

He doffed a soft, light brown felt hat when the big boys came by with the colors.

He smiled a warm little smile when the little cadets, grammar school boys, bobbed past him unevenly, trying their best to march as well as the big ones.

He Hears Tribute

Earlier Col. Davis had heard a tribute to him read over the public

---

[154] Actually, some of the faculty who preferred to remain in San Diego County joined former Brown Military Academy headmaster Louis Bitterlin in opening San Diego Military Academy in the former Las Flores Inn in Solana Beach [729]. San Diego Military Academy closed in 1977 [730] and the site, on Academy Drive in Solana Beach, is now occupied by Santa Fe Christian Schools.

[155] For example, the bugle call for reveille at sunrise each morning also woke families in the newly-built homes across Diamond Street from the academy.

---

address system. While the band played the "The Anniversary Song," Col Davis' life story including the founding of the academy in 1910 was read to an audience of cadets and 500 parents and friends.

After the review the band marched to the front of the reviewing stand and played for Col Davis the old song, "Aura Lee".

Brown Military Academy will move to Glendora after commencement exercises today [524].

(SDHC #U-T 6/11/58)

Development of the southern and western portion of the College Campus property was soon underway, beginning with the demolition of the historic buildings dating to the days of the San Diego College of Letters[156]. A groundbreaking ceremony for the Pacific Plaza shopping center was held on May 17, 1960 [525], and stores were open within a year.

---

[156] The original plan was to retain and remodel the four reinforced concrete dormitory buildings in the north eastern portion of the College Campus as a 'geriatrics center' [623].

The *Evening Tribune* interviewed Davis a few days after his 90th birthday in 1963. They reported that he was now confined to his bed at his home at 4637 Lamont Street, and that it had been about a year since he could see and hear what was happening to what was left of the institution to which he had given 48 years of his life.

> Barracks C across the street was the last of the buildings he saw. Its appearance then did not leave a pleasant memory. Windows had been smashed and all the things vandals can do to an empty building had been done.
>
> "If they only knew how unutterably dear it is to him," said his wife, Bessie, with whom the colonel celebrated their 60th wedding anniversary Jan. 22.
>
> Only three buildings are left standing of what was once Brown Military Academy at the end of the 1958 school term and most of the property is now a shopping area.
>
> The colonel would like to remember the beauty instead of the broken windows [526].

On February 5, 1964, the *San Diego Union* reported that Col. Davis was ill at his home on Lamont [527]. He died on February 12 at the age of 90. The massive dormitory buildings just across Lamont Street that stood as monuments to the impressive growth of his 'baby school' but whose costs ultimately led to its financial collapse and sale were still standing at the time of his death, but these last remaining academy

Barracks C, Brown Military Academy, December 1965.

buildings were also demolished by the end of 1965.

After some years' delay construction began on the Plaza Apartment complex, covering the balance of the former academy property not already occupied by Pacific Plaza[157]. The Plaza apartments were opened in 1970, converted to condominiums in 1980, and are now (in 2013) a major residential center with a population far exceeding the 400 – 500 cadets who once boarded on the campus of the San Diego Army and Navy Academy and its successor, Brown Military Academy, when they occupied the same property in the heart of Pacific Beach. Pacific Plaza underwent a major redevelopment in 1980s and is now one of the most important retail centers in Pacific Beach. The only reminder of the military academy on the site is a memorial to honor Brown Military Academy, the 'West Point of the West', outside the Great Plaza Buffet, near where Capt. Davis first held classes and drills for his original 13 little dazed students in 1910.

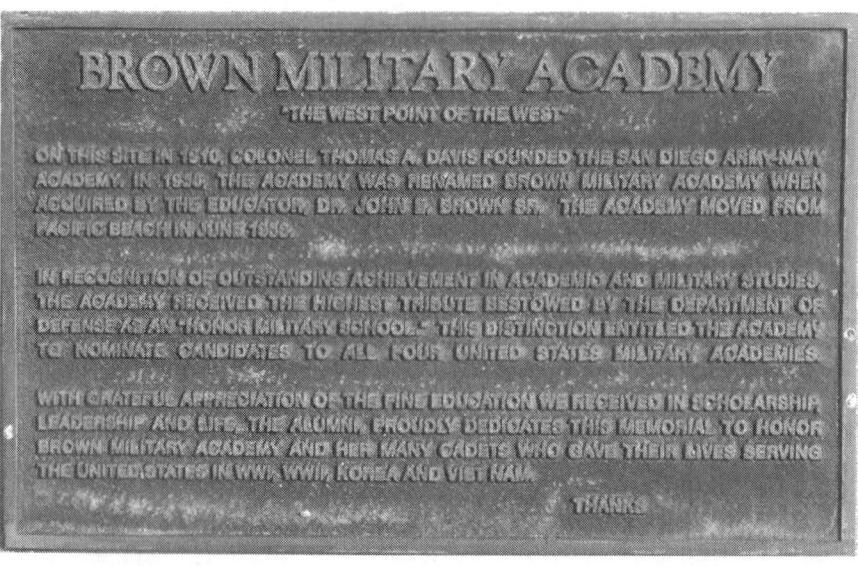

---

[157] The Plaza Apartments covered the property formerly owned by the academy in Acre Lot 64 and the northeastern quarter of the College Campus property.

9 Kate Sessions

Kate Sessions is one of the most recognized figures in San Diego history. A horticulturist best remembered as the 'Mother of Balboa Park', she is credited with transforming the scrub-covered lands of the 1200-acre park into a landscaped beauty spot. Today she is honored with a statue and plaque at the entrance to the park to which passers-by often add a clipping from one of the many nearby plantings, possibly one that she herself had introduced.

Kate Sessions is also honored in Pacific Beach where a monument and plaque at the northwest corner of Garnet Avenue and Pico Street stands on the site of her former nursery, and where the Kate O. Sessions Memorial Park and Kate Sessions Elementary School in the Mount Soledad foothills pay tribute to her status as the 'Number One Citizen' of the community which became her final home [528].

Kate Olivia Sessions was born in San Francisco in 1857 and moved to Oakland in 1868. She attended the University of California in nearby Berkeley, graduating in 1881 with a degree in chemistry. She originally came to San Diego in 1884 at the age of 26 to take over as principal of the Russ School when the original principal abruptly resigned in 1883. Her arrival was noted in the *San Diego Union* on January 15, 1884:

> Miss Kate O. Sessions and Miss Lettie E. Bentley, experienced teachers from Oakland, arrived by the Orizaba[158] on Sunday, under engagement to the Trustees of this School District, the former as Principal and the latter as Assistant, of the city schools [529].

However, the original principal reconsidered his resignation and was reinstated a few months later and Miss Sessions was reduced to

---

[158] The Orizaba was a side-wheel steamer operated by the Pacific Coast Steamship Company on a regular route between San Francisco and San Diego, calling at Port Harford, Santa Barbara and San Pedro.

Assistant Principal. After another year at the Russ School she resigned and taught briefly in San Gabriel before returning to San Diego to embark on the vocation for which she has become legendary.

From her early childhood Kate Sessions had shown an interest in flowers and plants, collecting and preserving specimens she found around her home. She had continued to show this interest while in San Diego and had made the acquaintance of people with similar interests, including businessman and rancher Solon Blaisdell and his wife. In 1885 the Blaisdells had the opportunity to buy the only existing nursery and floral business in San Diego and invited Miss Sessions to enter into a partnership to help operate it. She accepted their offer and they assumed ownership of the San Diego Nursery on Fifth Street in downtown San Diego.

1885 was also the year when the Great Boom began in San Diego and within months thousands of new residents were pouring into town. Businesses of all kinds, including nurseries, flourished. In 1886 when Babcock and Story laid out the Coronado Beach subdivision and auctioned off lots, the Blaisdells and Kate Sessions purchased an entire block near the ferry landing as a site to expand their nursery. When their partnership was dissolved a year later the assets were divided equitably, with Miss Sessions retaining the San Diego Nursery business on Fifth Street [14].

Miss Sessions' interests as a florist and nursery owner coincided with an interest in civic affairs, especially efforts to improve the appearance of the city through landscaping. She was secretary of the Society for the Improvement and Beautifying of San Diego [530] and chairman of its special street-tree planting committee [531]. She was also a member of the Woman's Home Association and was appointed to their committee to arrange for an annual flower festival [532]. To further her ideas for beautifying the city with trees, she petitioned the Common Council for the use of a portion of the City Park as an experimental nursery and garden. The council agreed and on February 9, 1892, approved Ordinance No. 153 granting K. O. Sessions permission to use and occupy a 32-acre plot near the northwest corner of the park for a period not exceeding ten years on condition that each year she would plant 100 'choice and varied sorts of trees and care for the same' and also furnish 300 'ornimental [sic] trees in crocks or boxes to be used by the City'. In addition to the trees furnished to the city she was also allowed to cultivate and grow plants and cut flowers for sale [533].

In 1903 Miss Sessions began acquiring property in Mission Hills, then open country on the north side of town, and eventually she bought or leased most of the area between Stephens and Lark Streets north of Lewis Street.   By 1905 her nursery operations had been relocated from the City Park to Mission Hills with a sales yard at the corner of Stevens and Lewis [534].   The Mission Hills nursery thrived but the development of the area for housing, encouraged by the opening of a streetcar line in 1909 and its extension in 1913 increasingly encroached on the nursery's growing fields and lath-houses.   The increase in property values also led to increased assessments and higher taxes, which Miss Sessions vigorously opposed[159]. As a result, she began looking for another area with the soil and climate, and open space, required for her nursery operation but with easy access to her downtown customers, and she found what she was looking for in Pacific Beach.

Pueblo Lot 1785 is located in the Mount Soledad foothills above Pacific Beach, on the northern side of the original Pacific Beach subdivision[160].   Pueblo Lot 1785 was itself divided roughly in half north-to-south, with the eastern 86 acres having been 'set apart' for the city and the western 74 acres divided into two equal 37-acre parcels. In 1912 Kate Sessions and her brother Frank acquired the two parcels in the western portion of Pueblo Lot 1785, Kate purchasing the southern 37 acres from Annie Collins [535] and Frank obtaining the northern 37 acres from M. and Etta Hall [536][161].

Shortly after the Sessions acquired the western portion of Pueblo Lot 1785, Frank also obtained a lease on the city's portion, which adjoined their property on the east. Resolution No. 12324 adopted on December 2, 1912, authorized the Common Council to lease Frank Sessions the eastern portion of Pueblo Lot 1785 for a term of 5 years for

---

[159] Her frustration boiled over in 1914 when her appeal for a reduction of assessment was disallowed. The *Evening Tribune* reported that 'Miss Sessions took to heart the refusal to such an extent that in words somewhat harsh, she undertook to express her feeling of disapproval of not only the work of the assessor but of the councilmen that reviewed that work. She was allowed to speak until she had satisfied herself.' [632].

[160] The southern boundary of Pueblo Lot 1785 is Loring Street, or where Loring would be if it ran straight between Foothill Boulevard and Soledad Road. The western boundary is where a northerly extension of Ingraham Street would run if it ran straight into the foothills.

[161] Frank Sessions apparently fell behind on the payments for his half of this property and the Halls sued and forced a public auction at the courthouse door on April 27, 1916, at which they placed the winning bid of $4850. After the required one-year waiting period had passed without redemption by the debtor the property was deeded to the Halls on April 28, 1917 [634], and on the same day the Halls granted it to Kate (not Frank) Sessions [627], who then became the owner of the entire western portion of Pueblo Lot 1785.

---

a total rental of $200 [537].   The terms of this lease were so favorable that San Diego Mayor James E. Wadham objected, remarking that he would pay twice that much himself.   He complained that 'Miss Sessions, who expects to use the land for a nursery, has had free use of city park some years for the same purpose on the ground that she was improving it', according to the December 8, 1912, *San Diego Union* [538].   The *Union* speculated that the mayor would veto the measure, and that the council would then override his veto but there is no indication in the Record of the Common Council that the mayor actually acted on his dissatisfaction.   On the contrary, on January 15, 1913, a little over a month later, the council adopted another resolution granting Frank Sessions permission to install a pumping plant on the northeast corner of the Pacific Beach reservoir site [539][162].   The Fairbanks Morse pump raised water 100 feet from the city reservoir to a new reservoir Frank Sessions had built at the northeastern corner of his 37-acre parcel, the highest point within the pueblo lot and well situated to store water for irrigation.

As the mayor had expected, the Sessions developed the northern and eastern portions of the pueblo lot as a nursery and growing fields. Frank Sessions relocated his poinsettia fields from Mission Hills and by the winter of 1914–1915 the *Union* reported that whole hillside was a mass of brilliant red easily discernible from the city [540].

However, Miss Sessions had other plans for the southwestern quarter of the pueblo lot.   In 1913 she submitted a subdivision map for Soledad Terrace, dividing the 37-acre parcel into 28 lots connected by Los Altos Road, an access loop from Soledad Road [541].   Most of the lots were between one and two acres, larger than the residential lots and smaller than the agricultural acre lots in the nearby Pacific Beach subdivision.   Miss Sessions apparently expected they would appeal to buyers interested in planting gardens[163].

Miss Sessions also brought her encouragement of civic improvement, particularly the landscaping of public spaces, to Pacific Beach.   The *Evening Tribune* reported on November 30, 1914, that citizens of Pacific Beach were becoming enthused over the 'city beautiful' proposition and would hold a mass meeting to set a date for

---

[162] The Pacific Beach reservoir site is Acre Lot 6, on the eastern edge of Pueblo Lot 1784, adjacent to the property Kate Sessions had acquired in the southwestern quarter of Pueblo Lot 1785.   The reservoir had been built and operated by the Pacific Beach Company and sold to the city in 1906 [631], and is still in use today.

[163] A 1932 article in the *Union* looking back at the landmarks of her life mentioned that the war had put a damper on her delightful plans for a community of garden growers [629].

Originally Pacific Beach

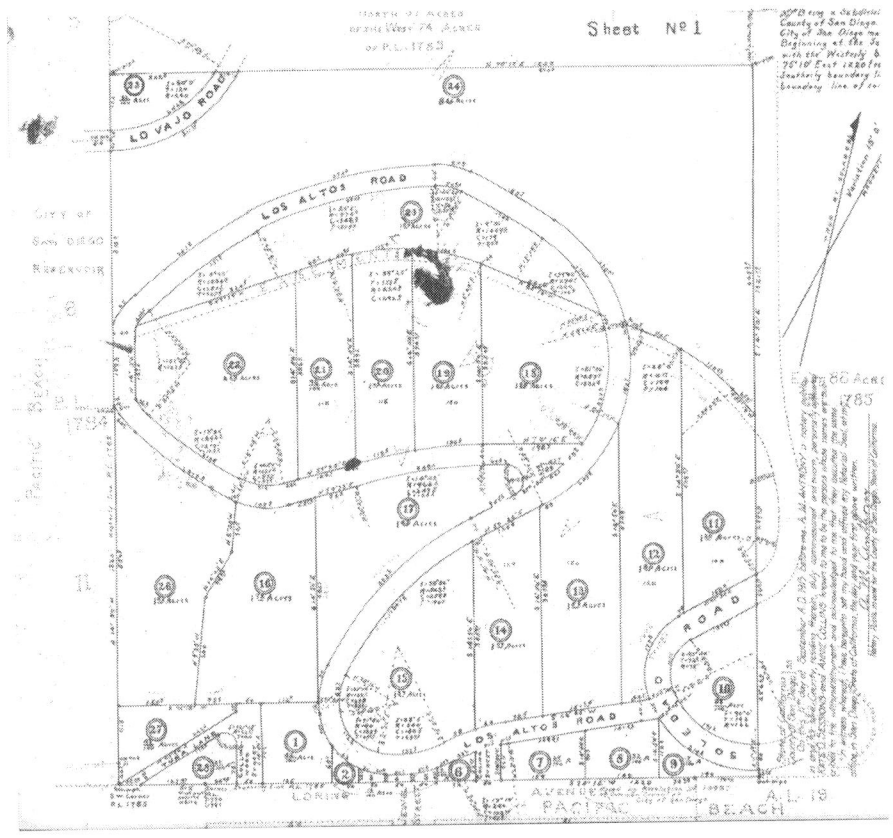

a 'clean up' day and discuss plans to improve the general surroundings of the beach. Among the speakers would be Miss K. O. Sessions, leading florist of San Diego, who would talk on the subject of beautifying a suburban town [542].

In April 1915 the *San Diego Union* announced that the San Diego Floral Association would make a 'pilgrimage' to Soledad Terrace, Pacific Beach, to inspect the gardens and greenhouses of Frank Sessions and Miss Kate Sessions ('Those who do not go in their own machines can take the 2:30 La Jolla car from Fourth and C streets') [543]. After at least a hundred members of the San Diego Floral Association and 'other lovers of flowers' visited Soledad Terrace, made a tour of the gardens and gathered in one of the lath-houses for punch and cakes, Miss Sessions told them of her plans for that section of San Diego. The *Union* explained that the tract had been divided into acre gardens with the idea of interesting homeseekers who would specialize in some particular plant or flower and supplying the market with home grown blooms instead of shipping them in from Los Angeles. The Sessions had already planted five acres to rose geraniums and another five acres to bergamot mint, 'being the pioneers in this section to raise smelly plants commercially'[164]. If this experiment proved successful, much larger tracts would be planted and other kinds of plants added [540].

Another plan was the completion of the road to the top of Mount Soledad, which was expected to 'take rank with Point Loma or Grossmont as a point of interest to tourists'. The *Evening Tribune* had reported in 1913 that A. H. Frost, president of the San Diego Beach Company and Clark Bailey, a capitalist from La Jolla, had just completed a very important and expensive highway from Pacific Beach to the top of Mt. Soledad [544]. This highway was apparently not as complete as that article suggested, however, and nearly three years later the April 10, 1916, *Evening Tribune* announced

> The new road up Soledad mountain, Pacific Beach, is to be dedicated, or christened, or something of that sort, when the Floral association makes its first trip up there Tuesday afternoon.
> They are first going to Miss Kate Sessions' gardens at Soledad terrace, and will then go up to the top, over the new road just completed, where there is a wonderful view of the city, ocean and mountains.
> Any wishing to go may take autos from the chamber of commerce at 1:30 Tuesday for a small sum, or may go to Pacific Beach station on the 1:30 La Jolla train, and take autos the rest of the way [545].

The *Union's* report a few days later stated that the San Diego Floral Association had 'celebrated the completing of the new road' with an out-door meeting, going to the top of Soledad mountain, above Pacific Beach, guided by Miss Kate Sessions. The celebration included planting five Torrey pines and three Mount Diablo big cone pines, each planted by a San Diego pioneer or other dignitary (or in the case of one tree, two five-year-old boys from Pacific Beach) [546].

The Sessions owned the western portion of Pueblo Lot 1785 and leased most of the rest from the city, but as their five-year lease came to an end they began scaling back their investment. In 1917 Kate Sessions offered to donate the private reservoir at the northeast corner of their property to the city and to sell the pumping plant built on the city's reservoir site for $1800 [547]; the reservoir was deeded to the city on May 22, 1918 [548]. The Sessions also began selling off portions of their growing fields to other nurseries; in December 1922 a 10-acre parcel along Soledad Road south of the reservoir was deeded to Walter Lans and another 4-acre parcel further to the south on Soledad Road,

---

[164] These 'smelly plants' were to be processed in a new 'still' installed in the Foreign Arts building at the Exposition by the California Floral Perfumery Company, according an article in the April 11, 1915, *San Diego Union* [630].

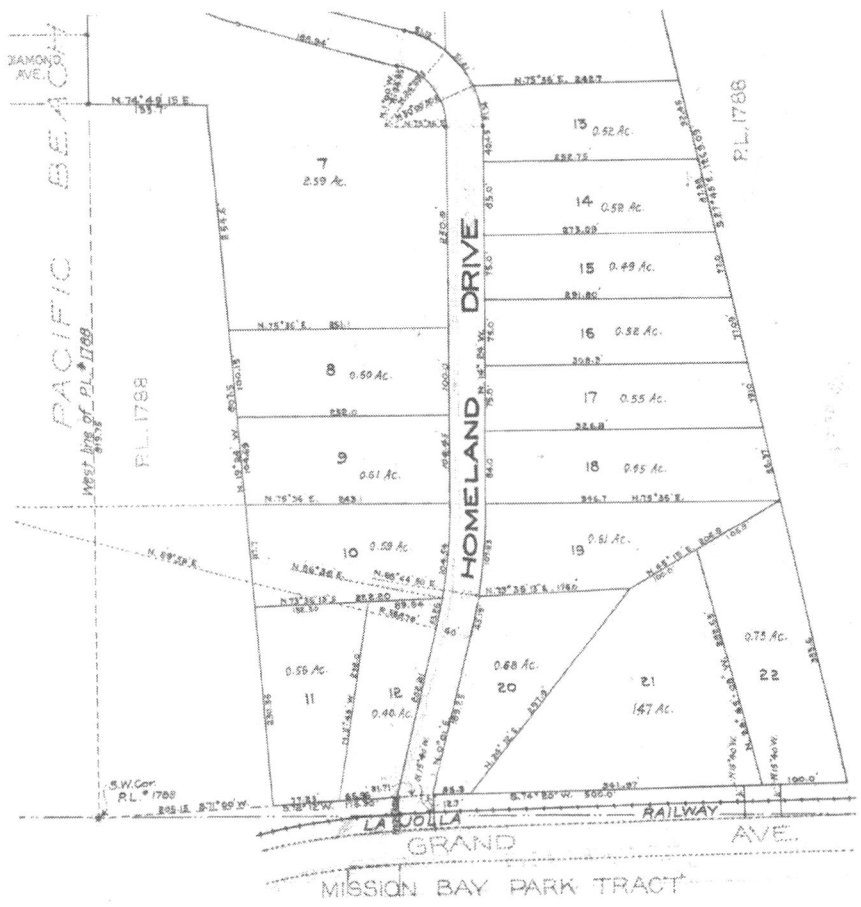

bordering Soledad Terrace, to the Westergaard Bros. of the Rose Court Floral Co. [549].

Although the Sessions had relocated their growing fields to Pacific Beach the Kate Sessions Nursery sales office remained in Mission Hills under the supervision of her assistant Pasquale (Anton) Antonicelli. Kate Sessions (and Frank Sessions and his family) also continued to live in Mission Hills. In 1924 Miss Sessions purchased lots 17 to 22 in the Homeland Villas No. 2 tract near the southwest corner of Pueblo Lot 1788, just east of the Pacific Beach subdivision[165] [550]. At the same

---

[165] Rose Creek runs through this property, along the line separating lots 19 and 20 from lots 21 and 22. Like the Mission Bay Park tract to the south, the subdivision map for Homeland Villas No. 2 does not appear to recognize the existence of this stream even though it had frequently flooded and inundated the surrounding area during winter rains.

time, Anton Antonicelli bought lots 9 to 12 [551], although he sold his lots to Miss Sessions the following year [552]. These acquisitions provided her with a plot of nearly 7 acres on the north side of Grand (later Balboa, now Garnet) Avenue, which at that time was part of the main highway to Los Angeles and points north (via Pacific Beach and La Jolla), and it was to this location that she and Antonicelli moved her remaining nursery operations from Mission Hills. The City Directory for 1926 lists addresses for Kate Sessions' nursery at 4016 Randolph Street[166] (Mission Hills) and 2520 Grand Avenue (Pacific Beach). The 1927 directory also lists two addresses, 2600 Grand and 4016 Randolph. In 1928 and 1929 the only address listed for the Kate Sessions nursery was 4016 Randolph (with growing fields at Pacific Beach) but, beginning in 1930, the address was 2590 Grand Avenue, where it remained until the 1940s. The 2590 Grand location, on the west side of Homeland Drive (now Pico Street), is where the monument to her Pacific Beach nursery now stands and where she planted the tipuana tree that has grown to become her 'living monument'.

At about the same time that she moved the last of her nursery operations to Pacific Beach, Kate Sessions herself also took up residence in Pacific Beach. The March 10, 1927, *San Diego Union* reported that the two-story cement house of Miss Kate O. Sessions, on the brow of Mount Soledad, had been 'enclosed'. The report added that the location commanded a wonderful view which could never be obstructed [553]. The new home was on lot 22 of her Soledad Terrace tract.

Guided tours of Miss Sessions gardens and nursery became regular events for the Floral Association and other horticultural organizations. In 1932 the 'charming estate of the famous horticulturist, Miss Kate O. Sessions' was included in a tour of San Diego garden spots arranged for visitors to the Olympic Games in Los Angeles and the *San Diego Union* noted that:

> In passing it might be stressed that to visit Miss Sessions' garden on a personally conducted tour is to get one of the most deliciously "different" pleasures California offers to the flower-minded. Miss Sessions makes her loved "children" come alive, each in turn, as she describes them with little humorous stories and gay wit intertwined with accurate and priceless

---

[166] The 4016 Randolph address was at the corner of Randolph and Washington, across the street from the Calvary Cemetery (now known as Mission Hills Pioneer Park, the gravestones, but not the graves, of hundreds of San Diego pioneers having been removed). The present (2013) Mission Hills Nursery ('Since 1910 – Continuing Kate Session's Tradition') is in the northern half of the same block, at Randolph and Fort Stockton Drive.

information [554].

The 86-acre city property adjacent to the Sessions' property on the east side of Pueblo Lot 1785 had remained undeveloped since the expiration of Frank Sessions' lease in 1917. In 1933, Pacific Beach residents petitioned the city to designate a 2-acre exclave at the southwest corner of the city land as a park to be known as 'Color Park'[167]. According to the August 15, 1933, *San Diego Union* the park would be planted with two 'exotics', an ever-blooming blue plumbago, a native of South Africa, and bougainvillea, a native of Brazil, as well as the native Matilija poppy and two native oak trees. The native evergreen shrubs already on the property would be maintained [555]. The exotic plants were expected to provide the color, sky blue and purple, and to be visible 'as a gorgeous splotch clear across the bay, which won't hurt anybody at all', according to a follow-up article in the May 15, 1934, *Union* [556].

The Color Park was approved and dedicated in 1935 and in 1937 the *Union* reported that Boy Scouts, under the capable direction of Miss Kate O. Sessions, were clearing weeds that were threatening to choke the young plants and shrubs. The shrubs and plants were expected to bear profuse blooms of red, white and blue when matured and had been provided by Miss Sessions, Pacific Beach's No. 1 citizen [557].

The Kate Sessions nursery not only sold plants and trees to retail customers and provided landscaping services to private residences but also donated plants and landscaping service to civic organizations. In Pacific Beach she supplied the plants for landscaping the new fire station [558] and school [559], and was made an honorary member of the ZLAC Rowing Club for her efforts in beautifying their sandy bay-front location [560]. More important than these tangible contributions, Kate Sessions provided inspiration and leadership to community groups such as the Pacific Beach Garden Club. As the *San Diego Union* put it, Pacific Beach had 'soil, climate and Miss Kate Sessions'; the soil was deep and workable, the climate was exceptionally mild and delightful, and these attributes brought Kate Sessions to Pacific Beach, 'the Miss Sessions, woman horticulturist of national and international

---

[167] The land proposed for the park was isolated from the remainder of the city property by Soledad Road, the northern continuation of Lamont Street that looped around the steep hill at the end of Lamont before resuming its course along the western edge of the city land toward the summit of Mount Soledad. Soledad Road was realigned in 1961, shortening the route by cutting through the hillside beyond Lamont. Kate Sessions Way and an alley south of the Soledad Club now mark the earlier route. The former Color Park was in the space between this alley and the yards of the neighborhood to the south, which mark the boundary of the city land.

reputation. A "plant mother" influencing every garden in San Diego county, her presence is of inestimable value to Pacific Beach' [561].

By 1937 Kate Sessions had been a presence in Pacific Beach for 25 years and a full-time resident for 10 years. 1937 was also the 50th anniversary of the founding of Pacific Beach, the Opening Sale by the Pacific Beach Company on December 12, 1887, and the Pacific Beach Chamber of Commerce planned a Golden Jubilee dinner to be held on November 1 at the large mess hall at Brown Military Academy. The celebration would feature a testimonial to Kate Sessions; the president of the chamber explained in the October 17 *Union* that 'Miss Sessions, because of her devotion to Pacific Beach's interests through the years, and her unfaltering confidence in its future, by common consent has earned the distinction of being the community's foremost citizen' [562]. The celebration dinner, rescheduled for November 8, Kate Sessions' 80th birthday, was attended by over 500 people, including many 'old-time' Pacific Beach residents. San Diego civic leader Julius Wangenheim honored Miss Sessions, recalling her early days as a school teacher; 'Apparently she decided it was easier to get something out of the good earth than into the heads of young San Diegans. Wherever she moved, beautiful things sprang up. San Diegans owe her a great debt' [563].

On December 3, 1939, Kate Sessions fell and broke her hip (while watering plants in her garden) and was taken to Scripps Hospital in La Jolla. While in the hospital her health deteriorated and she died of pneumonia on March 24, 1940, Easter Sunday. She is buried in Mt. Hope Cemetery alongside her brother Frank and their parents. Their graves are shaded by a twisted juniper, her favorite tree according to biographer Elizabeth MacPhail [528].

Kate Sessions' property holdings in Pacific Beach passed to her cousin Alice Carroll and were gradually sold off. The home that she built in 1927 with the 'wonderful view which can never be obstructed' is still standing today (2013) but the large lots in the surrounding subdivision that she laid out hoping to attract gardeners have mostly been re-divided and filled in with large homes with swimming pools and tennis courts. The nursery on Rose Creek was acquired by A. Maude Thomas of La Jolla, who, according to the *San Diego Union*, had 'hoped to carry on Miss Sessions good work for the plant lovers of San Diego' [564]. However, most of the nursery site, including the sales office (and tipuana tree), along with much of the rest of the Homeland Villas No. 2 tract and the eastern part of Pacific Beach, was expropriated by the United States government in 1941 to use for housing defense workers [565][168].   Mrs. Thomas moved on to the Anderson nursery on Rosecrans Street.

The tipuana tree continues to grow at the site of the former nursery.   In 1941 Max Matousek, who had been a foreman at her nursery, wrote to the *Union's* Public Forum encouraging all tree-lovers to see the tipuana tree planted by Kate Sessions at 2590 Balboa Ave in Pacific Beach.   It would be in flower the next week-end, a mass of golden yellow, a living monument to Kate Sessions [566].   In 1961 a California Historic Monument commemorating the life and influence of Kate Sessions was dedicated on the nursery site, under the branches of the tipuana tree at the corner of what is now Garnet Avenue and Pico Street [567].

Kate Sessions Elementary School was opened on January 3, 1956, on a site not far from her Soledad Terrace home and nursery site[169]. Many of the new students lived in homes built on the property she had once owned in the western half of Pueblo Lot 1785.

The eastern half of Pueblo Lot 1785 had long been city property. In 1935 the 2-acre plot in the southwest corner of the city land had been dedicated as Color Park and in 1948 the entire area became a city park called Soledad Terrace Park [568].   Without Miss Sessions' supervision the original Color Park had become neglected and according to a September 5, 1956, article in the *Sentinel*, a Pacific Beach weekly, was in a 'state of ruin', a 'casualty of the late war period'.   The article noted that Color Park was the last undertaking of Kate Sessions' life, and the only one left unaccomplished, and asked what could be more appropriate than to dedicate a revived and completed Kate O. Sessions Color Park on the 100th anniversary of her birth [569].   On the 100th anniversary of her birth, November 8, 1957, this last undertaking was accomplished.   The eastern portion of Pueblo Lot 1785, formerly Soledad Terrace Park, which the Sessions had once leased from the city and which adjoined their former nursery growing fields and her Soledad Terrace garden subdivision, was dedicated as Kate O. Sessions Memorial Park.

---

[168] The property formerly owned by Kate Sessions on the east side of Homeland Drive (Pico Street), lots 17 - 22, was not part of the government expropriation in 1941. Much of this property is between the banks of Rose Creek.

[169] The author was among the 499 students opening Kate Sessions Elementary School that day.

KATE OLIVIA SESSIONS' NURSERY SITE

1857 - 1940

THIS PLAQUE COMMEMORATES THE LIFE AND INFLUENCE OF A WOMAN WHO ENVISIONED SAN DIEGO BEAUTIFUL. ON THIS SITE SHE OPERATED A NURSERY AND GAINED WORLD RENOWN AS A HORTICULTURIST. SHE WAS THE FIRST WOMAN TO RECEIVE THE INTERNATIONAL MEYER MEDAL IN GENETICS.

CALIFORNIA REGISTERED HISTORICAL LANDMARK NO. 764

PLAQUE PLACED BY THE CALIFORNIA STATE PARK COMMISSION IN COOPERATION WITH THE PACIFIC BEACH WOMAN'S CLUB.
JULY 7, 1961

10 The Housing Projects

Reuben Fleet was a former army airman who had trained at Rockwell Field on North Island in 1917 and went on to found Consolidated Aircraft in Buffalo, New York, in 1923. Consolidated relied primarily on military contracts and in order to improve his prospects with the United States Navy, and in particular for a projected 'flying boat' design, Fleet moved the company, and hundreds of employees, to San Diego in 1935. The initial Consolidated Aircraft plant was built on land reclaimed from San Diego Bay along Pacific Highway in 1935 and was followed by further additions in 1938 as the Consolidated PBY flying boat proved successful and the Navy increased orders.

By the late 1930s the international situation had become tense as Germany and Japan militarized and began moving aggressively against their neighbors. In preparation for the possibility of war the United States began planning an enlargement of the Army Air Corps, including a fleet of 4-engine, long-range, high-altitude heavy bombers. Boeing had designed the B-17 'Flying Fortress' in 1935 and started production in 1937. In 1939 Consolidated developed an alternative design which became the B-24 'Liberator', capable of carrying a heavier bomb load at faster speeds and higher altitude over a longer range. Production of the B-24 in San Diego began in 1940 and surged almost immediately as additional orders came in from Britain and France, both then at war with Germany. To accommodate the increased production Consolidated built additional plants and hired thousands of new workers beginning in 1940. By the fall of 1941 employment was up to 25,000. Another 20,000 employees were added in the following year [570].

According to the 1940 census San Diego then had a population of 203,000, far too few for tens of thousands of additional workers to be recruited from the local area alone. Instead, tens of thousands of people moved to San Diego to work for Consolidated and other defense-related industries. At the same time Navy and Marine Corps bases in the San Diego area had begun mobilizing in anticipation of war, increasing the population of military personnel and their dependents. The sudden arrival of these new residents put a serious strain on local resources, particularly housing.

In October 1940 Congress passed the Lanham Defense Housing

Act in an effort to provide adequate housing for defense workers. Among the first, and ultimately the largest, of these projects was Linda Vista, a 'city within a city' on what was then the uninhabited northern side of Mission Valley. Construction of Linda Vista began in March 1941 and it eventually grew to 4846 family units and 20,000 residents [571]. However, even this huge construction project was not sufficient to keep up with the continuing influx of workers and the government sought other tracts of relatively open land within a reasonable distance of the defense plants. One such area was Pacific Beach.

On August 25, 1941, the United States of America filed an action to condemn and acquire title to four tracts of land in the eastern portion of Pacific Beach 'for the purpose of using said site for housing for persons engaged in national defense activities and their families' [572]. The complaint for condemnation listed 280 defendants including the City and County of San Diego, the State of California, the San Diego Beach Company, the Pacific Beach Company, utility companies, mortgage companies and hundreds of individual Pacific Beach property owners. The four tracts were described by metes and bounds and the property to be acquired was more particularly described as 273 separate parcels, most of which were defined by lot and block numbers in the Pacific Beach, Mission Bay Park or Homeland Villas No. 2 subdivisions.

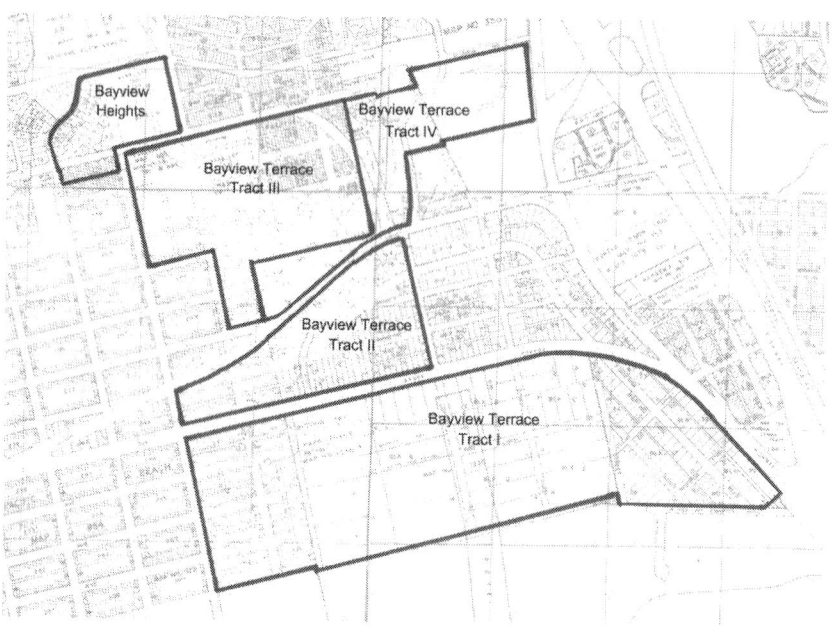

The *San Diego Union* reported that 1000 new homes would be built on the site before the end of 1941 at a total cost of approximately $3,300,000. Unlike the 3000 new homes under construction in Linda Vista the homes in Pacific Beach were built under a provision of the Lanham act which would require their removal in five years 'unless a housing shortage or national emergency exists at that time'. The houses were described as 'demountable' and constructed of four-foot plywood modules. Although the joints would be tightly sealed the various parts could easily be dismantled for shipment to another site. They were designed to meet the demands of the low wage earner and families in the low income brackets who were now housed in sub-standard dwellings.

The homes would not have garages but the anticipated parking problem would be solved by 'parking compounds' where occupants could leave their cars, requiring no more than a 500-foot walk from the farthest house. A school, with classrooms designed to double as craft rooms in the evening and with an auditorium for general meetings, dramatics and social activities, would be built facing the bay. The school playground would have modern equipment and a lighted baseball diamond and there would be access to the beach for swimming and boating.

> Particular thought has been given to street design for the project, which will be divided by Garnet and Balboa aves. Project roads have been designed with the idea of minimizing the traffic problem and providing maximum safety for children who will reside in the area.
> The square block pattern for the streets will be abandoned and park walks will interconnect all units, which will consist of court groups.
> The site is bounded by Pacific highway on the east, Mission bay on the south, Olney st. on the west and runs 1500 feet north of Balboa ave. The nursery which the late Kate Sessions, prominent San Diego horticulturist, owned is included in the site, and the blooming acacia trees, long a landmark in San Diego, will be preserved in a proper setting. [573]

On December 21, 1941, the *Union* reported that the 1000-unit demountable homes project in Pacific Beach due for occupancy January 1 would be called Bayview Terrace [574]. On January 2 the news was that the 1000 demountable units in Bayview Terrace were virtually complete and applications for leases would be accepted within two weeks. Rentals would average $2.50 a month less than Linda Vista, where rents ranged from $27.50 to $35.00 a month [575].

The Bayview Terrace housing development was declared complete and ready for occupancy on January 24, 1942. The *San Diego Union* reported that there were 200 one-bedroom units, 600 two-bedroom units and 200 with three bedrooms available for defense workers. Rents for the one-bedroom units would range from $23 to $25 a month, for those with two bedrooms, $25.50 to $30 a month, and for the larger ones $28 to $30 a month. There were single family detached houses, duplex buildings and multiple family buildings, all one-story type, planned to be light, airy and cheerful. Kitchens were equipped with electric refrigerator, gas range, automatic water heater, combination kitchen sink and laundry trays, drainboard, and kitchen cabinet. All homes were heated by gas. An addition charge of $1.60 a month was made for water, while gas and electricity were metered individually [576].

Two weeks later the *Union* noted that 250 families had already moved in to the Bayview project and that federal authorities had given the green light to construction of 600 more permanent defense housing units and 3100 demountable units in the San Diego area. There was no definite word as to where the new buildings would be located but it was thought that the demountable homes would be added to the existing defense housing projects, including Bayview Terrace [577].

In fact 127 more demountable homes were built in an additional tract adjacent to Bayview Terrace, west of Pendleton, south of Beryl, east of Noyes and north of Chalcedony Streets (and including the half-block on the south side of Chalcedony between Olney and Noyes Streets). The property was acquired in June 1942 and although the new tract was formally known as Bayview Heights[170] it was generally treated as a part of Bayview Terrace, which was thereafter said to consist of 1127 homes.

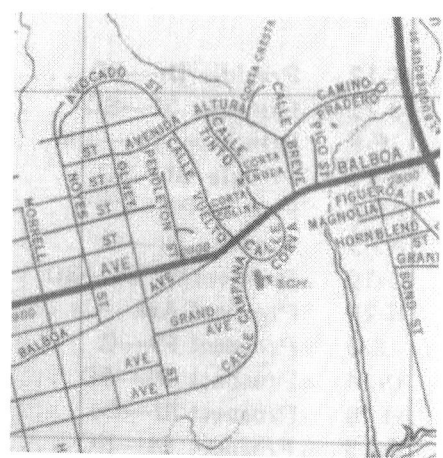

The new school was also completed in record time. According to the April 15, 1942, *San Diego Union* Bayview Terrace Elementary school in the housing project for defense workers at Pacific Beach 'opened yesterday with 270 pupils answering to roll call'. Only 10 of the 24 rooms had been opened and they were only taking children from the first to sixth grades but the two kindergarten rooms and the

---

[170] One difference between Bayview Terrace and Bayview Heights is that the roofs of the demountable homes in the former were darker and the latter were lighter, a feature which distinguishes the two projects in aerial photos of the area.

Originally Pacific Beach

cafeteria, kitchen and auditorium were expected to be opened in September. The youngsters had been attending Pacific Beach Elementary school under crowded conditions that necessitated double sessions. Although built and owned by the federal government, the school had been leased to the city board of education and it would operate as a public school [578].

A month later the students themselves weighed in with articles in the News of the Schools section of the May 10 *San Diego Union*. Rosemary Roe, Gr. 6, Bayview Terrace, wrote that

> The newly opened Bayview Terrace school is in the Bayview Terrace defense project, Pacific Beach. The building is arranged in three double wings off of a long main building. At the west end there is a hangar-shaped auditorium. At the east end there are two kindergarten rooms. Everyone likes the way the school is arranged.

Carol Sloan, Gr.6, Bayview Terrace, wrote

> The rooms are long and wide, with many windows on the east side and transoms above the blackboard on the west side. We have a blackboard at the south end of the room that is almost the width of the room. The blackboard on the west side is just half the length of the room.
>
> At the back, which is toward the north, we have two large cupboards, many drawers of all sizes, a nice big bookcase, and a closet in which to keep our coats. We have a sink, too, which is very handy as we have soap and cold running water.
>
> The room is painted white. The cupboards and the teacher's desk are painted a rusty red. There is an electric clock in the front of the room, and we have an automatic heater [579].

From the 1920s to 1970s San Diego city directories included a street index which listed each address on each street in the city along with the name of the resident. The city directories also included a name

Aerial view of Bayview Terrace (and Bayview Heights) housing project, looking north. The long buildings at the edge of the project at center right, next to Rose Creek, belong to the Bayview Terrace school. Bayview Heights is at top left. (SDHC #10356-2)

index which listed all city residents by name, and in 1942 these listings included the resident's occupation. The street index and name index together make it possible to determine the occupation of the resident at any street address. In 1942 the city directory listed the new streets in the Bayview Terrace project for the first time along with the hundreds of new addresses on these streets and on the existing streets which extended into the projects. The city directory listings for the names of residents at a random sample of 20 of the 102 addresses on Calle Tinto in the Bayview Terrace project in 1942 showed that all were aircraft workers and all but one were employed by Consolidated Aircraft (one worked at Solar Aircraft). In another sample the residents of all eight addresses on Diamond Street east of Pendleton Street (2281 to 2288 Diamond, within the Bayview Terrace project) were listed as 'aircrftwkr CACorp'.

The influx of defense workers and the need to provide for their housing had been recognized by 1941 and construction of public

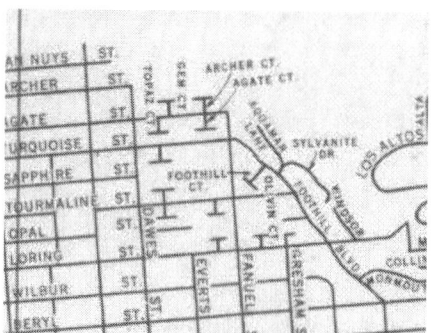

housing projects like Bayview Terrace was well underway before the attack on Pearl Harbor on December 7, 1941, and the subsequent declaration of war against Japan and the other Axis powers. With the onset of war the buildup of the defense-related population of San Diego accelerated and led to a further demand for low-cost and rapidly-constructed homes within a reasonable distance of the downtown industries. Once again property was found in Pacific Beach, this time in the northwestern section of the community in the area around what was then the junior high school and is now Pacific Beach Elementary School. The Los Altos Terrace project began in July 1942 with the acquisition of a tract of land extending from Loring to Archer Street and between Dawes Street and the Mt. Soledad foothills, excepting two entire blocks and a few other properties with existing homes, and the school property itself [580].

On March 27, 1943, the *San Diego Union* reported that 428 houses were under construction in the Los Altos project and that rentals were expected to start in about three weeks [581]. By May 5 the *Union* was able to report that the new Los Altos project at Pacific Beach, consisting of 428 units of 1, 2 and 3-bedroom dwellings, had been opened for occupancy. Couples were being permitted to occupy the single-bedroom units, with others going to families with children [582].

Originally Pacific Beach

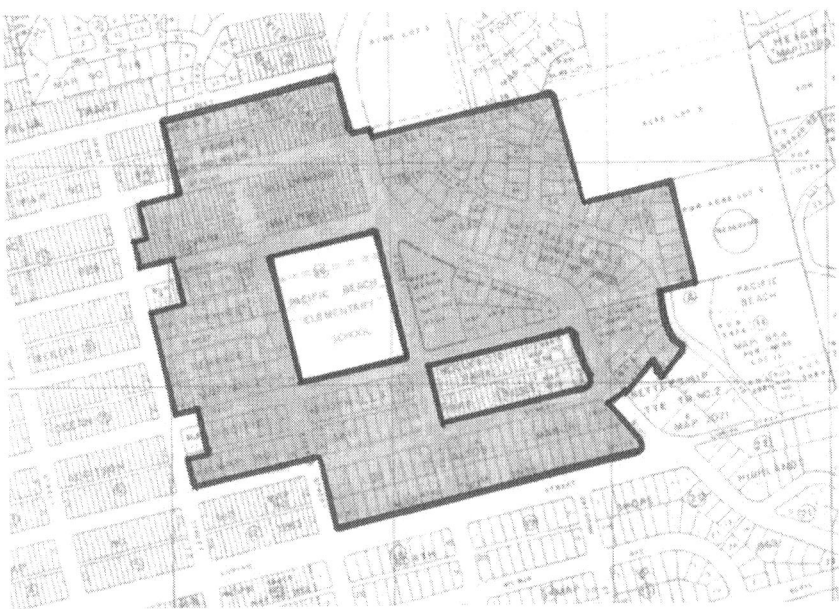

In addition to the demountable homes themselves the Federal Public Housing Authority also provided more substantial buildings for community-wide use. The *San Diego Union* reported on August 22, 1943, that contracts had been let for a community activities building and a child care building in the Los Altos housing project at Pacific Beach and for a child care building at 'Bay Terrace' [583][171].

Although the Bayview Terrace and Los Altos Terrace projects had been developed for civilian defense workers, the war had also led to a huge increase in the military population of the San Diego area who also required housing and in 1944 Pacific Beach was selected as the site of a project to build 232 homes for naval personnel. On November 30, 1944, the United States government condemned a tract of land between Fortuna and La Playa Avenues and Haines and Jewell Streets [584]. The *San Diego Union* reported on December 22, 1944, that work had started at the site of what would become the Cyane Naval Housing project [585]. On April 7, 1945, a second tract along Shasta Street was

---

[171] While the demountable homes are long gone, the child care buildings are still in operation in the 21st century. The Los Altos Childrens Center is located next to Pacific Beach Elementary School on Turquoise Street and Bayview Child Development Center is at the northwest corner of Garnet Avenue and Soledad Mountain Road. The Bayview Terrace project made use of the former A. B. Cairnes home just north of the child care building and facilities at the new Bayview Terrace school a block to the south instead of building a new community center in 1943.

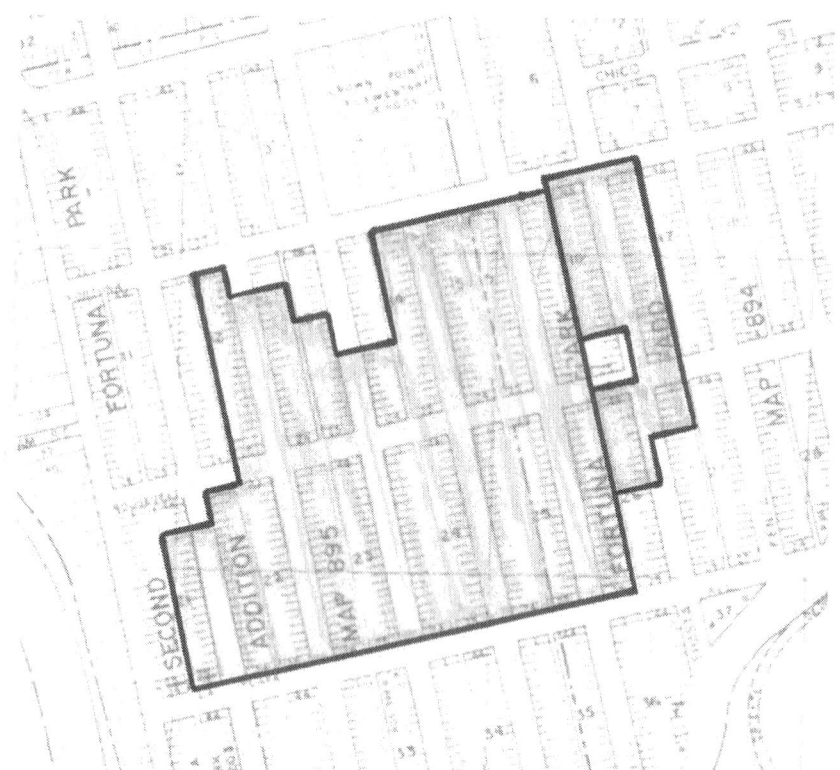

condemned and added to the eastern side of the Cyane project [586].

In April 1945 the *San Diego Union* reported that the federal public housing authority had reclassified the demountable war housing as 'permanent', meaning demountable units would not be demolished after the war and would either be retained on their present sites or removed to other locations. Although denounced by realty and apartment house interests, who called the houses 'eyesores', the announcement was generally popular with residents of the public housing projects, many of whom expressed a desire to remain [587].

The expropriation of property for the Bayview Terrace project had extended nearly to the shore of Mission Bay and as far east as Pacific Highway but most of the home construction had been concentrated in the northern and western areas and no homes were built in the immediate vicinity of the bay. Nevertheless, the government had refused to release unused land even after the war ended and by 1947 this policy interfered with the city's desire to dredge Mission Bay and build up its shoreline. According to the December 13, 1947, *San Diego Union*, if the city built up the shoreline as planned it would leave the Bayview Terrace area at 'low swamp level, without drainage' [588]. A few months later the government housing agency did relinquish the unused tidelands and the city renewed its effort to acquire them [589].

Drainage also became an issue in 1951, when winter storms again struck the area. A portion of Bayview Terrace was located near Rose Creek and, like the railway and racetrack before it, was vulnerable to flooding when the creek rose after heavy rainfall upstream. The December 31, 1951, *Union* reported that Rose Canyon Creek overflowed its banks and flooded several houses in the Bayview Terrace Housing Project and at least one family used a rowboat to get away. Fortunately the water receded by afternoon and the residents moved back into their homes [590]. However, less than three weeks later another storm caused renewed flooding. The January 19, 1952, *Union* included a photo of Camino Pradero in the Bayview Terrace housing project, inundated with water which had overflowed the banks of Rose Canyon Creek as it inched toward floor level [591].

While the public housing projects provided immediate relief for an acute housing shortage in the early years of the defense industry build-up, the demand for housing also increased commercial housing development in Pacific Beach during the 1940s and 1950s. City directories show the number of addresses on Diamond Street, for example, increased from 60 in 1940 to 125 in 1945, 225 in 1950 and 350 in 1955 (not counting the 40 addresses on Diamond Street within the Bayview Terrace project after 1941). On Reed Avenue the comparable numbers were 25 in 1940, 85 in 1945, 185 in 1950 and 350 in 1955. Other sections of Pacific Beach saw similar rates of growth. Many of the new residents were defense workers who had moved to San Diego during the war and decided to stay. Some of these new homeowners had first come to Pacific Beach as residents of the Bayview Terrace project.

The growing population of Pacific Beach included families with children and the growing number of children led to a need for additional schools. The government had built Bayview Terrace Elementary as part of the initial construction of the Bayview Terrace project but other school expansion had been curtailed by war-time restrictions. In 1946 the San Diego school board proposed an 'emergency' building program which included funds for one new school, Crown Point Elementary in Pacific Beach [592]. In July 1946 the board authorized the purchase of the site, between Ingraham, Fortuna and Jewell Streets and Pacific Beach Drive, just north of the Cyane Navy Housing project [593]. Construction began in March 1947 with completion expected before the school year began in September, but construction delays prevented the school from opening until the 525 pupils began classes in the still uncompleted school on January 5, 1948 [594].

Plans for a high school in Pacific Beach were approved in 1951 and construction of Mission Bay High School[172] began in 1952 on a portion of the land south of Grand Avenue that had originally been acquired by the government for the Bayview Terrace project. Construction was funded by federal funds allocated for assistance in defense-impacted areas [595]. Students began classes on September 14, 1953 [596]. Grand Avenue (formerly Ivy Avenue), which had been the right-of-way of the Los Angeles and San Diego Beach Railway between 1907 and 1917, was extended across Rose Creek and connected to Pacific Highway, in part to accommodate the increased traffic caused by the new high school.

With the increased supply of standard housing and a decline of defense jobs after the war the demand for the demountable units diminished. In 1955 the Public Housing Administration announced that the demountable houses in Bayview Terrace were for sale. The announcement noted that they were designed and built to be taken apart, moved and reassembled and suggested uses such as non-dwelling shelters for storage and beach or mountain vacation cabins. In more rural areas, where zoning and building codes were not too stringent, they could be modified for regular home use. Prices were $300 for a one-bedroom single, $600 for a duplex and $950 for a triplex. Payment was to be in cash on taking title and they were to be removed within 90 days [597]. A month later 343 demountable units were offered for sale and removal from the Los Altos housing project in the section bounded by Loring, Dawes and Agate streets and Foothill Boulevard. They would be sold at $350 for one-bedroom units, $450 for two-bedroom and $470 for three-bedroom units. Occupants could buy the units where they lived or terminate their tenancy within 15 days [598]. The October 8, 1955, *Union* reported that 798 demountable units from Bayview Terrace were to be offered for sale on December 1 [599].

San Diego city directories again document the rapid decline of the public housing projects in Pacific Beach during the 1950s. Of the 102 addresses on Calle Tinto in the Bayview Terrace project, for example, there were 15 vacancies listed in the 1953-54 city directory, 20 in 1955, and 50 in 1956. By 1957, the city directory only listed 13 addresses on Calle Tinto, all vacant, six in 1958, and none thereafter, although Calle Tinto itself continued to appear in the city directory for several more

---

[172] Pacific Beach business leaders protested the name and threatened not to vote for any more school bonds if the school was not named Pacific Beach High. The school board decided that Pacific Beach's name was already attached to elementary and junior high schools and that the new school would serve considerable territory outside Pacific Beach and stayed with their original choice [635].

years. Sylvanite Street in the Los Altos project had 39 addresses in 1953-54; six were vacant in 1955 and by 1956 there were no addresses listed on Sylvanite Street. Sylvanite Street disappeared from maps and city directories in the 1960s, replaced by portions of Castle Hills and Windsor Drives.

The Public Housing Administration had intended to sell the land to private interests once the demountable housing units had been removed but the February 2, 1956, *Union* reported that the army had placed a hold on property in the Bayview Terrace project in order to survey it for possible use as an antiaircraft gun installation [600]. A month later the army agreed to abandon its plans and instead to consider a site on Point Loma [601]. On June 17 the *Union* reported that 6 ½ acres of Bayview Terrace land fronting on Grand Avenue would be sold on June 25 [602] and on June 26 the *Union* announced that the low bids had been taken under study [603].

Land in the former Los Altos project was offered for sale in July of 1956. The July 15 *San Diego Union* contained a notice that surplus vacant land zoned R-1 in the heart of Pacific Beach residential section was for sale. Approximately 72 acres divided into 11 items of the Los Altos project were available for immediate construction. All dwelling buildings on the project had been sold and would be removed prior to passing title [604]. Three remaining parcels, aggregating more than 40 acres, in the former Los Altos housing project were offered for sale in November [605].

The developers who purchased the surplus property in the former Los Altos project did proceed with the construction of new homes. The July 26, 1959, *San Diego Union* noted that one such tract, Hollywood Park, along the north side of Turquoise Street across from Pacific Beach Elementary School, featured a contemporary design which some builders said would not sell in a subdivision development. This latest modern design included wood siding combined with concrete block, open planning in the interior and extensive use of glass walls [606]. The Hollywood Park homes did sell, and most are still standing today.

On the other hand, the majority of the land in the Bayview Terrace project has never been returned to private ownership. The *Union* reported on August 14, 1957, that the Defense Department had approved 1000 Capehart military housing units for the San Diego area. One hundred of the units would be built at the Miramar Naval Air Station but the remainder would be divided between the 'old Bayview Terrace war housing project' and Linda Vista. Under the Capehart housing program, homes would be financed and built by private contractors and the government would take out mortgages and eventually acquire ownership of the units by making payments using the rental allowance of their military occupants [607]. Final approval of the project and transfer of the land from the Public Housing Administration to the Navy was reached in November 1958 [608]. Site preparation and construction, including the realignment and renaming of most of the streets in the former housing project, began in 1959 and residents were moving in by 1960. The homes in what is now known as the Admiral Hartman Community were renovated in the early 2000s. The extensive area of single-family homes of a uniform design laid out along streets that 'abandon the square block pattern' more closely resemble a suburban housing development than the community of high-density residential units built on rectangular blocks that most of the rest of Pacific Beach has become.

The Bayview Terrace housing project is remembered by some for its connection to the sensational Black Dahlia murder case. The nude body of Elizabeth Short (Beth, Betty), drained of blood and carefully cut in half, was found in Los Angeles on January 15, 1947. The link to Pacific Beach was that the 22-year-old Miss Short had spent the month prior to her murder as a guest at the home of Elvern French at 2750 Camino Pradero. According to the January 17 *San Diego Union* she had met Mrs. French's daughter at a downtown theater early in December 1946 and, assuming she was destitute, Miss French had invited her home, where she remained until January 7 [609]. On January 20 the *Union* reported that police were questioning a red-headed man in the 'Black Dahlia'[173] slaying case who 'readily admitted' knowing the 22-year-old model but 'stuck to his story' that he had last seen her when he had driven her to Los Angeles a week before she was murdered. That left unexplained the report of two waitresses at a drive-in café at Pacific Highway and Balboa Street in Pacific Beach who were positive they had seen the model with a red-headed man just hours before she was murdered. 'She sat in that chair last Tuesday about 5 p.m. with a red-headed man,' one of the waitresses asserted. 'They sat and drank beer and laughed and talked for about a half-hour and then left' [610]. In the end the authorities were never able to identify a suspect in the Black Dahlia case; the fact that the killer escaped justice combined with a glamorous victim and a lurid crime scene has made this crime notorious, often called Southern California's answer to London's Jack the Ripper.

Bayview Terrace also was the scene of a murder notable for its senselessness and for the extensive legal maneuvering that followed.

---

[173] According to the *Union*, the 'jet-haired' Miss Short was called the Black Dahlia 'because of her fondness for sheer black clothing'.

Elmer Edwin Frazee, a 59-year-old watchman at Bayview Terrace, was shot three times in the head inside the project office on November 24, 1945. William Jerome Phyle, a 32-year-old ex-army paratrooper, was found the next day in Escondido with the victim's missing government truck, and readily admitted killing him and stealing $1.25 from his wallet, saying his only regret was that he didn't empty the whole gun into Frazee. Convicted and sentenced to death, Phyle 'dodged the gas chamber' 11 times over the next six years by claiming insanity, his appeals going all the way to the United States Supreme Court. He was finally executed on February 29, 1952, the *San Diego Union* reporting that he 'walked calmly to the San Quentin gas chamber with a cigaret in his mouth' [611].

The Cyane Navy Housing site in Crown Point survived into the 1960s. The April 2, 1964, *San Diego Union* reported that the Navy would dispose of 264 'substandard family housing units' at Cyane Navy Housing in Pacific Beach. The plan was for the closing to be 'by attrition'; the present occupants would not be moved or evicted but any vacant units would not be reassigned to personnel. The vacancy rate was already almost 50 per cent and once completely vacant the housing would be demolished and the land would be used for other Navy purposes [612]. However, the Navy declared the property surplus and it was taken over by the General Services Administration in 1965, and by 1966 the 66 4-unit buildings had been razed and the site cleaned up [613]. The government traded the majority of the site to a private developer in exchange for property near Moffett Field in the San Francisco Bay area in 1966, and it is now mostly taken up by the Bay Pointe and Avalon Mission Bay apartments. Another portion of the land along Shasta Street was transferred to the school district in 1972 for use as a facility for handicapped children [614] and is now owned by the ARC of San Diego and used to support people with disabilities.

After presiding over the phenomenal growth of Consolidated Aircraft in San Diego and launching production of the B-24 'Liberator', Reuben Fleet sold his interest in the company to Vultee Aircraft at the end of 1941 and retired from management. In 1943 the two companies merged to become Consolidated Vultee Aircraft, or Convair, and in 1954 Convair in turn was acquired by General Dynamics. Following the enormous success of the B-24[174] Convair had limited success after

---

[174] 6724 B-24 bombers were built in San Diego alone from 1940 to 1945; when those built in other facilities across the country are considered the total number of B-24s produced was 18,481.

the war with its huge 10-engine B-36 'Peacemaker' bomber, but increasingly failed to generate successful designs of its own and maintained production by subcontracting for other aircraft companies.

In 1995 General Dynamics announced the closing of its San Diego operation and in 1996 the huge plants between the airport and Pacific Highway that once supported tens of thousands of San Diegans, and nearly all the residents of the Bayview Terrace and Los Altos housing projects in Pacific Beach, were demolished. Today there are virtually no aircraft workers in San Diego and the only physical reminder of Consolidated Aircraft is the former parts plant on the east side of Pacific Highway north of Witherby Street, now occupied by SPAWAR, the Space and Naval Warfare Systems Command.

Downtown San Diego's Gaslamp Quarter, where the streets are lined with buildings from the late nineteenth and early twentieth centuries, is called the 'Historic Heart of San Diego'. An even earlier era is preserved (or restored) in Old Town San Diego State Historic Park. In Pacific Beach there is little to remind one of the past. If Pacific Beach has a historic heart it might be the College Campus, originally set aside for San Diego's first college in 1888 and later home to a military academy which flourished on the site for nearly 50 years. The academy has itself been gone for 50 years and the property is occupied by condominiums and a shopping center, and a small monument noting its history. Another monument, and a city park and elementary school, commemorate Kate Sessions, the renowned horticulturist and Pacific Beach resident from the early years. Across the street from the Kate Sessions monument is the Rose Creek Cottage, a single room from Braemar Manor which was salvaged and moved across town after the Scripps mansion was demolished to make way for a hotel. A few ranch houses still standing among newer homes on city streets mark the locations of the former lemon ranches which once covered parts of Pacific Beach. Other industries and institutions which were important to early-day Pacific Beach, like the railroad, racetrack and asbestos works, have disappeared without a trace. But even in Pacific Beach, where reminders of the past are mostly gone, it has not really been forgotten.

References

[1]   W. E. Smythe, History of San Diego 1542 - 1908, Volume II. The Modern City, San Diego: The History Company, 1908.

[2]   *Articles of Incorporation of the Pacific Beach Company,* 1887.

[3]   *San Diego Union,* July 31, 1887.

[4]   *San Diego Union,* December 4, 1887.

[5]   *San Diego Union,* December 8, 1887.

[6]   *San Diego Union,* December 9, 1887.

[7]   *San Diego Union,* December 13, 1887.

[8]   *San Diego Union,* December 12, 1887.

[9]   *San Diego Union,* December 17, 1887.

[10]   *San Diego Union,* April 30, 1888.

[11]   *Pacific Beach, San Diego, Cal. Subdivided for The Pacific Beach Company by H. K. Wheeler, C. E.,* October 1887.

[12]   *San Diego Union,* February 19, 1888.

[13]   *Price List of San Diego College Lots,* April 26,1888.

[14]   *Monteith's Directory of San Diego and Vicinity for 1889-90,* San Diego: John C. Monteith, 1889-90.

[15]   *San Diego Union,* August 29, 1889.

[16]   *Map 697, Pacific Beach, San Diego, Cal. Subdivided for The Pacific Beach Company, October 1887 by H. K. Wheeler, C. E.,* San Diego, 1892.

[17]   J. R. Thomas, *Letter to Rev. J. W. Whitney,* Escondido, California, February 26, 1892.

[18]   *Directory of San Diego City, Coronado and National City,* San Diego, Calif.: S. H. Olmsted and A. A. Bynon, 1892-93.

[19]   *San Diego City and County Directory,* San Diego, California: The Olmsted Co., Printers, 1895.

[20]   *Map 791, Amended Map of Pacific Beach,* 1894.

[21]   *San Diego County Property Records, Deed Book 255, Page 423,* November 30, 1896.

[22]   *Map 854, Map of Pacific Beach, Subdivided for the Pacific Beach Co., October 1887,* 1898.

[23]   *San Diego County Property Records, Deed Book 280, Page 363,* October 3, 1898.

[24]   *San Diego County Property Records, Deed Book 277, Page 72,* October 3, 1898.

[25]   *San Diego County Property Records, Deed Book 274, Page 494*, October 3, 1898.

[26]   *San Diego County Property Records, Deed Book 275, Page 222*, October 3, 1898.

[27]   *USGS Topographic Map, La Jolla Quadrangle, 1903.*

[28]   M. Wagner, "Harr Wagner: Biographical Notes," *The Western Journal of Education*, vol. XLII, no. 10, pp. 3 - 6, October, 1936.

[29]   *The Golden Era*, March 1887.

[30]   V. Granstaff, *Harr Wagner, California Educational Publicist*, Los Angeles: A dissertation submitted in partial satisfaction of the requirements for the degree Doctor of Education, 1956.

[31]   *The Golden Era*, May 1887.

[32]   *The Golden Era*, June 1887.

[33]   *Articles of Incorporation of the San Diego College Company*, 1887.

[34]   *The Presbyterian Ministerial Directory (Northern)*, 1898.

[35]   J. M. Guinn, A History of California and an Extended History of Its South Coast Counties, Los Angeles, CA: Historic Record Company, 1907.

[36]   *The Golden Era*, November 1887.

[37]   *San Diego Union*, September 4, 1887.

[38]   J. Smith, "Gilded Shams: Observatory on San Miguel Mountain (Part One)," *San Diego Reader*, September 6, 2007.

[39]   *San Diego Union*, October 9, 1887.

[40]   *San Diego County Property Records, Deed Book 141, Page 488*, January 25, 1889.

[41]   *San Diego Union*, January 28, 1888.

[42]   *San Diego Union*, January 29, 1888.

[43]   *San Diego Daily Bee*, January 29, 1888.

[44]   *The Golden Era*, September/October 1888.

[45]   *The Golden Era*, September 1889.

[46]   *San Diego Union*, October 18, 1888.

[47]   *San Diego Union*, October 26, 1888.

[48]   *San Diego Union*, January 4, 1889.

[49]   *First Annual Catalogue of San Diego College of Letters at Pacific Beach, San Diego, Cal*, San Diego, Cal.: A. F. Clark, Printer, Collegiate Year 1888-89.

[50]   *The College Rambler*, June 12, 1889.

[51]   *San Diego County Property Records, Deed Book 129, Page 463*, July 12, 1888.

[52]   *San Diego County Property Records, Deed Book 133, Page 499,*

September 22, 1888.

[53]   *San Diego County Property Records, Deed Book 146, Page 434,* March 25, 1889.

[54]   *San Diego County Property Records, Deed Book 155, Page 42,* September 2, 1889.

[55]   *San Diego Union,* February 5, 1889.

[56]   *San Diego Union,* February 9, 1889.

[57]   *San Diego Union,* February 15, 1889.

[58]   *San Diego Union,* February 16, 1889.

[59]   *San Diego Union,* February 23, 1889.

[60]   *San Diego Union,* February 24, 1889.

[61]   *San Diego Union,* March 3, 1889.

[62]   *San Diego Union,* April 9, 1889.

[63]   *San Diego Union,* April 28, 1889.

[64]   *San Diego Union,* May 7, 1889.

[65]   *In the Superior Court of the County of San Diego Cecil S. Sprecher vs Eunice S. Sprecher, Case No. 4965,* June 23, 1890.

[66]   *Testimony taken by Court Commissioner in the case of C. S. Sprecher, Plaintiff, vs. Eunice Sprecher, Defendent,* San Diego, California, December 1, 1890.

[67]   *San Diego Union,* December 3, 1890.

[68]   *San Diego Union,* June 19, 1889.

[69]   *San Diego Union,* June 20, 1889.

[70]   *The Golden Era,* June 1889.

[71]   *San Diego Union,* June 21, 1889.

[72]   *The Golden Era,* September 1889.

[73]   *San Diego Union,* August 25, 1889.

[74]   *San Diego Union,* September13, 1889.

[75]   *San Diego Union,* January 5, 1890.

[76]   *San Diego Union,* January 10, 1890.

[77]   *San Diego Union,* January 17, 1890.

[78]   *San Diego Union,* June 18, 1890.

[79]   *San Diego Union,* June 20, 1890.

[80]   *The Golden Era,* July 1890.

[81]   *San Diego Union,* July 13, 1890.

[82]   *The Great Southwest,* July 1890.

[83]   *The West American Scientist,* August 1890.

[84]   *The West American Scientist,* September 1890.

[85]   *The West American Scientist,* December 1890.

[86]   *San Diego Union,* October 31, 1890.

[87]   *San Diego Union,* November 16, 1890.

[88]   *San Diego Union,* December 21, 1890.

[89]   *San Diego Union,* January 4, 1891.

[90]   *San Diego Union,* March 5, 1891.

[91]   *San Diego Union,* May 29, 1891.

[92]   *San Diego Union,* July 15, 1891.

[93]   *San Diego Union,* July 23, 1891.

[94]   *San Diego Union,* August 18, 1891.

[95]   *San Diego County Property Records, Deed Book 202, Page 331,* July 23, 1892.

[96]   *In the Superior Court of the County of San Diego, In the Matter of The San Diego College Company, an Insolvent Debtor,* October 19, 1891.

[97]   *San Diego Union,* October 20, 1891.

[98]   *San Diego County Property Records, Deed Book 219, Page 147,* November 24, 1894.

[99]   *San Diego County Property Records, Deed Book 219, Page 143,* November 24, 1894.

[100]   *Supreme Court of California, Thomas et al vs San Diego College Co et al, No. 19,560,* February 25, 1896.

[101]   *San Diego Union,* April 29, 1896.

[102]   *Evening Tribune,* December 23, 1896.

[103]   *Evening Tribune,* June 4, 1897.

[104]   *San Diego Union,* March 2, 1898.

[105]   *San Diego County Property Records, Deed Book 271, Page 1,* March 15, 1898.

[106]   *San Diego Union,* July 10, 1898.

[107]   *San Diego Union,* July 17, 1898.

[108]   *San Diego Union,* October 21, 1898.

[109]   *San Diego County Property Records, Deed Book 390, Page 38,* April 13, 1905.

[110]   *San Diego Union,* May 14, 1899.

[111]   *San Diego Union,* June 27, 1899.

[112]   *San Diego Union,* August 13, 1899.

[113]   *San Diego City Directory,* San Diego, Cal.: San Diego Directory Co., 1901.

[114]   *Evening Tribune,* March 8, 1901.

[115]   *San Diego Union,* August 6, 1901.

[116]   *Evening Tribune*, March 14, 1903.

[117]   *Evening Tribune*, March 16, 1903.

[118]   *San Diego Union*, January 9, 1904.

[119]   *Evening Tribune*, January 5, 1904.

[120]   *San Diego Union*, November 5, 1903.

[121]   *San Diego Union*, April 13, 1904.

[122]   *Evening Tribune*, July 6, 1904.

[123]   *San Diego Union*, May 4, 1905.

[124]   *San Diego Union*, May 4, 1906.

[125]   *San Diego Union*, July 19, 1907.

[126]   *San Diego Union*, August 20, 1958.

[127]   Presbyterian Ministerial Directory (Northern), 1898.

[128]   R. Held, "A Momentous 100 Years - The Story of San Diego High School," *The Journal of San Diego History*, vol. 28, no. 2, 1982.

[129]   P. G. Bell, A Portraiture of the Life of Samuel Sprecher, D.D., LL.D, Philadelphia, PA: Lutheran Publication Society, 1907.

[130]   *San Diego Union*, July 4, 1895.

[131]   *Los Angeles Herald*, June 25, 1893.

[132]   *San Diego Union*, November 9, 1897.

[133]   *San Francisco Call*, August 11, 1897.

[134]   D. Tripi, "Join the LJES PTO," Garth Conboy, August 2008. [Online]. Available: http://www2.sandi.net/ljes/Handbook2009.pdf. [Accessed 20 July 2012].

[135]   *San Diego Union*, March 30, 1899.

[136]   *Pacific Education Journal*, Oakland: Department of Public Instruction, 1892.

[137]   *San Diego Union*, July 16, 1894.

[138]   *Southern California Practitioner*, June 1898.

[139]   *Victoria Daily Colonist*, March 1, 1898.

[140]   *San Francisco Call*, California Digital Newspaper Collection, Center for Bibliographic Studies and Research, University, March 7, 1898.

[141]   J. B. Clapp and E. F. Edgett, Plays of the Present, New York: The Dunlap Society, 1902.

[142]   *Articles of Incorporation of the San Diego and Old Town Street Railroad Company*, 1886.

[143]   R. P. Middlebrook, "High Iron to La Jolla," *The Journal of San Diego History*, vol. 7, no. 1, January 1961.

[144]   K. F. Schumacher, "La Jolla Zephyr," *Dispatcher - Railway Historical Society of San Diego, Calif.*, 30 September 1962.

---

[145]   *San Diego Union,* December 3, 1887.

[146]   *Articles of Incorporation of the San Diego and Pacific Beach Railway Company,* 1887.

[147]   *San Diego Union,* September 27, 1887.

[148]   *San Diego Union,* December 11, 1887.

[149]   *San Diego Union,* January 8, 1888.

[150]   *San Diego Union,* February 19, 1888.

[151]   *San Diego Union,* March 3, 1888.

[152]   *San Diego Union,* April 6, 1888.

[153]   *San Diego Union,* April 17, 1888.

[154]   *San Diego Union,* April 19, 1888.

[155]   *San Diego Union,* April 25, 1888.

[156]   *San Diego Union,* April 29, 1888.

[157]   R. V. Dodge, "La Jolla Lines Roster," *Dispatcher - Railway Historical Society of San Diego, Calif.,* 30 September 1962.

[158]   *San Diego Union,* April 21, 1888.

[159]   *San Diego Union,* June 13, 1888.

[160]   *San Diego Union,* June 24, 1888.

[161]   *San Diego Union,* July 8, 1888.

[162]   *San Diego Union,* July 14, 1888.

[163]   *San Diego Union,* May 6, 1888.

[164]   *San Diego Union,* July 14, 1888.

[165]   *San Diego Union,* September 27, 1891.

[166]   *San Diego Union,* July 17, 1892.

[167]   *San Diego Union,* July 19, 1892.

[168]   *San Diego Union,* July 20, 1892.

[169]   *San Diego Union,* February 16, 1889.

[170]   *San Diego Union,* October 18, 1893.

[171]   *San Diego Union,* December 14, 1893.

[172]   *San Diego Union,* December 19, 1893.

[173]   *San Diego Union,* March 8, 1894.

[174]   *San Diego Union,* March 13, 1894.

[175]   *San Diego Union,* March 22, 1894.

[176]   *San Diego Union,* March 27, 1894.

[177]   *San Diego Union,* April 2, 1894.

[178]   *San Diego Union,* May 14, 1894.

[179]   *San Diego Union,* May 16, 1894.

[180]   H. S. F. Randolph, La Jolla Year by Year, La Jolla, California, 1955.

[181]   *San Diego Union,* June 15, 1894.

[182]   *San Diego Union,* February 4, 1897.

[183]   *San Diego Union,* December 22, 1898.

[184]   R. V. Dodge, Rails of the Silver Gate, San Marino, California: Golden West Books, 1960.

[185]   *San Diego Union,* March 30, 1906.

[186]   *San Diego Union,* January 7, 1907.

[187]   *San Diego Union,* January 13, 1907.

[188]   *San Diego Union,* November 17, 1919.

[189]   *San Diego Union,* December 17, 1889.

[190]   *San Francisco Chronicle,* December 18, 1889.

[191]   *San Diego Union,* December 25, 1889.

[192]   *San Diego Union,* February 24, 1891.

[193]   *San Diego Union,* February 26, 1891.

[194]   *San Diego Union,* January 17, 1895.

[195]   *San Diego Union,* January 17, 1908.

[196]   *San Diego Union,* July 1, 1917.

[197]   *Articles of Incorporation for the Southern California Breeders Association,* July 6, 1887.

[198]   *San Diego Union,* July 20, 1887.

[199]   *San Diego Union,* July 31, 1887.

[200]   *San Diego Union,* August 4, 1887.

[201]   *San Diego Union,* September 11, 1887.

[202]   *San Diego Union,* October 16, 1887.

[203]   *San Diego Union,* November 10, 1887.

[204]   *San Diego Union,* November 15, 1887.

[205]   *San Diego Union,* November 16, 1887.

[206]   *San Diego Union,* April 3, 1888.

[207]   *San Diego Union,* April 11, 1888.

[208]   *San Diego Union,* April 22, 1888.

[209]   *San Diego Union,* May 2, 1888.

[210]   *San Diego Union,* May 3, 1888.

[211]   *San Diego Union,* May 4, 1888.

[212]   *San Diego Union,* July 1, 1888.

[213]   *San Diego Union,* September 11, 1888.

[214]   *San Diego Union,* July 30, 1888.

[215]   *San Diego Union,* October 7, 1888.

[216]   *San Diego Union,* October 21, 1888.

[217]   *San Diego Union,* October 27, 1888.

[218]   *San Diego Union,* October 28, 1888.

[219]   *San Diego Union,* October 30, 1888.

[220]   *San Diego Union,* November 11, 1888.

[221]   *San Diego Union,* November 13, 1888.

[222]   *San Diego Union,* November 23, 1888.

[223]   *San Diego Union,* December 20, 1888.

[224]   *San Diego Union,* December 25, 1888.

[225]   *San Diego Union,* December 27, 1888.

[226]   *San Diego Union,* December 29, 1888.

[227]   *San Diego Union,* March 3, 1889.

[228]   *San Diego Union,* April 14, 1889.

[229]   *San Diego Union,* June 20, 1889.

[230]   *San Diego Union,* December 17, 1889.

[231]   *San Diego Union,* October 25, 1890.

[232]   *San Diego Union,* October 30, 1890.

[233]   *San Diego Union,* November 27, 1891.

[234]   *San Diego Union,* December 17, 1891.

[235]   *San Diego Union,* December 20, 1891.

[236]   *San Diego Union,* December 23, 1891.

[237]   *In the Superior Court of the County of San Diego Kate T. Cobb v. Southern California Breeders Association,* 1890.

[238]   *Alfred R. Schulenburg vs S. D., O.T. & P.B. Railroad Co., Deposition of E. W. Britt,* September, 1895.

[239]   *In the Superior Court of the County of San Diego Albert R. Schulenburg vs San Diego, Old Town & Pacific Beach Railroad Co.,* March 14,1895.

[240]   *In the Superior Court of the County of San Diego Albert R. Schulenburg vs San Diego, Old Town & Pacific Beach Railroad Co. No. 8676,* March 27, 1895.

[241]   *San Diego Union,* October 30, 1896.

[242]   *San Diego Union,* May 29, 1897.

[243]   *Evening Tribune,* January 29, 1898.

[244]   *San Diego Union,* September 18, 1898.

[245]   *San Diego Union,* November 22, 1898.

[246]   *San Diego Union,* November 26, 1898.

[247]   *San Diego Union,* June 20, 1899.

[248]   *San Diego Union,* July 1, 1899.

[249]   *San Diego Union,* May 10, 1903.

[250]   *San Diego Union,* June 19, 1903.

[251]   *Articles of Incorporation, Belmont Breeders Association,* June 30, 1903.

[252]   *San Diego Union,* July 1, 1903.

[253]   *San Diego Union,* July 23, 1903.

[254]   *San Diego Union,* September 2, 1903.

[255]   *Evening Tribune,* September 18, 1903.

[256]   *San Diego Union,* September 19, 1903.

[257]   *Articles of Incorporation, American Saddle-Horse Breeding Farm,* September 21, 1903.

[258]   *San Francisco Daily Call,* June 4, 1904.

[259]   *San Diego County Property Records, Deed Book 354, Page 420,* November 2, 1904.

[260]   *San Diego Union,* June 17, 1905.

[261]   *Evening Tribune,* September 27, 1905.

[262]   *San Diego Union,* March 10, 1906.

[263]   *San Diego Union,* October 20, 1906.

[264]   *Articles of Incorporation, Mission Bay Park Company,* November 8, 1906.

[265]   *San Diego Union,* November 22, 1906.

[266]   *San Diego County Property Records, Deed Book 420, Page 128,* November 5, 1907.

[267]   *Articles of Incorporation of Ye Olde Mission Inn Company,* 1907.

[268]   *San Diego Union,* February 3, 1908.

[269]   *Evening Tribune,* November 27, 1908.

[270]   *San Diego Union,* November 28, 1908.

[271]   *San Diego County Property Records, Deed Book 453, Page 69,* November 30, 1908.

[272]   *San Diego County Property Records, Deed Book 461, Page 260,* November 30, 1908.

[273]   *Evening Tribune,* July 22, 1910.

[274]   *San Diego Union,* October 18, 1910.

[275]   *San Diego County Property Records, Deed Book 607, Page 167,* April 29, 1913.

[276]   *San Diego Sun,* February 2, 1931.

[277]   *San Diego County Property Records, Deed Book 146, Page 85,* September 24, 1888.

[278]   *San Diego Union,* September 29, 1888.

[279]   *San Diego Union,* October 17, 1888.

[280]   *San Diego Union,* January 19, 1889.

[281]   *San Diego Union,* April 18, 1889.

[282]   *San Diego Union,* July 20, 1889.

[283]   *San Diego Union,* January 5, 1890.

[284]   *San Diego Union,* May 28, 1890.

[285]   *San Diego Union,* May 30, 1890.

[286]   *San Diego Union,* June 18, 1890.

[287]   *San Diego Union,* July 6, 1890.

[288]   *Articles of Incorporation of the John D. Hoff Asbestos Company,* 1890.

[289]   *The Golden Era,* April/May 1890.

[290]   *The Golden Era,* June 1890.

[291]   *The Golden Era,* November/December 1890.

[292]   *The Golden Era,* December 1890.

[293]   S. H. Adams, The Great American Fraud, Chicago: P. F. Collier & Son, 1905.

[294]   *San Diego County Property Records, Deed Book 203, Page 229,* July 16, 1892.

[295]   *San Diego County Property Records, Deed Book 203, Page 447,* August 29, 1892.

[296]   *Directory of San Diego City and County,* San Diego: John Thom, 1893-94.

[297]   *San Diego County Property Records, Deed Book 203, Page 228,* July 15, 1892.

[298]   *San Diego County Property Records, Deed Book 203, Page 286,* March 31, 1892.

[299]   *San Diego County Property Records, Deed Book 203, Page 234,* March 28, 1892.

[300]   *San Diego County Property Records, Deed Book 143, Page 299,* February 26, 1889.

[301]   *San Diego Union,* March 13, 1956.

[302]   *San Diego Union,* February 16, 1954.

[303]   *San Diego Union,* March 2, 1892.

[304]   *San Diego Union,* March 27, 1892.

[305]   *San Diego Union,* April 21, 1892.

[306]   *San Diego Union,* July 31, 1892.

[307]   *San Diego Union,* January 1, 1894.

[308]   *San Diego Union,* January 1, 1895.

[309]   *San Diego Union,* December 13, 1895.

[310]   *San Diego County Property Records, Deed Book 243, Page 211,* Sepetember 20, 1895.

[311]   *San Diego County Property Records, Deed Book 243, Page 321,* October

19, 1895.

[312]   *San Diego County Property Records, Deed Book 243, Page 459,* November 20, 1895.

[313]   *San Diego Union,* January 1, 1896.

[314]   *The San Diego Weekly Union,* May 21, 1896.

[315]   *San Diego Union,* May 26, 1896.

[316]   *San Diego Union,* June 20, 1896.

[317]   *San Diego Union,* July 11, 1896.

[318]   *San Diego Union,* January 12, 1897.

[319]   *San Diego Union,* April 7, 1897.

[320]   *San Diego Union,* July 19, 1897.

[321]   *San Diego Union,* August 4, 1897.

[322]   *San Diego Union,* September 8, 1897.

[323]   *San Diego Union,* October 18, 1897.

[324]   *San Diego County Property Records, Deed Book 228, Page 426,* February 28, 1894.

[325]   *San Diego Union,* November 12, 1897.

[326]   *San Diego Union,* December 8, 1897.

[327]   *San Diego Union,* December 15, 1897.

[328]   *San Diego Union,* February 13, 1898.

[329]   *San Diego Union,* August 4, 1897.

[330]   *San Diego Union,* February 24, 1898.

[331]   *San Diego Union,* July 18, 1898.

[332]   *San Diego Union,* August 6, 1898.

[333]   *San Diego Union,* August 8, 1898.

[334]   *San Diego Union,* August 14, 1898.

[335]   *San Diego Union,* October 27, 1898.

[336]   *San Diego Union,* December 19, 1898.

[337]   *San Diego Union,* February 6, 1899.

[338]   *The San Diego Weekly Union,* May 18, 1899.

[339]   *San Diego Union,* June 26, 1899.

[340]   *San Diego Union,* October 8, 1899.

[341]   *San Diego Union,* January 1, 1900.

[342]   *San Diego Union,* January 18, 1900.

[343]   *Evening Tribune,* March 8, 1900.

[344]   *Evening Tribune,* April 11, 1900.

[345]   *Evening Tribune,* June 13, 1900.

[346]   *San Diego Union,* July 31, 1900.

[347]   *Evening Tribune,* January 29, 1901.

[348]   *San Diego Union,* April 3, 1901.

[349]   *Evening Tribune,* April 12, 1901.

[350]   *Evening Tribune,* April 23, 1901.

[351]   *Evening Tribune,* June 17, 1901.

[352]   *San Diego Union,* July 18, 1901.

[353]   *San Diego Union,* August 21, 1901.

[354]   *San Diego Union,* October 14, 1901.

[355]   *San Diego Union,* December 1, 1901.

[356]   *Evening Tribune,* April 19, 1902.

[357]   *San Diego Union,* July 11, 1902.

[358]   *Evening Tribune,* July 15, 1902.

[359]   *San Diego Union,* November 4, 1902.

[360]   *Evening Tribune,* November 8, 1902.

[361]   *San Diego Union,* January 10, 1903.

[362]   *San Diego Union,* April 30, 1903.

[363]   *Evening Tribune,* April 30, 1903.

[364]   *Evening Tribune,* May 20, 1903.

[365]   *Evening Tribune,* July 7, 1903.

[366]   *San Diego Union,* August 15, 1903.

[367]   *Evening Tribune,* April 27, 1904.

[368]   *San Diego County Property Records, Deed Book 345, Page 356,* May 31, 1904.

[369]   *Evening Tribune,* April 13, 1904.

[370]   *San Diego Union,* April 12, 1906.

[371]   *San Diego Union,* January 8, 1907.

[372]   *San Diego Union,* January 20, 1907.

[373]   *San Diego County Property Records, Deed Book 337, Page 140,* November 3, 1903.

[374]   *The San Diego Weekly Union,* February 14, 1907.

[375]   *San Diego County Property Records, Deed Book 224, Page 283,* May 8, 1893.

[376]   *Interview with George Waddell Brooks, September 7, 1961,* San Diego History Center.

[377]   *Map 1045, Map of Blocks 53 and 66 Being a Sub-division of Lot 20, Pacific Beach, San Diego, Cal.,* December 1906.

[378]   *San Diego County Property Records, Deed Book 424, Page 215,* September 23, 1907.

[379]   *San Diego Weekly Union,* October 3, 1907.

[380]   *San Diego Union,* February 10, 1908.

[381]   *Map 1099, Map of Blocks 90 and 105 Being a Sub-division of Lot 34, Pacific Beach, San Diego, Cal,* October 1907.

[382]   *Map 1873, Kendrick's Addition to San Diego Beach, A Sudivision of Acre Lot 47 Pacific Beach (Map 854) except the easterly 80 feet thereof.,* December 1925.

[383]   *Map 1917, Pacific Pines, Being a Subdivision of Acre Lots 61 and 62 of Pacific Beach,* May 1926.

[384]   *Map 1933, Map of C. M. Doty's Addition, Being a Subdivision of Lot 19 of Pacific Beach,* June 1926.

[385]   *Map 2430, Lamont Terrace, Being a subdivision of a portion of Acre Lot 33 of Pacific Beach,* September 1947.

[386]   *Map 2386, Chalcedony Terrace, Being a subdivision of portions of Acre Lot 36 of Pacific Beach,* February 1947.

[387]   *Map 2439, Chalcedony Terrace Addition, Being a subdivision of portions of Acre Lot 36 of Pacific Beach,* October 1947.

[388]   M. McClain, "The Scripps Family's San Diego Experiment," *The Journal of San Diego History,* vol. 56, no. 1-2, 2010.

[389]   *San Diego County Property Records, Deed Book 172, Page 352,* January 17, 1891.

[390]   *San Diego County Property Records, Deed Book 173, Page 479,* January 22, 1891.

[391]   *San Diego County Property Records, Deed Book 175, Page 102,* January 31, 1891.

[392]   *San Diego County Property Records, Deed Book 211, Page 79,* December 2, 1890.

[393]   *San Diego Union,* January 7, 1891.

[394]   *Evening Tribune,* December 6, 1938.

[395]   *San Diego County Property Records, Deed Book 169, Page 493,* October 30, 1890.

[396]   *San Diego County Property Records, Deed Book 194, Page 421,* October 28, 1891.

[397]   *Marriage License and Certificate, San Diego County, California; F. T. Scripps and Emma Jessop,* December 23, 1893.

[398]   *San Diego County Property Records, Deed Book 250, Page 432,* April 29, 1896.

[399]   *San Diego County Property Records, Deed Book 52, Page 118,* November 3, 1885.

[400]   *San Diego County Property Records, Deed Book 97, Page 83,* August 6, 1887.

[401]   *San Diego County Property Records, Deed Book 284, Page 265,* December 29, 1899.

[402]   *San Diego County Property Records, Deed Book 292, Page 467,* August 3, 1900.

[403]   *San Diegan - Sun,* October 5, 1900.

[404]   *Evening Tribune,* November 21, 1900.

[405]   *San Diego Union,* April 27, 1905.

[406]   S. E. J. Scripps, "Walks in My Garden," *The California Garden,* vol. 1, no. 4, 1909.

[407]   *San Diego County Property Records, Deed Book 324, Page 484,* June 16, 1903.

[408]   *Map 898, Map of Ocean Front, a subdivision of Lots 43 and 44 Pacific Beach,* June 1903.

[409]   *San Diego County Property Records, Deed Book 336, Page 76,* November 19, 1903.

[410]   *San Diego County Property Records, Deed Book 337, Page 384,* January 4, 1904.

[411]   *San Diego County Property Records, Deed Book 340 Page 359,* April 6, 1904.

[412]   *San Diego County Property Records, Deed Book 341, Page 128,* February 4, 1904.

[413]   *Map 1098, Map of Braemar, Being a Sub-division of acre Lots 69 and 70, all of Block 387 excepting Lots 33 and 34, Pacific Beach, a re-subdivision of a portion of Broulett's Addition, in Pueblo Lot 1793; also a portion of Lot 71, Pacific Beach, and PL 1803,* October 1907.

[414]   *San Diego Union,* October 4, 1907.

[415]   *Evening Tribune,* June 22, 1903.

[416]   *Evening Tribune,* April 27, 1904.

[417]   *Evening Tribune,* February 13, 1904.

[418]   *Evening Tribune,* June 6, 1906.

[419]   *San Diego Union,* August 20, 1906.

[420]   *San Diego Union,* October 19, 1906.

[421]   *San Diego Union,* January 20, 1907.

[422]   *The California Garden,* August 1910.

[423]   *San Diego Weekly Union,* August 18, 1910.

[424]   *The California Garden,* September 1914.

[425]   *San Diego Union,* July 30, 1911.

[426]   *San Diego Union,* December 2, 1911.

[427]   *San Diego Union,* December 22, 1912.

[428]   *Evening Tribune,* May 30, 1913.

[429]   *Evening Tribune,* October 17, 1921.

[430]   *Evening Tribune,* July 21, 1923.

[431]   *Evening Tribune,* April 28, 1925.

[432]   *Evening Tribune,* March 31, 1926.

[433]   *Common Council Book 51 of Resolutions, Page 369,* May 3, 1926.

[434]   *Map 1927, Map of Braemar Extension,* June, 1926.

[435]   *San Diego County Property Records, Deed Book 1237, Page 41,* June 12, 1926.

[436]   *San Diego Union,* July 18, 1926.

[437]   *Braemar, A setting of enduring charm for your permanent home,* Barney & Rife, Selling Agents, 1926.

[438]   *San Diego County Property Records, Deed Book 1297, Page 445,* January 10, 1927.

[439]   *San Diego Union,* October 17, 1926.

[440]   *Evening Tribune,* November 6, 1926.

[441]   *San Diego Union,* October 25, 1926.

[442]   M. McClain, "ZLAC Rowing Club, 1892-2007," *The Journal of San Diego History,* vol. 53, no. 3, 2007.

[443]   *San Diego Union,* June 24, 1926.

[444]   *San Diego Union,* September 20, 1942.

[445]   *Evening Tribune,* May 26, 1928.

[446]   *San Diego Union,* April 28, 1929.

[447]   *Evening Tribune,* May 2, 1931.

[448]   *Evening Tribune,* May 22, 1931.

[449]   *Evening Tribune,* May 9, 1931.

[450]   *San Diego Union,* October 28, 1934.

[451]   *Evening Tribune,* May 20, 1933.

[452]   *San Diego Union,* May 19, 1935.

[453]   *San Diego Union,* September 28, 1935.

[454]   *Evening Tribune,* January 2, 1936.

[455]   *San Diego Union,* July 29, 1936.

[456]   *San Diego Union,* June 3, 1937.

[457]   *San Diego Union,* May 31, 1959.

[458]   *San Diego Union,* January 26, 1960.

[459]   *Evening Tribune,* October 29, 1986.

[460]   *San Diego Union,* August 25, 1976.

[461]   *San Diego Union,* August 22, 1926.

[462]   *San Diego Union,* February 23, 1909.

[463]   *Interview with Col. Thomas A. Davis, July 19, 1957,* San Diego History Center.

[464]   *Evening Tribune,* November 22, 1910.

[465]   *San Diego Union,* November 24, 1910.

[466]   *San Diego Union,* January 22, 1911.

[467]   *San Diego Union,* June 18, 1911.

[468]   *Evening Tribune,* August 17, 1911.

[469]   *San Diego Union,* July 30, 1911.

[470]   *San Diego Union,* September 2, 1911.

[471]   *San Diego Union,* August 18, 1912.

[472]   *San Diego Union,* March 12, 1916.

[473]   *San Diego Union,* January 1, 1917.

[474]   *San Diego Union,* December 14, 1917.

[475]   *Evening Tribune,* January 14, 1920.

[476]   *San Diego Union,* February 1, 1921.

[477]   *San Diego Union,* February 15, 1921.

[478]   *San Diego Union,* June 10, 1921.

[479]   *San Diego County Property Records, Deed Book 962, Page 412,* October 24, 1923.

[480]   *San Diego Union,* August 5, 1921.

[481]   *San Diego Union,* November 25, 1924.

[482]   *San Diego Union,* October 24, 1925.

[483]   *San Diego Union,* September 11, 1926.

[484]   *San Diego Union,* November 13, 1926.

[485]   *San Diego Union,* January 1, 1927.

[486]   *San Diego Union,* November 9, 1927.

[487]   *San Diego Union,* August 5, 1928.

[488]   *Evening Tribune,* August 27, 1928.

[489]   *San Diego Union,* November 25, 1928.

[490]   *San Diego Union,* May 29, 1929.

[491]   *Evening Tribune,* May 21, 1958.

[492]   *Evening Tribune,* August 27, 1929.

[493]   *San Diego Union,* September 19, 1929.

[494]   *Evening Tribune,* January 1, 1930.

[495]   *San Diego Union,* January 12, 1930.

[496]   *San Diego Union,* January 16, 1930.

[497]   *Evening Tribune,* May 13, 1930.

[498]   *San Diego Union,* June 15, 1930.

[499]   *Evening Tribune,* November 22, 1930.

[500]   *San Diego Union,* January 1, 1931.

[501]   *San Diego Union,* November 23, 1931.

[502]   *Evening Tribune,* June 20, 1932.

[503]   *San Diego Union,* January 6, 1933.

[504]   "Army and Navy Academy History and Traditions," [Online]. Available: http://www.armyandnavyacademy.org/about-ana-military-academy/school-history-traditions. [Accessed 2012].

[505]   *San Diego County Property Records, Deed Book 1770, Page 461,* June 11, 1930.

[506]   *San Diego County Property Records, Deed Book 1821, Page 402,* November 15, 1930.

[507]   *San Diego County Official Records, Book 6, Page 193,* June 18, 1931.

[508]   *San Diego County Official Records, Book 405, Page 175,* August 23, 1932.

[509]   *San Diego Union,* November 24, 1935.

[510]   *The Cadet,* Pacific Beach, California: San Diego Army and Navy Academy, 1936.

[511]   *San Diego County Official Records, Book 480, Page 321,* March 18, 1936.

[512]   *San Diego Union,* August 2, 1936.

[513]   *San Diego Union,* August 8, 1936.

[514]   *San Diego Union,* August 14, 1936.

[515]   *San Diego Union,* March 16,1937.

[516]   *Evening Tribune,* April 5, 1937.

[517]   *San Diego Union,* April 3, 1937.

[518]   *San Diego Union,* August 29, 1937.

[519]   *San Diego Union,* June 6, 1937.

[520]   *San Diego Union,* January 1, 1938.

[521]   *San Diego Union,* December 18, 1938.

[522]   *San Diego Union,* March 31, 1939.

[523]   *San Diego Union,* February 9, 1958.

[524]   *Evening Tribune,* June 11, 1958.

[525]   *San Diego Union,* May 17, 1960.

[526]   *Evening Tribune,* July 2, 1963.

[527]   *San Diego Union,* February 5, 1964.

[528]   E. C. MacPhail, *Kate Sessions Pioneer Horticulturist,* San Diego: San Diego Historical Society, 1976.

[529]   *San Diego Union,* January 15, 1884.

[530]   *Maxwell's Directory of San Diego City and County,* San Diego, Cal.: Geo. W. Maxwell, 1887.

[531]   *San Diego Union,* October 12, 1887.

[532]   *San Diego Union,* March 15, 1888.

[533]   *San Diego Common Council, Book 20 of Resolutions, Page 435,* February 9, 1892.

[534]   *Dana Burks' San Diego City and County Directory,* San Diego, Cal.: San Diego Directory Co., 1905.

[535]   *San Diego County Property Records, Deed Book 581, Page 375,* November 1, 1912.

[536]   *San Diego County Property Records, Deed Book 569, Page 139,* July 29, 1912.

[537]   *Common Council Book 20 of Resolutions, Page 26,* December 2, 1912.

[538]   *San Diego Union,* December 8, 1912.

[539]   *Common Council Book 20 of Resolutions, Page 205,* January 15, 1913.

[540]   *San Diego Union,* April 25, 1915.

[541]   *Map 1618, Soledad Terrace,* September 11, 1913.

[542]   *Evening Tribune,* November 30, 1914.

[543]   *San Diego Union,* April 19, 1915.

[544]   *Evening Tribune,* September 6, 1913.

[545]   *Evening Tribune,* April 10, 1916.

[546]   *San Diego Union,* April 14, 1916.

[547]   *Evening Tribune,* April 23, 1917.

[548]   *San Diego County Official Records, Book 754, Page 450,* April 3, 1918.

[549]   *San Diego County Property Records, Deed Book 919, Page 288,* December 4, 1922.

[550]   *San Diego County Property Records, Deed Book 982, Page 142,* March 28, 1924.

[551]   *San Diego County Property Records, Deed Book 982, Page 141,* March 28, 1924.

[552]   *San Diego County Property Records, Deed Book 1899, Page 187,* February 19, 1925.

[553]   *San Diego Union,* March 10, 1927.

[554]   *San Diego Union,* August 16, 1932.

[555]   *San Diego Union,* August 15, 1933.

[556]   *San Diego Union,* May 15, 1934.

[557]   *San Diego Union,* August 8, 1937.

[558]   *Evening Tribune,* October 26, 1934.

[559]   *San Diego Union,* August 3, 1926.

[560]   *San Diego Union,* May 31, 1936.

[561]   *San Diego Union,* May 16, 1937.

[562]   *San Diego Union,* October 17, 1937.

[563]   *San Diego Union,* November 9, 1937.

[564]   *San Diego Union,* January 18, 1942.

[565]   *San Diego County Property Records, Deed Book 1233, Page 170,* August 26, 1941.

[566]   *San Diego Union,* June 24, 1941.

[567]   *San Diego Union,* July 7, 1961.

[568]   *San Diego Union,* August 5, 1948.

[569]   *The Sentinel,* September 5, 1956.

[570]   W. Wagner, Reuben Fleet and The Story of Consolidated Aircraft, Fallbrook, California: Aero Publishers, 1976.

[571]   *San Diego Union,* February 13, 1944.

[572]   *San Diego County Official Records, Book 1233, Page 170,* August 27, 1941.

[573]   *San Diego Union,* August 24, 1941.

[574]   *San Diego Union,* December 21, 1941.

[575]   *San Diego Union,* January 2, 1942.

[576]   *San Diego Union,* January 25, 1942.

[577]   *San Diego Union,* February 10, 1942.

[578]   *San Diego Union,* April 15, 1942.

[579]   *San Diego Union,* May 10, 1942.

[580]   *San Diego County Official Records, Book 1381, Page 1,* July 11, 1942.

[581]   *San Diego Union,* March 27, 1943.

[582]   *San Diego Union,* May 5, 1943.

[583]   *San Diego Union,* August 22, 1943.

[584]   *San Diego County Official Records, Book 1781, Page 250,* November 30, 1944.

[585]   *San Diego Union,* December 22, 1944.

[586]   *San Diego County Official Records, Book 1856, Page 248,* April 7, 1945.

[587]   *San Diego Union,* April 28, 1945.

[588]   *San Diego Union,* December 13, 1947.

[589]   *San Diego Union,* July 2, 1948.

[590]   *San Diego Union,* December 31, 1951.

[591]   *San Diego Union,* January 19, 1952.

[592]   *San Diego Union,* April 21, 1946.

[593]   *San Diego Union,* July 17, 1946.

[594]   *San Diego Union,* January 6, 1948.

[595]   *San Diego Union,* October 22, 1952.

[596]   *San Diego Union,* September 13, 1953.

[597]   *San Diego Union,* July 31, 1955.

[598]   *San Diego Union,* August 27, 1955.

[599]   *San Diego Union,* October 8, 1955.

[600]   *San Diego Union,* February 2, 1956.

[601]   *San Diego Union,* March 6, 1956.

[602]   *San Diego Union,* June 17, 1956.

[603]   *San Diego Union,* June 26, 1956.

[604]   *San Diego Union,* July 15, 1956.

[605]   *San Diego Union,* November 14, 1956.

[606]   *San Diego Union,* July 26, 1959.

[607]   *San Diego Union,* August 14, 1957.

[608]   *San Diego Union,* November 11, 1958.

[609]   *San Diego Union,* January 17, 1947.

[610]   *San Diego Union,* January 20, 1947.

[611]   *San Diego Union,* March 1, 1952.

[612]   *San Diego Union,* April 2, 1964.

[613]   *San Diego Union,* June 22, 1966.

[614]   *San Diego Union,* January 31, 1972.

[615]   E. S. Robinson, *The Presbyterian Ministerial Directory,* Oxford, Ohio: The Ministerial Directory Company, 1898.

[616]   *San Diego Union,* September 3, 1888.

[617]   *Evening Tribune,* September 16, 1908.

[618]   *Evening Tribune,* December 31, 1912.

[619]   *In the Superior Court of the County of San Diego Jane P. Rowe vs A. G. Gassen and the City of San Diego, California.*

[620]   *San Diego County Property Records, Deed Book 1169, Page 275,* November 9, 1925.

[621]   *San Diego Common Council, Book 45 of Resolutions, Page 6, Resolution Ordering Work No. 36444,* January 11, 1926.

[622]   *San Diego Common Council, Book 56 of Resolutions, Page 342, Resolution Ordering Work No. 56561,* June 8, 1931.

[623]   *North Shores Sentinel,* July 9, 1958.

[624]   *Letter from Thomas A. Davis, President, B.M.A. to Mrs. Edith Steele,* In the files of the San Diego History Center, February 1, 1941.

[625]   *Pacific Beach Presyterian Church Web Site (http://www.pbpres.org/history.html).*

[626]   *United States Census, Enumeration District 37-50, Supervisor's District 21, Sheet No. 8B,* San Diego, California, 1930.

[627]   *San Diego County Property Records, Deed Book 736, Page 100,* April 28,

1917.

[628]   *In the Superior Court of the County of San Diego, In the matter of the application of Folsom Bros. Company, a corporation, for a change of its corporate name.,* January 27, 1911.

[629]   *San Diego Union,* March 27, 1932.

[630]   *San Diego Union,* April 11, 1915.

[631]   *San Diego County Property Records, Deed Book 384, Page 173,* February 9, 1906.

[632]   *Evening Tribune,* April 15, 1914.

[633]   *New York Times,* April 11, 1897.

[634]   *San Diego County Property Records, Deed Book 734, Page 277,* April 28, 1917.

[635]   *San Diego Union,* December 3, 1952.

[636]   *San Diego County Property Records, Deed Book 270, Page 237,* May 28, 1898.

[637]   *San Diego County Property Records, Deed Book 304, Page 461,* February 19, 1901.

[638]   *San Diego County Property Records, Deed Book 198, Page 362,* May 7, 1892.

[639]   *San Diego County Property Records, Deed Book 262, Page 39,* March 8, 1897.

[640]   *San Diego County Property Records, Deed Book 197, Page 253,* March 1, 1892.

[641]   *San Diego County Property Records, Deed Book 199, Page 180,* March 15, 1892.

[642]   *San Diego County Property Records, Deed Book 195, Page 76,* February 12, 1892.

[643]   *San Diego County Property Records, Deed Book 197, Page 80,* March 4, 1892.

[644]   *San Diego County Property Records, Deed Book 202, Page 182,* June 28, 1892.

[645]   *San Diego County Property Records, Deed Book 197, Page 266,* April 19, 1892.

[646]   *San Diego County Property Records, Deed Book 228, Page 133,* February 28, 1894.

[647]   *San Diego County Property Records, Deed Book 251, Page 312,* June 10, 1896.

[648]   *San Diego County Property Records, Deed Book 228, Page 435,* May 22, 1893.

[649]   *San Diego County Property Records, Deed Book 192, Page 49,* October 3, 1891.

[650]   *San Diego County Property Records, Deed Book 214, Page 90,* September 26, 1893.

[651]   *San Diego County Property Records, Deed Book 329, Page 346,* June 13, 1903.

[652]   *San Diego Union,* April 27, 1904.

[653]   *The San Diego Weekly Union,* February 11, 1897.

[654]   *San Diego County Property Records, Deed Book 321, Page 283,* July 31, 1902.

[655]   *Salt Lake Tribune,* September 25, 1912.

[656]   *San Francisco Call,* September 19, 1911.

[657]   *San Diego County Property Records, Deed Book 912, Page 62,* September 2, 1922.

[658]   *San Diego Union,* May 23, 1899.

[659]   *San Diego County Property Records, Deed Book 320, Page 163,* April 15, 1902.

[660]   *San Diego County Property Records, Deed Book 197, Page 127,* February 25, 1892.

[661]   *San Diego County Property Records, Deed Book 276, Page 8,* January 24, 1899.

[662]   *San Diego Union,* December 13, 1891.

[663]   *San Diego County Property Records, Deed Book 227, Page 258,* April 4, 1894.

[664]   *San Diego County Property Records, Deed Book 308, Page 451,* July 25, 1901.

[665]   *San Diego County Property Records, Deed Book 314, Page 245,* November 21, 1901.

[666]   *San Diego County Property Records, Deed Book 266, Page 45,* November 22, 1897.

[667]   *San Diego County Property Records, Deed Book 246, Page 60,* October 29, 1895.

[668]   *San Diego County Property Records, Deed Book 285, Page 384,* February 1, 1900.

[669]   *San Diego County Property Records, Deed Book 411, Page 266,* April 11, 1907.

[670]   *San Diego County Property Records, Deed Book 384, Page 331,* April 9, 1906.

[671]   *San Diego County Official Records, Book 917, Page 138,* December 5, 1922.

[672]   *San Diego County Property Records, Deed Book 615, Page 210,* August 19, 1908.

[673]   *Map 931, Map of Subdivision of Acre Lots 17, 18, & 35 at Pacific Beach,*

November 1904.

[674]   *San Diego County Property Records, Deed Book 323, Page 474,* July 23, 1903.

[675]   *San Diego County Property Records, Deed Book 224, Page 283,* May 8, 1893.

[676]   *San Diego County Property Records, Deed Book 224, Page 287,* November 25, 1893.

[677]   *San Diego County Property Records, Deed Book 270, Page 293,* June 8, 1898.

[678]   *San Diego County Property Records, Deed Book 321, Page 46,* August 16, 1902.

[679]   *San Diego County Property Records, Deed Book 323, Page 271,* July 10, 1903.

[680]   *Map 924, Hauser's Subdivision of Acre Lot 49 of Pacific Beach,* August 1904.

[681]   *San Diego County Property Records, Deed Book 222, Page 6,* June 14, 1893.

[682]   *San Diego County Property Records, Deed Book 195, Page 155,* February 16, 1892.

[683]   *Map 1263, Map of Hollywood Park, Being a sub-division of a portion of Acre Lots 7, 8, 9 and 10 Pacific Beach,* March 1910.

[684]   *Map 1203, Turners Sea Shell Park, Being a sub-division of W 1/2 of SW 1/4 of SW 1/4 of Pueblo Lot 1800,* August 1909.

[685]   *San Diego County Property Records, Deed Book 198, Page 248,* April 5, 1892.

[686]   *San Diego County Property Records, Deed Book 326, Page 409,* March 18, 1903.

[687]   *San Diego County Property Records, Deed Book 222, Page 59,* June 6 1893.

[688]   *San Diego County Property Records, Deed Book 214, Page 90,* September 26, 1893.

[689]   *San Diego County Property Records, Deed Book 967, Page 351,* January 25, 1924.

[690]   *San Diego County Property Records, Deed Book 1418, Page 468,* February 7, 1928.

[691]   *Map 894, Map of Fortuna Park Addition Being a subdivision of the Easterly 1/2 of P. L. 1800 San Diego, Cal.,* January 1903.

[692]   *Map 895, Map of Second Fortuna Park Addition Being a subdivision of the westerly 1/2 of PL 1800 San Diego, Cal.,* April 1903.

[693]   *Map 1627, Congress Heights Addition,* January 1914.

[694]   *In the Superior Court of the State of California in and for the County of San Diego Andrew F. MacFarland vs Ella Clem MacFarland, Case No. 29651.*

[695]   *San Diego Common Council, Book 5 of Resolutions, Page 311,* February 4, 1895.

[696]   *San Diego Union,* May 11, 1906.

[697]   *San Diego Union,* June 7, 1890.

[698]   *San Diego County Property Records, Deed Book 193, Page 424,* February 3, 1892.

[700]   "http://usfencinghalloffame.com/roll-of-honor/400-hattan-ella-jaguarina," [Online]. [Accessed 2012].

[701]   *Evening Tribune,* April 11, 1896.

[702]   *San Diego Union,* August 26, 1954.

[703]   *San Diego County Property Records, Deed Book 52, Page 119,* November 12, 1885.

[704]   *San Diego County Property Records, Deed Book 97, Page 84,* August 9, 1887.

[705]   Z. B. Locker, "Whatever Happened to Izard Street?," *The Journal of San Diego History,* vol. 22, no. 2, 1976.

[706]   *San Diego Union,* October 11, 1977.

[707]   *Record of Board of Aldermen #12,* October 29, 1900 - November 4, 1901.

[708]   *San Diego County Property Records, Deed Book 153, Page 152,* February 19, 1889.

[709]   *San Diego County Property Records, Deed Book 1180, Page 358,* May 9, 1925.

[710]   *Map 1699, First Addition to Braemar,* October, 1917.

[711]   *San Diego Union,* January 23, 1964.

[712]   *San Diego Union,* January 22, 1916.

[713]   *San Diego Union,* January 7, 1910.

[714]   *San Diego County Property Records, Deed Book 1266, Page 446,* October 22, 1926.

[715]   *San Diego County Property Records, Deed Book 1199, Page 270,* July 20, 1926.

[716]   S. Bugbee and K. Flanigan, San Diego's Historic Gaslamp Quarter: Then and Now, San Diego, California: Tecolote Publications, 1989.

[717]   S. Storey M.P., To the Golden Land: Sketches of a Trip to Southern California, London: Walter Scott, 24 Warwick Lane, Paternoster Row, 1889.

[718]   E. G. Gudde, California Place Names: A Geographical Dictionary, Berkeley and Los Angeles, California: University of California Press, 1969, p. 204.

[719]   G. W. James, Rose Hartwick Thorpe and the Story of 'Curfew Shall Not Ring Tonight', Pasadena, CA: The Radiant Life Press, 1916.

[720]   A. F. True and R. H. Sievers, *A Preliminary Study of the Forced Curing*

of *Lemons as Practiced in California,* Washington, DC: Government Printing Office, 1912.

[721]   *San Diego Union,* September 12, 1938.

[722]   *San Diego County Property Records, Deed Book 283, Page 49,* November 9, 1899.

[723]   *San Diego County Property Records, Deed Book 308, Page 217,* April 13, 1901.

[724]   *San Diego County Property Records, Deed Book 332, Page 198,* September 29, 1903.

[725]   *San Diego County Property Records, Deed Book 326, Page 79,* December 27, 1902.

[726]   *San Diego Union,* July 3, 1890.

[727]   *San Diego Union,* October 19, 1891.

[728]   *San Diego Union,* April 23, 1957.

[729]   *Encinitas Coast Dispatch,* August 7, 1958.

[730]   *San Diego Union,* August 22, 1977.

[731]   Hinsdale Public Library, "Hinsdale History," 2009. [Online]. Available: http://www.hinsdalelibrary.info/about-us/hinsdale-history/. [Accessed 2 11 2013].

[732]   *San Diego County Property Records, Deed Book 207, Page 33,* September 15, 1892.

[733]   *San Diego County Property Records, Deed Book 250, Page 14,* February 28, 1896.

[734]   *San Diego County Property Records, Deed Book 252, Page 353,* October 2, 1896.

[735]   *San Diego Union,* January 14, 1951.

[736]   Dept. of Entomology, Cornell University, "Rodolia cardinalis, Vedalia Beetle," [Online]. Available: http://www.biocontrol.entomology.cornell.edu/predators/Rodolia.html. [Accessed 2013].

[737]   *Los Angeles Herald,* December 29, 1894.

Illustrations

A last look at Brown Military Academy, a former Pacific Beach   Cover
landmark. J. C. Webster Photo.

Outside the Pacific Beach Company office, Fifth and   Opposite Page 1
E Streets, San Diego, 1888. San Diego History Center
Photograph Collection #3797.

Pueblo Lots in the Pacific Beach Area, from Map of the Pueblo   1
Lands of San Diego California, May 1870. Office of the San Diego
County Recorder.

Central portion of map of Pacific Beach, San Diego, Cal.   8-9
Subdivided for The Pacific Beach Company, Oct. 1887 by H. K.
Wheeler, C. E. Map Library of the San Diego History Center #1669.

Map 697, Pacific Beach, San Diego, Cal. Subdivided for The Pacific   14
Beach Company, October 1887 By H. K. Wheeler C. E. Filed
January 8, 1892. Office of the San Diego County Recorder.

Map 791, Amended Map of Pacific Beach Being a Subdivision of   15
Pueblo Lots 1784, 1792, 1791, 1790, 1789, 1796, 1795, 1794, 1793,
1799 and Part of 1803. Filed December 29, 1894. Office of the San
Diego County Recorder.

Map 854, Map of Pacific Beach Subdivided for the Pacific Beach Co   16
October 1887. Filed September 28, 1898. Office of the San Diego
County Recorder.

Laying the Cornerstone, San Diego College of Letters. From *Harr*   23
Wagner, California Educational Publicist by Viola Granstaff (1956).
San Diego Central Library California Room.

Samuel Sprecher D.D., LL.D., Taken during the 66th year of his   25
age. From *A Portraiture of the Life of Samuel Sprecher, D.D., LL. D.* by
P. G. Bell (1907).

Faculty and students of San Diego College of Letters in front of the   26
original college building, 1888. San Diego History Center
Photograph Collection #9800.

Detail of College of Letters photo   27

Roasted Ox! - Advertisement for 'Immolation Sale' of real estate by the San Diego College of Letters Company. *San Diego Union*, February 15, 1889. — 30

Postcard of Hotel Balboa, Pacific Beach, San Diego, Cal. — 47

Miss Olive Hoff, the new "Cissy". *The San Francisco Call*, March 7, 1898. California Digital Newspaper Collection, Center for Bibliographic Studies and Research, University of California, Riverside, <http://cdnc.ucr.edu>. — 50

The Sea Serpent! Is Due at Pacific Beach, advertisement by San Diego, Old Town and Pacific Beach RR. *San Diego Union*, July 15, 1888. — 57

The route of the San Diego, Pacific Beach and La Jolla Railway through Pacific Beach as surveyed in 1901 - 1902. This map also pinpoints the locations of the approximately 50 buildings in Pacific Beach at the time. U.S. Geological Survey, La Jolla quadrangle, Edition of Dec. 1903, reprinted Jan. 1909. — 60

Los Angeles and San Diego Beach Railway train steaming through Pacific Beach about 1914. San Diego History Center Photograph Collection #91:18564-1666. — 64

Base Ball, Philadelphia vs. San Diego, Opening of the Pacific Beach Driving Park. *San Diego Union*, November 10, 1887. — 71

Box Score of Philadelphia vs. San Diego baseball game. *San Diego Union*, November 16, 1887. — 72

Pacific Beach Driving Park - Two Great Extra Days, including Sword Combat on Horseback between Jaguarina and Capt. Wiedemann. *San Diego Union*, October 28, 1888. — 76

View of Pacific Beach Racetrack from the east. The grandstand and club house are in the foreground with central Pacific Beach in the background. San Diego History Center Photograph Collection #344. — 88

Map 1120, Mission Bay Park Tract, filed February 1907. Office of the San Diego County Recorder. — 89

Postcard of Rancho 101 Motel, 6596 Pacific Highway, San Diego 9, Cal., incorporating the former judges' stand from the racetrack (with flag). — 93

The First Liberty Pole Ever Erected on San Miguel, July 4, 1890; 99
cartoon spoofing A. H. Isham's trek to the top of Mt. Miguel with
Alonzo Horton and Mary Proctor to stage an Independence Day
fireworks extravaganza. *The Golden Era*, June 1890. San Diego
Central Library California Room.

Two of the full-page advertisements for The Story & Isham 100
Commercial Company, general agents for the John D. Hoff
Asbestos Company. *The Golden Era*, April - May 1890 (left) and
June 1890 (right). San Diego Central Library California Room.

John D. Hoff, the asbestos entrepreneur. *The Golden Era*, November 102
and December, 1890. San Diego Central Library California Room.

Detail from U. S. Coast and Geodetic Survey chart of the Pacific 107
Coast from False Bay to La Jolla dated 1889. The area across the
tracks and the creek from the racetrack may represent the Hoff
Asbestos Works.

Parcel map of the area where Pueblo Lots 1788, 1789 and 1797 meet 109
at the eastern edge of the Pacific Beach subdivision, indicating the
possible location of the John D. Hoff Asbestos Company
manufacturing facility. Office of the San Diego County Recorder.

Map showing locations of lemon ranches in Pacific Beach in 1900. 129

Panoramic view of Pacific Beach from Bunker Hill in about 1906 137
showing the lemon ranches in Acre Lots 30 and 53. San Diego
History Center Photograph Collection #283.

View from College Campus showing lemon orchards on the 138
corners of Garnet and Lamont in 1904. San Diego History Center
Photograph Collection #23535.

View from College Campus showing lemon orchards on the 138
corners of Garnet and Jewell in 1904. San Diego History Center
Photograph Collection #266.

View from College Campus in 1908 showing decline of lemon 139
orchards on the corners of Garnet and Lamont. San Diego History
Center Photograph Collection #395-A.

View from College Campus after 1912. The former lemon orchards 139
on the corners of Garnet and Jewell are dead or dying. San Diego
History Center Photograph Collection #14589.

Braemar Manor, the Scripps Mansion in Pacific Beach, prior to 1926   150
renovations. Photo is dated 1920. San Diego History Center
Photograph Collection #93:18888.

Map 1097, Braemar subdivision, filed December 1907. Office of the   153
San Diego County Recorder.

Advertisement for Talent Worker's Fair to be held at F. T. Scripps'   154
Garden, Pacific Beach, August 17-18, 1910. *San Diego Union*,
August 15, 1910.

Braemar Manor, the Scripps Mansion in Pacific Beach, after 1926   156
renovations. San Diego History Center Photograph Collection #87-
16174.

Map 1927, Braemar Extension subdivision, filed July 1926. Office   158
of the San Diego County Recorder.

Artist's conception of Braemar subdivision, from an advertising   159
poster by Barney & Rife, 1926. San Diego History Center Library
#AD1049-078 F5D6.

Lawn and gardens at Braemar Manor, with the Scripps' private   161
beach and Mission Bay in the background, dated 1929. San Diego
History Center Photograph Collection #2380-5.

Replica Mayflower, the 'pirate ship' for garden fetes at Braemar   162
Manor. San Diego History Center Photograph Collection #2380-2.

Sketch of 'artistic entrance gates' which once marked the approach   166
to the Braemar residential tract.

Braemar entrance gates today.   167

Parents, Attention! Advertisement for San Diego Army and Navy   170
Academy in *San Diego Union*, February 14, 1911.

San Diego Army and Navy Academy; the Senior Arch. *The Cadet*   178
(yearbook of the San Diego Army and Navy Academy), 1936.

Aerial view of Brown Military Academy and vicinity. San Diego   187
History Center Photograph Collection #83:14603-1, annotations by
author.

Col. Davis watches the last parade at the military academy he   190
founded nearly 50 years earlier before it moved to Glendora in
1958. *Evening Tribune*, June 11, 1958. San Diego History Center
Photograph Collection #U-T 6/11/58.

Demolition of Barracks C of the former Brown Military Academy,   191
December 1965. J. C. Webster Photo.

Memorial to Brown Military Academy, the 'West Point of the   192
West', in the parking lot of Pacific Plaza, 2013.

Statue of Kate Sessions south of Laurel Street and west of the   193
Cabrillo Bridge in Balboa Park. In this photo she is holding fresh
cuttings of Bird of Paradise, one of the species she introduced to
Balboa Park and San Diego.

Map 1618, Soledad Terrace subdivision, filed by Kate Sessions in   197
1913. Office of the San Diego County Recorder.

Map 1359, Homeland Villas No. 2 subdivision. Office of the San   199
Diego County Recorder.

Monument to Kate Session on the site of her nursery sales office at   204
Garnet and Pico Streets in Pacific Beach.

Map of Pacific Beach showing location of Bayview Terrace housing   206
tracts.

Map of northeastern portion of Pacific Beach showing streets   208
created for the Bayview Terrace public housing project.

Aerial photo of Bayview Terrace public housing project. San Diego   209
History Center Photograph Collection #10356-2.

Map of a portion of northwest Pacific Beach showing streets   210
created for the Los Altos public housing project.

Map of Pacific Beach showing location of Los Altos housing tract.   211

Map of southern Pacific Beach showing location of Cyane Naval   212
public housing project.

The author, and a parade at Brown Military Academy,   Back Cover
1953. J. C. Webster Photo.

Made in the USA
San Bernardino, CA
19 December 2015